# CYBERHENGE

# CYBERHENGE

Modern Pagans on the Internet

## Douglas E. Cowan

ROUTLEDGE
New York • London

Published in 2005 by
Routledge
270 Madison Avenue
New York, NY 10006

Published in Great Britain by
Routledge
2 Park Square
Milton Park, Abingdon
Oxon OX14 4RN U.K.

Copyright © 2005 by Routledge

Routledge is an imprint of the Taylor & Francis Group.

Printed in the United States of America on acid-free paper.

Library of Congress Cataloging-in-Publication Data

Cowan, Douglas E.
    Cyberhenge : modern Pagans on the Internet / Douglas E. Cowan.
        p. cm.
    Includes bibliographical references and index.
    ISBN 0-415-96910-7 (hb : alk. paper)—ISBN 0-415-96911-5 (pb : alk.
paper)
        1. Internet—Religious aspects—Neopaganism.    2. Cyberspace—
Religious aspects—Neopaganism.    I. Title.

    BP605.N46C69 2004
    299'.94—dc22

                                                            2004019665

For Joie,
*res ipsa loquitur*

# Table of Contents

# Introduction

A cowan is a person who is curious about the Old Ways, but may not know much (or anything) about them, or about this particular coven. In other words, a beginner. Cowans do not attend classes or rituals, but are welcome to come and chat and ask questions. Cowans may wear a {C} before their name if they wish. Should a cowan wish to study more in-depth, s/he needs to make their intention known to a member of The Synod, who will then ask the cowan to become a postulant.

members.tripod.com/~Silver_Web_Coven

By definition, cowans cannot part the mists of Avalon. In Marion Zimmer Bradley's brilliantly evocative novel (1982), parting the mists that separate the holy isle from the mundane world is a responsibility and a privilege reserved for a high priestess of the Goddess, an acknowledged adept of the Old Ways. Instead, as the Internet operators of the Silver Web Coven suggest, "a cowan is a person who is curious about the Old Ways"—in this case, the ways in which modern Pagans are translating their religious beliefs and practices onto the newest of human communication technologies, the World Wide Web.

Having done earlier research into the phenomenon of new religious movements on the Internet, which I freely admit did little more than scratch the surface (Cowan and Hadden 2004b), I came to *Cyberhenge* with certain expectations about what I would find during a more detailed exploration of modern Paganism on the Web. In many ways, though, *Cyberhenge* was a surprise to me, something I suspect most useful works of scholarship are. And I was as surprised by what I did not find as what I did. At the most basic level, despite industry rhetoric about the vast creative potential represented by the Internet, despite the claims of modern Pagan enthusiasts that "computers are like demigods in a box" (Telesco and Knight 2001: xiii), the majority of what transpires online remains decidedly mundane. E-mail rules, conversation takes place, but online Pagan ritual, for example, barely makes a showing.

As a colleague pointed out while we were discussing this book, however, a time-honored tradition in sociology—and, I would argue, one of its chief satisfactions—is the bursting of popular bubbles. To learn that something is not as it is commonly perceived is, to me, infinitely more interesting than simply confirming popular perception. "Social scientists love nothing so much as irony," write Rodney Stark and William Sims Bainbridge (1997: 2), and as my father would say, "Never were truer words spoken," for there is plenty of irony on the modern Pagan Internet.

Not surprisingly, like a host of other religious groups and adherents around the world, many modern Pagans are using the Internet in sincere attempts to create new forms of community, some of which were unimaginable little more than a decade ago. Wiccans, Witches, Druids, and Asatruar who would never have had the opportunity to interact off-line now forge relationships in the thousands of discussion groups on Internet portals such as Yahoo! and MSN, in site-based chat rooms, and on the ubiquitous alt.-type discussion forums. All of this suggests that there is a vast communal conversation taking place on the Web, and in some ways there is. Surprisingly, though, with the exception of alt.-forums, relatively few of these groups prove at all durable; many have only a handful of participants and most post less than one message per month per member. Not surprisingly, there are a plethora of modern Pagan Web sites on the Internet, everything from elaborate information sites to dedicated search engines and "cyberstores," from attempts at fully orbed "cybercovens" to very plain examples of "my Wiccan Web page." Surprisingly, though less so when considered against the larger modern Pagan context, there is little that is particularly creative; that is, many sites simply replicate off-line and online resources with no attempt to improve or adapt them. As I have argued elsewhere, at this point in the technological infancy of popular Internet communications, the world online remains little more than a cybershadow, an electronic reflection of life off-line. What modern Paganism on the Internet does demonstrate, however, is how new information spaces are being colonized by religion and its practitioners, how these spaces provide alternative, hitherto unavailable venues for the performance and instantiation of often marginalized religious identities, and how potential for the electronic evolution in religious traditions such as modern Paganism is supported by the very architecture and philosophy of the World Wide Web.

Given the number of reviews one sees on Web sites such as Amazon.com, often complaining that a scholarly work was not what readers expected or wanted, I think it equally important to say what this book is *not* about. First, *Cyberhenge* is not about how to practice modern Paganism on the World Wide Web; those mists remain firmly in place and this cowan will make no attempt to dispel them. Second, this is not a compendium of modern Pagan presence online; the fluid nature of the Internet and the speed with which Web sites appear and disappear renders any such attempt futile at best. Third, obviously, as a cowan, this is not an insider's perspective; I leave the range of epistemological and methodological issues with which anthropologists, sociologists, and ethnographers who are also modern Pagans will have to contend to them. Though some popular modern Pagan authors have warned would-be Wiccans, for example, that "all books written by non-Wiccans about Wicca" should be avoided (Cunningham 1993: 6), it is worth pointing out that emic perspectives have just as many blind spots as etic ones, they differ only in terms of what they see and what they don't.

One of the challenges in writing a book like this is the number of interlocking and interpenetrating concepts that must be considered, discussed, and often held in creative tension. To that end, a number of theoretical perspectives are deployed here, though with little attempt to weave a master narrative beyond the connection each makes with some aspect of the modern Pagan Internet. Without these, though, any analysis of the Internet as a site for modern Pagan innovation—or that uses modern Paganism as a way of interpreting religion on the Internet—runs the risk of following the lead of many books that try to examine religion online, but become little more than Web site catalogues, barely distinguishable editions of *The Traveler's Guide to the _____ Religion on the Web*. As I discuss each of these intervailing perspectives over the course of the book, I have tried to include enough background material and contextualization so that readers who are not intimately familiar with either modern Paganism as a new religious movement or the Internet as an innovative venue for religious practice will not feel completely at sea.

There are a number of people whose specific contributions I would like to acknowledge. First and foremost is Damian Treffs, my initial editor at Routledge, who showed tremendous enthusiasm for this project from the moment I suggested it to him. I know we both wish that he could have seen *Cyberhenge* through to conclusion. For conversations on religion and the Internet going back a few years now, and which I hope will continue for some time into the future, I am indebted to my colleague at the University of Waterloo, Lorne Dawson. Paul Thomas and Glenn Young, graduate students at the University of Missouri-Kansas City, read all or part of the draft manuscript and offered inevitably helpful suggestions. I would like to say that any errors of judgment in this book are their responsibility. . . but we all know that just isn't the case.

Last, I would like to acknowledge the hundreds of modern Pagan seekers who chose to perform on the Internet stage, and whose performance—whether leading role or bit part—found its way into the researches of a curious cowan. Theirs is a fascinating play, filled with irony and humor, with hyperbole and sincerity, with a touch of tragedy here and there, but always with a clear sense of the ongoing human search for the Divine.

# CHAPTER 1

# The Modern Pagan Internet
## *From Hyperbole to Reality and Back Again*

> Cyberspace is a technological doorway to the astral plane . . . Once we
> enter Cyberspace, we are no longer in the physical plane; we literally stand
> in a place between the worlds, one with heightened potential to be as sa-
> cred as any circle cast upon the ground.
> Lisa McSherry (2002: 5)

### Screenshots from the Modern Pagan Web

"A bit wild and a touch edgy" reads the front page of the JaguarMoon Cyber
Coven Web site, "so be prepared to get shocked by viewpoints other than your
own" (www.jaguarmoon.org). Off-line, the site's owner, Lisa McSherry, is a
modern Pagan and an author who claims to have written "several books exploring the Internet from a Pagan perspective" (McSherry 2003). Online, however, in her persona as Lady Maat (which she sometimes spells Ma'at), she
presides as the High Priestess of JaguarMoon, a *cybercoven* dedicated to teaching "Wicca in a nonthreatening manner" (McSherry n.d. [d]). Later in this book
I will have more to say about the concept of the cybercoven and the ways it is reshaping more traditional understandings of modern Pagan community. Briefly,
though, McSherry defines it as "a group of people of an earth-based faith or belief system who interact primarily, if not solely, through the Internet and/or the
World Wide Web" (McSherry n.d. [c]; cf. 2002: 8–10). Although members of
JaguarMoon may also belong to an off-line coven or other ritual working group,
McSherry offers her online version so that Web visitors interested in modern
Paganism will, at the very least, "be able to discern the difference between

someone who knows what they are talking about and a B.S. artist" (McSherry n.d. [d]). Participants in her training program are expected to dedicate a year and a day of online study to a wide variety of modern Pagan topics, but they are assured that in the end they will receive "a thorough education in almost every aspect of being a Witch" (McSherry n.d. [a]). JaguarMoon's "system of training witches is a proven one," she continues, and promises that those who complete the course "will finish the year with the tools to discern true knowledge amongst the 'new age' hocus-pocus."

In *The Cyber Spellbook*, popular Pagan authors Sirona Knight and Patricia Telesco (2002) devote nearly 30 pages to a variety of gods and goddesses drawn from pantheons around the world, and they attribute to each deity properties and powers suitable for invocation on the Web. Anna Perenna, for example, "is a Roman Goddess of cyber sexuality and fertility," and Annapurna, the "Great Hindu Mother Goddess . . . can make your Web site profitable, within the cyber world" (Knight and Telesco 2002: 51). Morgana, on the other hand, "is a Celtic Goddess of fertility and war who can help you reconfigure your [computer] system," and Mother Mary, "the Christian archetype of the Mother Goddess" is useful "when creating new businesses, crafting new ideas, and signing contracts" (Knight and Telesco 2002: 70). Few religious figures—well known or otherwise—escape their notice. Nwyvre, the "Celtic God of space and the firmament" according to Knight and Telesco, "is a good choice for UFO and contact experiences" (2002: 72), and even the Buddha, the "enlightened one," is pressed into service. "A God of solar energy and zero point energy," they write, "he embodies the wisdom of solar power and 'free' energy in calculators, radios, toys, laptops, homes, and automobiles" (Knight and Telesco 2002: 56).

Not everyone, however, is enthusiastic about Knight and Telesco's reimagining of a cybernetic Areopagus, where the electronic altar of whatever god or goddess one requires at that moment is no more than a few mouse clicks away. In fact, some regard it as just the kind of "'new age' hocus-pocus" that McSherry warns her cybercoven members about. A reviewer for *newWitch*, a magazine for teen Witches, regards *The Cyber Spellbook* as another example of Knight's (and, by implication, Telesco's) "special brand of condescending tripe" (Shanks 2003: 69; for a similar review of Telesco and Knight 2001, see Fisher 2002). This reviewer, a computer professional and modern Pagan on whom "technology long ago lost any romantic hold," has little patience and less respect "for people who write barely readable but highly marketable claptrap" (Shanks 2003: 69) that seeks to wed trendy technology and traditional religion. Out of a possible five, he rather begrudgingly gives the book a rating of "one broomstick." All is not lost for the cyber-Wiccan authors, though, because readers' reviews on Amazon.com—arguably a form of interactive book discussion club that allows far more people to express their opinions online than dedicated chat rooms—were much more positive. "All witches with fully functioning and open minds will want this book handy," writes one online reviewer (Grant 2002), though "half-brained Witches will hate it because it threatens their comfy little niche and beliefs."

Finally, consider the online Coven of the Whispering Brook (www.whisper-ingbrook.org). According to their site, this is "an all female eclectic Wiccan coven" whose main activity consists of weekly chat sessions in a Delphi forum (Whispering Brook n.d. [a]). Going online in May 2001, the Whispering Brook cybercoven includes members from New Zealand, California, and Mexico, and offers a "dedicant program" in which prospective members must participate before they will be considered for full admission. Lest anyone mistake them for just another modern Pagan chat group, however, Whispering Brook makes it very clear that it is an "online community that acts as a functioning coven. We are not a discussion group, we are not a chat room, we are much more than that. We are a family" (Whispering Brook n.d. [b]). Indeed, they have put a number of measures in place to ensure that the often tenuous nature of online communication and community does not affect what members regard as the serious, intentional nature of the group. For example, they offer something of an online modern Pagan illustration of the "strict church hypothesis," which posits that those religious organizations that demand more of their members in terms of commitment will be more successful in the long run (cf. Iannaccone 1994). Notwithstanding their claims *not* to be a chat group, the coven by-laws state that "Members must be present at chat. Chat is on Thursdays at 6:30pm PST [n.b., 2:30 p.m. the following day in New Zealand]. If you have two unexcused chat absences out of a consecutive four, then you will be gagged from the forum, or until you next show to chat . . . Coven members must check into the covenstead (forum) every few days. Once absent for a week, a reminder e-mail may be sent. Two weeks without visiting the coven may result in being dropped from the forum" (Whispering Brook n.d. [b])— which we assume means being released from the coven itself.

## From Hyperbole to Reality and Back Again

In these three brief snapshots of the modern Pagan Internet we are confronted with a number of issues that will concern us throughout this book. The free-wheeling, antinomian (and almost anarchic) character of modern Pagan belief and practice is challenged by Pagans' religious reimagining and often indiscriminate appropriation from other traditions—a process some critics have condemned as a form of "cultural strip mining" (Pike 2001: 134–37; cf. Aldred 2000). The hyperbole and exaggerated rhetoric in which so many claims for the power of the Internet seem to come cloaked is met by the reality that we are all ineluctably embodied, subject to the constraints of time and space, and that our ability to interact online is hardly a global phenomenon. Finally, the crisis of credibility and authority in both the online and off-line worlds meets a number of hardly surprising attempts to stake claims to the authenticity and legitimacy of one's own knowledge and expertise. Indeed, as we will encounter numerous times throughout the book, it is the Internet phenomenon of the "instant expert" (Berger and Ezzy 2004; Wright 2000) that both contributes to and limits the potential of the Web as a source for religious creativity and innovation.

Put simply, how do we know that Lisa McSherry has the wisdom and experience to provide "a thorough education in almost every aspect of being a Witch," to guide prospective Pagans on the very serious journey of spiritual discovery and exploration? She may very well have, but the ease with which a Web site can be created does nothing to establish or validate her credentials. In *The Wiccan Web* both Telesco and Knight (2001: 114–15) recognize what I have called elsewhere the Internet paradox: "more information available more quickly than ever before in human history, but with fewer controls on the quality, accuracy, and propriety of that information" (Cowan 2004: 258). While they are obviously not every modern Pagan's cup of magickal tea, both women offer their services, online and off-line, as experts in Wiccan belief, ritual, and practice. As I will argue more fully in Chapter 2, it is the open and relatively unrestricted creativity so highly valued by modern Pagans that allows for such a *laissez-faire* construction of both social and religious reality. While many authors offer lists of magickal correspondences between an often bewildering array of deities, minerals, plants, essential oils, planets and stars, food, incense, divination tools, and ritual practices, just as many declare that these correspondences must suit the individual practitioner to be efficacious. If they do not, then the individual should feel free to rearrange, reconstruct, or simply reinvent more appropriate parallels (see, for example, Cunningham 1988, 1993; Knight and Telesco 2002; NightMare 2001; RavenWolf 1993, 1998; Telesco and Knight 2001). "Since this idea is broaching on 'cutting edge' magic," write Telesco and Knight of their lists of cyberspatial correspondences (2001: 31), "what we're giving here are personal, instinctual associations . . . you may feel differently about these parts and should always trust your instincts over anything found in a book." Another author, who claims she employed sex magick to obtain her G4 Powerbook computer, writes that Witches uncertain of or apprehensive about the effects of their magick "can always precede any working with the following statement: 'If it is my best interest, and in the best interest of The Whole, let me be successful in this Working,' or something along those lines" (Firefox 2003).

As a preliminary caveat, however, this often exuberant attitude of religious individualism should not be construed as a lack of intentionality, sincerity, or seriousness on the part of modern Pagans. Indeed, quite the opposite. Though many of the more popular treatments of modern Pagan belief and practice might lead the uninitiated to conclude that these are little more than spiritual dilettantes, immature seekers unable to face the often harsh realities of the world around them (see, for example, Davis 1998; Faber 1996), as a growing number of other scholars have noted, men, women, and children from a wide variety of socioeconomic demographics populate the modern Pagan movement and have found it a remarkably fulfilling religious environment (see, for example, Adler 1986; Berger 1999; Berger, Leach, and Shaffer 2003; Greenwood 2000; Hutton 1999, 2003; Luhrmann 1989; Pike 2001; Salomonsen 2002; York 1995). Even a cursory review of a few of the more detailed emic treatments of modern Pagan belief and practice (see, for example, Bonewits 1989; Buckland 1995; Budapest 1989; Carr-Gomm 2002; Crowley 1994; Crowther 1998; Currott 1998; Farrar 1991; Farrar and Farrar 1981, 1984; Hopman and Bond 1996; RavenWolf 2003; Starhawk 1989; Vale and Sulak 2001) reveals clearly the depth of thought and self-reflection that exists within modern Paganism, as well as some of the internal tensions within the movement, that speak to the seriousness with which many modern Pagans regard their emerging religious tradition. This is not to say, of course, that there are *not* dilettantes, dabblers, and poseurs in the modern Pagan movement. There are, and the Internet has given many of these a forum for expression unimaginable just a decade ago; but such individuals are hardly limited to modern Paganism.

Thus, like many books, *Cyberhenge* is a study in contrasts. Seemingly incompatible domains of human behavior, innovation, and social construction are held in a variety of creative tensions, and out of those tensions often complex religious meanings come into view. Utilizing the multivalent emergence of modern Paganism in North America over the past few decades, this book examines and extends some of the discussions about the evolving relationship between religious belief and practice, and the metatechnology of the Internet and the World Wide Web. I use the term *metatechnology* here to highlight the reality that the hardware, software, and Internet service provision are, perhaps, the least remarkable characteristics of the various developing e-space cultures. That these cultures require the existence of Internet technologies and architecture is not in dispute; without the technologies the cultures themselves are impossible. These cultures far exceed, however, the now relatively commonplace electronics that make cyberspace possible. Cyberspace is *metatechnological* in that it is not the material world of hardware and wiring, not the interrelated command-and-control processes of software and programming, and not even the communications that take place between Internet users. Rather, it is that which is conceived and experienced in the interactive interstices between all three.

*Religion and Communications Technology*

As far as we know, religion has always been in the vanguard of social movements that have made use of new and innovative communication technologies.

The earliest examples of written texts are not laundry lists or civic compacts, but religious documents: solemn covenants between divinity and humanity; ritual instruction and ethical dicta according to which social life was organized; and wondrous, dynamic, often bloody cosmogonies preserved for communication within and across generations. As the shift was made from written text to printed text, and later from printed to mass-produced text, religious works were at every point in the forefront (Graham 1987). These shifts produced paradoxical, often contradictory results. For example, as printed religious texts established the notion of a "standard edition" (illustrated most obviously in the West by the appearance of the 1611 King James Bible as the "authorized version"), simply by expanding the available pool of readers mass-produced texts in vernacular languages opened up the range of possible interpretations. As readers became more familiar with the biblical texts, many were left unsatisfied by the dominant interpretations offered by established religious authorities. Although other factors are certainly at work in the emergence of religious movements such as the Church of Jesus Christ of Latter-day Saints, Christian Science, and Jehovah's Witnesses, that each offers radically different interpretations of the Bible is linked, at least in part, to the wider availability of the biblical text. Thus, in response to what he regarded as widespread apostasy, Joseph Smith produced *The Book of Mormon*, subtitled "Another Testament of Jesus Christ"; Mary Baker Eddy wrote *Science and Health with Key to the Scriptures* ([1875] 1971), the biblical commentary on which Christian Science depends; and Charles Taze Russell offered his interpretation of Holy Writ in the six-volume *Studies in the Scripture* (1906–1917).

With these cultural, technological, and religious dynamics in mind, one of the central issues we must consider is how the shift from mass-produced text to *hypertext* affects the proclamation of religious beliefs, the production and protection of religious doctrine, and the performance of religious ritual and practice. Because we are dealing with *texts*—whether they are entirely written or they integrate image, sound, and movement—there are a number of basic issues to consider here: (1) the nature of hypertext itself, which allows readers to access texts in highly individualistic ways; (2) the medium in which the hypertext is immersed, that is, the architecture of the Internet and how it facilitates transmission and replication of hypertext documents (especially the increasingly cut-and-paste character of information on the World Wide Web); (3) the difference between "content" and "creativity" in the electronic environment, including, as Castells notes (2001), the widening gap between those who provide online content and those who simply have Internet access; and (4) the interrelationship between online texts and off-line texts, which is a reflection of the inescapable connection between life in front of the computer screen and life away from it.

First, however well or poorly it is realized in actual usage, one of the realities of hypertext is a reader-driven nonlinearity. Although simple documents containing few links may be read in similar fashion, no matter how many readers find them on the Web, the more complex the hyperlinked textualization, the greater the number of possible combinations that may be followed to read the text or to move beyond it. Thus, online, there is no standard way in which a text must be approached, despite the occasional author's insistence that "this page must be read first" or "follow this path if you want to understand what I mean." Just as readers of mass-produced mystery novels have the option of reading the last chapter first—though this is obviously discouraged by mystery writers and runs directly counter to the purpose for which such novels are written—hypertext readers have the option of following myriad paths through the text and are often encouraged by Web designers to follow only such paths as make sense to them. Hypertext allows for the possibility, at least, of multiply coherent (indeed mutually exclusive) readings based on the ways in which Web visitors choose to navigate the various pages of a particular site, the stock of knowledge they bring to their Internet visit, and the ways in which the purpose for their visit changes in response to the information encountered (Kaplan 2000; Shields 2000).

Second, there is the architecture in which this multiply coherent hypertext is embedded. Once it advanced beyond simple communication and file sharing between a few select computers, emerging in the mid-1990s as what we know today as "the Internet," the architecture that supports (among other networks) the World Wide Web has one overriding protocol to which all others are rescindent: Data must get through. Both the physical structure of the Internet —servers, routers, trunks, and backbones—and the computer software that enables this structure—browsers, FTPs, and e-mail programs—interpret the inability of data to get through as a failure, a breakdown in the system. If the transmission of a data packet is blocked along one path, software and hardware cooperate to find another way to forward the packet. *Data must flow* is the prime directive of the Internet.

As numerous histories of the Internet attest either implicitly or explicitly (cf. Berners-Lee and Fischetti 2000; Castells 2001; Gillies and Cailliau 2000; Hafner and Lyon 1996; Hauben and Hauben 1997; Segaller 1999; Stoll 1990), the technological application that we know now as the World Wide Web (but which also includes other electronic communications networks such as Milnet [the United States military computer network], Telnet [an exclusively text-based network], and FTP [file transfer protocol, which facilitates the movement of computer files between terminals]) works expressly to defeat attempts at information enclosure. As I have noted elsewhere, arguing that in electronic "info wars" the Internet actually favors antagonistic countermovements, "the real value of the

Internet as a venue for countermovement propaganda is its amorphous breadth and the difficulty faced by any group in policing that which is propagated on the Web. That is, since the Internet is designed specifically to route data from one node to another by whatever means are available, it interprets attempts at censorship and control as instances of systemic failure" (Cowan 2004: 267). Moreover, most Web browsers allow site visitors not only to print hard copies of Web pages, but also to save those pages to one's hard drive complete with their hypertext source code. Cutting-and-pasting sections from one Web site and then reposting that material on a different site is now a common, almost absurdly simple procedure—a reality that has not escaped a remarkable number of modern Pagan site operators. Conscious of the fact, for example, that much of the Wiccan information on her Web sites does not originate with her— though casual visitors may not always be able to make that determination—Lisa McSherry (n.d. [b]) includes a disclaimer page apologizing for her unattributed use of Internet material and asking retroactive permission from authors to maintain their material on her sites. Addressing the quasi-anarchic conceptualization that many have about information on the World Wide Web (cf. DiBona, Ockman, and Stone 1999; Raymond 1999), and the attitude of limitless appropriation of spiritual and religious resources that informs much of modern Paganism, McSherry (n.d. [b]) writes in her defense (and implicitly in defense of others): "I fully admit that when I first went online I was not rigorous about noting where I got my information from, or who the author was. Please remember that it was not that long ago that the attitude on the 'Net and Web was to ignore copyrights and just spread information as widely as possible."

This problem highlights the third issue: the phenomenon of information replication on the Internet, as opposed to information origination, and the not insignificant difference between "content" and "creativity." Because the Internet's prime directive dictates that "information must flow," and there is no overarching process by which information can be vetted either before or after Web publication, the problem of all but indiscriminate reproduction will continue to be an important one in any analysis of religion and spirituality on the Web (cf. Cowan 2004). In this regard, for instance, consider the online "Book of Shadows," the basic ritual and conceptual text for many modern Pagans. Although subject to numerous fanciful interpretations about its origin, the Book of Shadows to which modern Wicca owes much of its belief structure, ritual practice, and ethical dicta was that compiled by Gerald Gardner and later redacted for wider audiences by Janet and Stewart Farrar (cf. Farrar and Farrar 1981, 1984; Hutton 1999). Not surprisingly, though, given the anarchic character of modern Paganism, "Book of Shadows" has become a considerably more elastic concept, and there is no single volume, no authoritative text to which all (or even most) modern Pagans turn. Whether compiled either individually or jointly (as the accepted sacred text of a particular coven), the Book of Shadows is a compendium of Pagan principles and ethics, ritual instructions, spell-workings, chants, incantations, invocations, herbal knowledge, divinatory lore, and a wide range of other magickal information. Online, Books of Shadows have become a fairly common component of modern Pagan "shovelware"—standard, often unattributed material drawn from a wide variety of sources and simply reposted to the Internet. The Coven of the New Moon, for example, which described itself as "a Online Coven created by and for teenagers" ([sic]; www.geocities.com/Athens/Rhodes/2544), includes information on candle magick, colors and correspondences, love amulets, and Wiccan terminology—all of which the site operator (who is not identified) attributes simply to "a Farrar book" (Coven of the New Moon n.d.). And, while Prarie [sic] Hearth Virtual Coven (http://prarie_hearth.tripod.com) restricts access to rituals and spells to coven members, a number of other topics are available for the casual online visitor: a history of Wicca, principles of Witchcraft, and a "Witch's Dictionary." Information on chakras, though, is drawn largely from RavenWolf's *To Ride a Silver Broomstick* (1993).

In addition to rituals, chants, and some abbreviated information on Pagan holidays, Coven Moonshae's Book of Shadows (www.dreamwater.org/moon-shae), includes eighty different spells, including one to prevail in a court case and another to attune traffic lights to the Wiccan's own particular travel plans. Because few of these are attributed, though, it is unclear where the majority of the spells originated. True to the "open source" character of much modern Paganism (see Chapter 2), Coven Moonshae encourages the free distribution of resources from its site and even includes a page on which site visitors can contribute their own spells. While the instructions for contributing spells are attributed to someone named Lady Moon Willow (n.d.), no such person exists in the online list of coven members. Additionally, a number of Coven Moonshae's spells clearly originate elsewhere. The "Freeze Them Out" spell, for example, which is intended to protect the practitioner "from an aggressive person" (Coven Moonshae n.d.) is also found in virtually identical form on at least three other sites (though, see also RavenWolf 1998: 211). The Candle and Cauldron e-zine (www.candleandcauldron.com) includes the spell, but states that the author is unknown. D'Magik, however, (www.dmagik.com), the online domain of a modern Pagan known simply as "Dee," attributes it to a woman named "Marilyn Warren." The point here is not who had the spell first, or who copied it from whom, but that it very likely originated with *none* of the modern Pagan Web authors who have included it on their sites. That is, it is simply Internet *content* that has been replicated, and represents no more *creativity* on the part of these particular site operators than the ability to click-and-drag icons from one computer directory to another.

Though his site is not limited to modern Paganism, on the Internet Sacred Text Archive (www.sacred-texts.com) John Hare has created an enormous on-line library of publicly available books and articles covering a wide variety of religions and religious topics. Although the material he posts is scrupulously attributed, Hare believes that information that is not covered by copyright or that authors have given permission to distribute should be available freely over the Web. Drawn originally from postings on electronic bulletin boards and re-formatted for Hare's site, the Book of Shadows section is extremely large, printing out at more than 2,000 pages. In his FAQ, however, Hare warns that some unscrupulous individuals have taken this portion of his site in its entirety, burned it onto a CD-ROM, and then offered it for sale through Internet auction sites such as Ebay.

Although not obviously drawn from material on Hare's site, another Book of Shadows that is offered for purchase online raises issues of information replication on the Web that challenge if not directly breach well-known concepts of intellectual property and copyright. Compiled by "Sapphire," whose Free Book of Shadows Web site (www.freebookofshadows.com; cf. Sapphire 2000) claims to be operated by "a small group of multimedia development professionals who wanted to devote their time to the creation of computer learning tools that genuinely helped individuals connect with the mysteries of life" (Magick Media Group 2003c), this Book of Shadows is available on CD-ROM for a $5.00 fee labeled "shipping and handling." In addition to more than 700 pages of modern Pagan shovelware, the CD contains a number of full-text books related to Western ceremonial magick, including, for example, the *Goetia, or Lesser Key of Solomon the King*, originally translated by members of the Hermetic Order of the Golden Dawn in the early twentieth century, and Aleister Crowley's *The Book of the Law*. While it could be argued that documents such as these are in the public domain (though both the *Goetia* [Liddell and Mathers 1995] and *The Book of the Law* [Crowley (1938) 1976] are still in commercial publication), neither the site operators nor the CD make any statement about copyright or reprint permission. Other items on the CD, however, including artwork and computer graphics which the compilers indicate are freely available for use on purchasers' own Web sites (Sapphire 2000), are of more questionable provenance. For example, the "Free Book of Shadows" includes three multimedia paintings by Russian artist Arseny Kostenko (www.darkside.ru/arts) and a number of Web graphics designed by American artist Robin Wood (www.robinwood.com), none of which indicates that permission to distribute was granted either Sapphire or her Magick Media group. In addition to the copyright notice prominently displayed at the beginning of the CD-ROM e-book, however, the "Terms of Service" to which purchasers "agree" indicate once again issues of knowledge enclosure, authority and authenticity, and the rather rampant commercialization of spiritual resources—hardly new concepts, but ones markedly exacerbated by the advent of the Internet. These terms declare that:

1. You agree not to resell the Book of Shadows or trade it in any manner.
2. You agree to take seriously the information contained in the CD-ROM. Some of these spells are very powerful and not to be taken lightly.
3. You agree that FreeBookofShadows.com or any of its staff is not responsible for the results of any use of the information contained on the CD-ROM. You understand that as a practiser [*sic*] of magick, you are responsible for your own actions and that harmful actions will be revisited three-fold. (Magick Media Group 2003b)

Similar conditions apply to another "free" Magick Media Group CD-ROM, "Mastering Sex Magick," which includes, among other things, the text of Sir Richard Burton's venerable *Kama Sutra of Vatsyayana*—once again with no copyright information or permission (Magick Media Group 2003a).

This process of replication points us, finally, to a fourth issue: the inevitable (and often problematic) relationship between off-line texts and online texts, and the rather mundane reality that lies behind much of the hyperbolic rhetoric about content production, the creativity inherent in Internet communications, and the effects of the World Wide Web on religious belief and practice. Several years prior to the invention of hypertext and a decade before the Internet was a household word in the technologized nations of the world, Theodore Roszak opined that computers were not unlike the sadly underdressed emperor in the well-known fairy tale. While admitting many of the benefits of the new technology, Roszak wrote that "the computer, like the too-susceptible emperor, has been overdressed in fabulous claims. Further, I believe that these claims have been deliberately propagated by elements in our society that are making some of the most morally questionable uses of computer power" (1994: xiii). And, like the computer, in the relatively few years of its existence the Internet has seen more than its share of overstatement—both utopian and dystopian—by industry enthusiasts and commercial entrepreneurs who want to ensure the largest possible market share for their particular products, by scholars who see in the World Wide Web exciting new frontiers for social research, by concerned observers who fear it will become an all-powerful tool to recruit the unwary into alternative and often unpopular religions, and by members of the modern Pagan movement itself who want to hold the Web up as a *cyberhenge*, the next great venue for the working of magick in the world. Let us briefly consider each of these cohorts in turn.

*Utopia and Dystopia: From Hyperbole to Reality . . .*

One of my favorite examples of the enthusiasm with which the Internet and the World Wide Web have been both embraced and promoted is from an article in a leading British Internet magazine, entitled "Instant Genius! Just add the Net" (Wright 2000). "Don't be ignorant," the author writes. "And don't spend more time learning something than you need to. Use the Net like Polyfilla and fill the gaps in your knowledge with ready-made, instant info bites. Just add a touch of brain power and mix until you dissolve the lumps. It's easy!" (Wright 2000: 51). The problem, of course, is this is exactly what many Internet users do, from university professors trawling the Net for syllabi and lecture notes to students both graduate and undergraduate, desperately seeking term papers; from Christian pastors downloading a year's worth of sermons to television pundits filling in notes for their on-camera remarks just minutes before the red light goes on; and from anxious Wiccans searching for freeze-them-out spells to evangelical Christians hunting down information with which to debunk those very same Wiccans. For those with access, the World Wide Web has become a library that is open 24 hours a day, 7 days a week. However, it is not knowledge hard won through long hours of study and reflection. It is not wisdom that has been gained through trial and experience. And there is no guarantee that the information one finds in that library can be trusted at all. Although these issues are hardly limited to the Internet, few problems with the World Wide Web are pointed out more often than the variable reliability of the information that is available. Used like this it is indeed brain spackle, and it creates the illusion of "instant experts," if certainly not the reality. It could be argued, of course, that as we become more familiar with the metatechnology of the Internet we will develop more sophisticated cognitive filters for the information that is available online. We will become more selective and more careful about how we approach information gathered from the World Wide Web. Although I have no doubt that this is true for some Internet users, the proportion of the Internet population for which it is true—itself a function of the relatively small number who actually use the Internet to search for information on a regular basis (see Pew Internet & American Life Project 2003; also Larsen 2001; Madden 2003)— remains to be seen. As television became more and more common, however, and as the expanded channel offerings of cable and satellite both increased and commercially concentrated televised product, there is little evidence that consumers of television news and entertainment have become any more discerning, or any less willing to believe the sensational over the sensible (cf. Postman 1986, 1992; Postman and Powers 1992). Similar arguments have been made from a variety of perspectives for print news media (see, for example, McChesney 1999; Rampton and Stauber 2003; Sommerville 1999). None of this, however, seems to dim the enthusiasm of those who see in the Internet the arrival of the next evolutionary step wrapped up in a metatechnological box.

In *Give Me That Online Religion*, sociologist Brenda Brasher (2001) makes a number of claims both for the general value of the Internet as a social technology and for religion on the Internet as a particular locus of innovative and salutary social practice. Few of her comments, however, move beyond a sense of evolutionary utopianism. "Online religion is the most portentous development for the future of religion to come out of the twentieth century," she writes (Brasher 2001: 17), while acknowledging the rather risky nature of such an assertion. "Using a computer for online religious activity," she even goes so far as to suggest, "could become the dominant form of religion and religious experience in the next century" (Brasher 2001: 19). Although she presents no empirical evidence to substantiate her claim, she contends that "as it widens the social foundation of religious life, cyberspace erodes the basis from which religion contributes to the destructive dynamics of xenophobia. In the process, it lessens potential interreligious hatred" (Brasher 2001: 6–7). Indeed, "as the latest site of cultural challenge and change, online religions (traditional and new) represent a stabilizing influence in the virtual domain" (Brasher 2001: 13). Communications consultant Jennifer Cobb writes similarly in *Cybergrace: The Search for God in the Digital World*, and, in a passage worth quoting at some length, declares:

> The reality of cyberspace transcends the dualism represented by the objectified mind and matter. Cyberspace is a messy and complex world of *experience*, both objective and subjective. The renewal of experience as a central feature of the world moves us beyond the hegemony of the Cartesian worldview. Though located at the level of the mind, cyberspace is fundamentally a world of process. As such, it has the potential for opening us to a new way of experiencing the world, a way that relies on a divine reality to give it meaning and substance. (Cobb 1998: 10)

Both Brasher and Cobb, however, ignore some rather fundamental realities about the Internet and the World Wide Web.

First, there is the reality of the digital divide (Castells 2001; Lenhart 2003; Loader 1998; Mossberger, Tolbert, and Stansbury 2003; Norris 2001; Wresch 1996), the fact that Internet access (and, increasingly, Web content production) is as subject to the varied processes of social stratification as other technological and cultural products. Although the Internet has grown at a remarkable rate since the invention of hypertext and the ready availability of Web browsers in the mid-1990s, still less than 10 percent of the world's population has access to it (Wellman and Haythornthwaite 2002). As Castells reminds us in *The Internet Galaxy*, the city of London has more Internet domains than the entire continent of Africa (2001: 264), and less than 1 percent of Africa's population has access to the Internet. He also notes that although, as a whole, access in the United States is increasing, a growing "ethnic digital divide" is "indicative of the fact that the Information Age is not blind to color" (Castells 2001: 249). Moreover, the most recent study by the Pew Internet & American Life Project (Lenhart 2003: 3) indicates that "the overall growth of the Internet population since late 2001" has "flattened," and no longer demonstrates the steady growth it had seen to that point.

Second, if throughout history and around the world religion has proved to be, shall we say, *less* than a stabilizing influence, why should we expect its presence on the Internet to function any differently? Those who go online are the same people who interact off-line. In fact, just like the "ethnic digital divide," it is clear that the Internet is not blind to all manner of human bias and prejudice. Put simply, there is plenty of hatred on the Net, religious and otherwise (Zickmund 1997). Consider, for example, Godhatesfags.com, the online domain of Topeka-based anti-gay activist Fred Phelps, the very model of Internet-based hate propaganda. Or consider Web sites for racist religious movements ranging from Richard Girnt Butler's Church of Jesus Christ Christian-Aryan Nations (www.twelvearyannations.org) to the virulently nationalist Hindu Unity (www.hinduunity.com), which are as easy to find online as sites that promote religious tolerance and understanding (for example, www.religious-movements.org; www.religioustolerance.org). Although the Aryan Nations is well known in the West, Hindu Unity is the Web presence of the Bajrang Dal, the youth wing of Vishva Hindu Parishad (see Hansen 1999; Jaffrelot 1993; Van der Veer 1994; Varshney 2002), and even maintains an online "hit list" of those it considers enemies of or traitors to the cause of a harshly xenophobic Hindu nationalism.

Third, there is the use to which empirical research indicates the Internet is put on a daily basis, which hardly supports the more enthusiastic portrayals of life online. In fact, quite the opposite. According to a number of reports from the Pew Internet & American Life Project (www.pewinternet.org/reports), while nearly 60 percent of those with Internet access in the United States actually go online daily, over 50 percent of them do so simply to send or retrieve e-mail—the single most common use of the World Wide Web. Conversely, less than 30 percent search for general information online, less than 20 percent look for answers to specific questions, and less than 10 percent choose to do their banking via computer. More significant for our purposes, however, is the finding that, on a daily basis, more than four times as many users check the weather over the Internet (17 percent) as search for religious or spiritual information online—at 4 percent, the same number as generate Internet content (Pew Internet & American Life Project 2003). And even this last figure does not adequately parse the problem. If a person checks her church Web site to confirm the time of the evening service ("religious information"), should this be considered the same as searching the Internet for an online prayer group related to that particular church ("spiritual information")?

And, finally, belief that the process of education and access to "correct" or "accurate" information can overcome a wide variety of social ills ignores the crucial reality that all educational philosophies, all heuristic frameworks according to which information is chosen, and all technologies by which those philosophies are enacted and that information disseminated are unavoidably embedded in a web of contested power relations (see, for example, Bourdieu 1984a, 1984b, 1997, 1998; Foucault 1970, 1978, 1982). One aspect of those relations is that, for all its appearance as the ultimate postmodern knowledge space, the Internet, the World Wide Web, and the computer technologies on which both depend are predicated on a very particular logical paradigm. As Theodore Roszak contends, "the computer is inherently a Cartesian device embedded in the assumptions of a single intellectual style within a single culture of the modern world. The very metaphors that surround it bespeak a conception of the mind as logical machinery" (1994: xxxv). How different, for example, would computer technology look if the intellectual paradigm within which it has been developed was based on Buddhist philosopher Nagarjuna's *reductio ad absurdum* arguments for phenomenological nonessentiality (Komito 1987) or the yogic sage Patanjali's beliefs that the world exists only to the extent (and only for as long as) the true Self (*purusha*) remains ignorant of itself (Eliade 1969)? Instead, precisely because of the intellectual paradigm within which they emerged, the computer and its metatechnological progeny maintain and reinforce an almost colonial attachment to Western rationalism and Cartesian logic.

Next, there are those who see the Internet through dystopian lenses, as a threat both to the social order and to personal freedom and spirituality. While evangelical Christian Douglas Groothuis notes quite correctly that "one of the pervasive lies of cyberspace culture is that increased exposure to information is, in itself, good for individuals and for society as a whole" (1997: 161), he locates a significant portion of the problem with the Internet in the worldview by which he believes much of the Web is informed. That is to say, any assessment of cyberspace—whether utopian or dystopian—that is not grounded in an evangelical Christian worldview will be flawed almost by definition. "The communication of information has become a modern idol," he concludes, "rendering the God of the Bible irrelevant" (Groothuis 1997: 161). In *Virtual Gods*, fellow Christian Tal Brooke (president of the evangelical Spiritual Counterfeits Project) exemplifies a dystopian vision of the Internet as the ultimate retreat from real life. "The final seamless sanctuary from reality," he writes (Brooke 1997: 176), "is indeed something that cyberspace—the beast that now stands in the town square of history—could offer in bounty, this garden of digital delights. The imagination can run free in the planes of cyberspace where digital reality is plastic and can be altered and reinvented at whim . . . Suddenly," though, Brooke concludes, "the patient has entered the darkest ward of the madhouse only to lock himself permanently in the inner chamber."

In the wake of the 1997 Heaven's Gate suicides, a number of commentators —both religious and secular—might have regarded Brooke's words as prophetic, for many located the blame for those deaths squarely on the virtual doorstep of the World Wide Web. Though the *New York Times* cautioned that "there is little evidence that the Net itself is acting as an instigator for cult be-havior" (Markoff 1997), the same article offered the more dystopian vision of anticult activist Rick Ross, who declared instead that "the Internet has proven a powerful recruitment tool for cults" (Ross, in Markoff 1997). In "Blaming the Web," *Newsweek* quoted Tal Brooke, who agreed with Ross. "I think the Net can be an effective cult recruiting tool," he opined. "It's like fishing with a lure" (Levy 1997; cf. Brooke 1997; Cowan and Hadden 2004b). Because the Heaven's Gate group owned computers, operated a moderately successful Web design company, and posted messages and group material to the Internet, the argu-ment seemed to be that the Web was guilty by association. In similar fashion, historian Hugh Urban (2000: 282) contends that Heaven's Gate "was one of the first [religious sects] to emerge as a true religion of and for the computer age." Though this claim is contradicted by the actual history of the group, Urban ar-gues that the Internet is a first-rate environment for the inception, incubation, and evolution of new religious movements. "First and most simply," he writes (Urban 2000: 283), "the Net is an ideal means of mass proselytization and rapid conversion—a missionary device which operates instantly, globally, and anonymously." Notwithstanding the reality that the Web operates in *none* of these ways necessarily, and despite the continuing popular perception that the unwary can be caught by the Net (cf. Berger and Ezzy 2004; Clark 2003), as a metatechnological tool for religious recruitment the Internet actually falls far short of even the mildest predictions (Dawson and Hennebry 1999). Urban continues, though, that "second, and more interesting, is the fact that the Internet, more than perhaps any other conventional medium, fosters the prac-tice of religious syncretism and the blending of many different traditions drawn from radically different and seemingly contradictory sources" (2000: 283). In this he *is* correct, and, as we will see, perhaps no more so than for mod-ern Pagans on the World Wide Web.

### And Back Again: Modern Pagans on the World Wide Web

"Going online," writes Lisa McSherry (2002: 4), "we immerse ourselves in a nonlinear environment, one that places us in a reality where we control our movements, while being transported to places unseen and unimagined. There is no tidy, rational way to move through Cyberspace." Quoting a Pagan broad-caster from Seattle, Macha NightMare, a faculty member at the Pagan Cherry Hill Seminary (www.cherryhillseminary.org), declares that the "Web is a living example of what we Witches are always yapping about: everything is con-nected, you can't do anything without affecting something else, and so on, and so on. The Web is the making of that ideal. I can connect my little Web docu-ments to any other resources in the entire world, without cost, without worry, and without restriction" (2001: 66). Wiccans Patricia Telesco and Sirona Knight regard the Internet as "one of the most far-reaching innovations affecting our culture today both spiritually and substantively . . . it holds tremendous potential for magic if we get past the bits 'n bytes long enough to see the possibilities. The use of the Internet provides virtually unlimited possibilities for Wiccans with access to it" (2001: xiii).

Like McSherry, Telesco and Knight seek to integrate not only the functions of the computer into their magick-making, but also the very hardware and software that facilitate those functions. For example, they encourage cyber-Wiccans to "dab your computer screen with insightful oils to help with Web Witching," suggesting further that "sandalwood and lavender are good choices" (Telesco and Knight 2001: 22). When blank, that same computer screen can serve as a scrying tool, like a crystal ball, though "you can power up the system to represent Spirit's flow through it" (Telesco and Knight 2001: 94). Even old, discarded computer equipment can serve a magickal purpose. Individual keys from an unused keyboard become divination tools akin to runes, bones, or yarrow stalks. Drawing or casting the "Caps Lock" key, for example, means one should "stop shouting or projecting your energy so much," while "Num Lock" indicates "You're too caught up in logical thinking" (Telesco and Knight 2001: 97, 98). Even the humble screwdriver is pressed into magickal service. Used as a divinatory pendulum, "since your computer's system is based on binary code, this particular form of divination is most successful if you limit it to yes-no answers" (Telesco and Knight 2001: 98). In their second book on the topic, *The Cyber Spellbook*, they opine that "without ongoing innovation the power of our Path fades into dogma. With this in mind, Cyber Magick becomes very important to our future" (Knight and Telesco 2002: 12). Here they continue integrating modern technology (though not limited to computers) into the magickal lifestyle. The computer mouse "is akin to a magic wand," while floppy disks "can be used as watchtower markers at the four directions of a magick Circle" (Knight and Telesco 2002: 86). "The keyboard represents the creative flow. You think about something, you type it, and then you see it—talk about manifesting power!" (Knight and Telesco 2002: 86). One might ask Knight and Telesco how a computer differs significantly from a typewriter or even a pencil in this regard, or point out to NightMare's informant that computer hardware and software are not without cost; indeed, for many people, e-mail is one of the most expensive ways to communicate. However, as I will discuss in the following two chapters, the more important issue is that *they* believe these things to be so and that they *act* on the basis of those beliefs.

*Cyberhenge* is predicated on the notion that if we are going to find the metatechnology of the Internet and the World Wide Web being used for purposes of religious innovation, invention, and experimentation, we are going to find it most clearly in traditions that not only allow for such dynamics theologically, ritually, and practically, but ones that actively encourage these dynamics and reward those participants who demonstrate proficiency in them. And if Internet advocates and enthusiasts who proclaim the cybernetic dissolution of boundaries and restrictions imposed by space, time, and culture are correct, what religious traditions are most likely to take advantage of that? There are few authentic examples of religious practice and community that exist entirely online, and even those that claim such an existence (e.g., the JaguarMoon cybercoven) cannot escape the problems of off-line embodiment. Put differently, it is unrealistic to suppose that online liturgies will one day replace the weekly mass at St. Catherine's Roman Catholic parish if only because the sheer *sensuality* of a Catholic mass, whether in Latin or the vernacular, cannot reasonably be equaled on a 19-inch monitor. Similarly, although online Hindu *puja* sites such as www.pujaroom.com might be interesting and useful in certain circumstances (see Dawson and Cowan 2004), like the Catholic mass, they can hardly replace the tactility and sensuousness of off-line *puja*— not least because critical ritual elements, such as cleaning, dressing, and feeding the deities, cannot be authentically recreated online. However, modern Paganism in its many guises appears well poised to step into this gap.

That religious groups, traditions, denominations, cults, sects, mystics and gurus, priests and priestesses, as well as individuals ranging from ordained Methodist clergy distraught over what they regard as the imminent demise of their denomination (see Cowan 2003b) to self-proclaimed religious *virtuousi* who believe they are in contact with sacred beings ranging from Zoroaster and Thoth to Hermes Trismegistus and the Virgin Mary (see, for example, Ellie Crystal at http://crystalinks.com) are using the Internet for reasons related to their religious faith is hardly in dispute. *How* they are using it, how their traditions are affected by it, and what religious traditions are most impacted by the Internet are much more important questions. And these are just a few examples of how the modern Pagan Internet has begun to emerge, how the lay lines —the avenues of power that many believe criss-cross the Earth like a web—of the modern Pagan cyberland are being charted.

### The Lay Lines of the Cyberland

In terms of the intersection between religion as a human phenomenon and the Internet (especially the World Wide Web) as a cultural architecture, the most obvious theoretical distinction is between *religion online* and *online religion*. Originally conceived as a dyad by Christopher Helland (2000; cf. Dawson and Cowan 2004; Hadden and Cowan 2000a; Young 2004), religion online meant the Internet as a vehicle for the provision of information about or by religious groups, movements, and traditions, whereas online religion regarded the World Wide Web as an interactive venue for religious practice, ritual, observance, and innovation. Since Helland's initial distinction, however, it has become clear that, by and large, these represent theoretical endpoints of a continuum rather than identifiable positions in empirical space. Though examples that cluster closer to the religion online end of the continuum are considerably easier to find, as the metatechnology of cyberspace has evolved, the nature of the space between these two poles has changed, creating an environment in which religious cybercommunity involves (and in some cases requires) some measure of both *religion online* and *online religion*. Although Chapter 3 will examine the cartography of modern Paganism and the modern Pagan Internet in more detail, here I would like to establish very briefly some of the contours of religion online and online religion, and how intersections between them suggest some of the intermediate outlines of modern Paganism on the World Wide Web.

Web sites devoted to providing information about or products related to a variety of modern Paganisms, but which neither encourage nor facilitate online participation in interactivities such as Pagan chat rooms, rituals, spell-working, or meditation/visualization practices populate the *religion online* end of the spectrum. Among these are dedicated Pagan search engines such as Avatarsearch (www.avatarsearch.com) and WitchCrawler (http://witchcrawler.com); online stores such as Spirit Tomes & Treasures (www.spirit-tomes.com), Earthspirits Emporium (http://earthspirits.org), and the Village Witchcraft Shoppe (www.villagewitchcraftshoppe.com); information sites related to well-known off-line groups such as Circle Sanctuary (www.circlesanctuary.org), the Church of All Worlds (www.caw.org), and Covenant of the Goddess (www.cog.org); the electronic version of off-line print magazines such as *Pangaia* (www.pangaia.com) and *SageWoman* (www.sagewoman.com); as well as personal information pages posted by a wide variety of modern Pagans ranging from the famous (Isaac Bonewits [www.neopagan.net] and Starhawk [www.starhawk.org]) to the not-yet-famous (James Hale [www.grawolph.com] and Serena Gale [www.geocities.com/Athens/Acropolis/8385]).

Among the myriad online offerings of modern Paganism, however, few sites rival the Witches' Voice. Also known as WitchVox (www.witchvox.com), the Witches' Voice is the online project of Fritz Jung and Wren Walker, and is still arguably the most extensive modern Pagan site on the Web. When Jeffrey Hadden and I first wrote about the Witches' Voice (Hadden and Cowan 2000a: 9–10), it claimed links to more than 3,000 Pagan Web pages and more than 31,000 related links overall. Three years later, the WitchVox site links to more than 5,000 Pagan Web pages and incorporates more than 46,000 related links, including personal Pagan pages as well as Pagan personals; an extensive list of covens and ritual working groups, both online and off-; shopping sites, Pagan news, general information, and a schedule of Pagan events from around the country and around the world. According to their mission statement, "The Witches' Voice is a proactive educational network providing news, information, services and resources for and about Pagans, Heathens, Witches, and

Wiccans" (WitchVox Staff 1997). In this regard, one of the sections by which we were most impressed was a set of pages designed to educate the general non-Pagan public about the various modern Paganisms. "These documents range from a sample letter that parents can send to elementary schools correcting misinformation about Wicca and Neopaganism in order to protect the rights of Wiccan/Neopagan children, to petitions asking for fairer treatment of non-traditional religious groups by the media" (Hadden and Cowan 2000a: 9). Elsewhere, though, Jung and Walker declare rather unequivocally that "WitchVox does NOT teach Witchcraft, Wicca, Heathenism or any forms of Paganism, nor do we give out spells, rituals, affirmations or charms" (WitchVox Staff 2003). Though it is a "dot.com" Web site, the Witches' Voice is justifiably proud of the fact that it is "banner-free" and accepts no advertising; site content is provided and maintenance costs offset by the modern Pagan community worldwide, and neither Walker nor Jung draw a salary for their work. As anyone knows who has either maintained or attempted to maintain even a simple Web site—let alone an enormously complex site such as WitchVox—this dedication alone speaks to the seriousness with which modern Pagans view not only their emerging religious traditions, but also the value of the World Wide Web as a vehicle for religion online, a way to communicate information about those traditions.

On the other hand, however useful (or not) attempts to create an entirely online version of an off-line coven prove to be—and there is not nearly the longitudinal data to evaluate that problem at present, though Chapter 4 will attempt some preliminary assessment—theoretically it is Web sites such as the JaguarMoon cybercoven that occupy the end of the continuum closer to *online religion*. That is, the Web provides (or attempts to provide) for all participants the primary locus of religious activity and, presumably, religious experience. This interaction is predicated on the notion that coven members, for example, will likely never meet off-line. Dedicant and initiate classes are conducted via e-mail; rituals take place in sacred groves and magickal circles that have been imaginatively constructed within the largely textual confines of chat rooms, multi-user domains (MUDs), and MUDs that are object-oriented (MOOs); and community administration and such interpersonal intimacy as evolves in the coven does so, at least at first glance, in a decidedly different way than it would off-line. The question remains, though, how viable entirely online covens (or any other intentional religious community) will be over time, and how that durability compares to similar groups organized off-line. McSherry, for example (2002: xi), indicates that she formed the JaguarMoon cybercoven after leaving another cybercoven, ShadowMoon, in 2000. In Chapter 4, I will also discuss how the concept of a "coven" has been elasticized somewhat as a result of going online, but it is worth pointing out here that, according to McSherry, the original ShadowMoon cybercoven "had more than a hundred members," yet "only half of them actually stayed through their year and a day of training" and "fewer than that became participants in the core coven" (2002: 81). This suggests, at least, that for a significant portion of the participants, the online experience by itself was not sufficient to generate the level of commitment necessary to create a viable, durable community—another subject to which we will return. Elsewhere, McSherry notes simply that ShadowMoon is "now defunct" (n.d. [d]).

Though initially research into the social psychology of Internet usage seemed to indicate that those who spent significant quantities of time online were less socially connected off-line (Kraut et al. 1998), which might suggest that they were seeking more significant social connections through the World Wide Web, more recent data challenge that notion and present a picture of Internet usage that favors extroverts and rewards those who integrate their online activities with their off-line lives (Kraut et al. 2002). Following this logic, it seems that those online religious communities—including but not limited to those that begin online—that move off-line and incorporate both domains will be more successful than those that attempt to provide for all their participants' religious needs solely over the Internet. In this regard, consider The House of Netjer, a reinvention of ancient Egyptian religion that began off-line, moved online, then expanded off-line and established a physical presence in the real world, in addition to online interaction. According to Krogh and Pillifant (2003, 2004), The House of Netjer now claims more than 400 members and organizes regular off-line events at which those who have only known each other electronically may interact in person.

Although it is simply an impression rather than an empirical statement, the majority of modern Pagan Web sites appear to ply the waters somewhere between religion online and online religion. On Internet portals such as Yahoo!, Delphi, and MSN, Pagan-oriented discussion groups number in the thousands, many offering information about spells, chants, correspondences, and divination with the expectation that the Internet may actually become a part of the divination or spellworking process. On Yahoo! alone, for example, more than 4,500 groups are listed under the rubric Pagan, more than 2,300 under Wicca, nearly 900 under Tarot, and more than 1,500 under Witchcraft. Even Druidry is represented: more than 300 Druid discussion groups exist for those who are interested. On MSN, more than 4,200 groups are listed under "Pagan," nearly 7,700 under "Wicca," and over 3,500 under "Witchcraft"! To be sure, on each of these portals some groups are more popular than others. Many have only a handful of members, whereas others number participants in the hundreds. Some see scores of posts daily; others go weeks, even months, between postings. That is, just like religious commitment off-line, online participation varies widely. Similarly, information about Wiccan rituals or seasonal festivals is integrated—however well or poorly—with attempts to perform some of these rituals online. 1001 Spells.com, for example (www.1001spells.com), is a multimedia site that claims to be the world's largest spell archive, but to which access is available only on the basis of a paid subscription. "Designed to look and act like a real book," reads the "Free Tour" portion of the site, "the Book of Shadows program takes full advantage of everything multimedia has to offer, including animated page turns and rich graphics for an unparalleled online experience" (1001 Spells 2002). Here, though, rather than a rich, tooled leather cover, creamy vellum pages, and text handwritten in India ink, the cyberwitch's Book of Shadows requires a computer, monitor, printer, cables, Internet access, and all the ergonomic paraphernalia that goes along with those. For the vast majority of users, this Book of Shadows is location-bound, chained to the computer desk and the power supply. Sitting beside a brook, on the other hand, reading or writing in one's Book of Shadows in the shade of a willow tree, is an experience denied those who access their spells online. As I noted above, in addition to their "Free Book of Shadows," the Magick Media Group also offers for sale (i.e., for the $5.00 shipping and handling fee) the "Mastering Sex Magick CD-ROM." "With clear instructions for harnessing and directing energies," reads the online promotional material (Magick Media Group 2003b), "we show in easy steps how you can get with [sic] you want by simply having sex— with a partner or by yourself. This is the most powerful magick ever, and now it can be yours." And, for those who want to know if love (or sex) is in the cards, stars, bones, or yarrow stalks, online divination sites incorporate prophetic tools and techniques ranging from tarot to runes, and from the I Ching, feng shui, and numerology to Western, Hindu, or Chinese astrology. On Tarot.com (www.tarot.com), for example, consumers pay for their services by purchasing Karma Coins®, which retail for 10 cents each and are also available in gift certificate form. According to the online information page (Tarot.com 2003), "Karma Coins keep monetary transactions out of the Tarot ritual," though a visitor to the site can spend as many as 70 Karma Coins on a full Tarot reading —a bargain by any reckoning.

**Click to Continue . . .**

The next two chapters consider in more detail aspects of modern Paganism and the modern Pagan Internet on which I have only touched briefly in this introduction. In many (arguably most) respects, online reality is little more than a cyber-shadow of the off-line world, an electronic reflection of real life, however important it has become to those with access to it. Because of this, though, some scholars argue that since little or no face-to-face contact takes place between participants there cannot be any real "community" established online. Chapter 2 begins by examining the various cultures of modern Paganism and asking how these cultures conceptualize the technologies that make online religious participation possible. As has already become obvious, I think, to speak of religious participation and practice from a modern Pagan perspective is to speak inevitably of magick—which, following some (but certainly not all) modern Pagans (Noble 2003), I spell with a "k" simply to differentiate it from stagecraft and legerdemain. Thus, as important as it is to understand how modern Pagans think about computer technology, it is equally important to understand how they regard magick, the energetic process that might fairly be called the heartbeat of the modern Pagan movement, as well as the notion of interrelatedness that both informs and underpins the rationality of magick from a Pagan perspective. In contrast to those who say that neither magick nor the concept of viable online community should be taken seriously, Chapter 3 argues that there are a number of compelling reasons to do both and that the claims of modern Pagans that the community they create online is as authentic as that which occurs off-line should hardly be dismissed out of hand. Not least here are the voices of modern Pagans themselves, many of whom believe very strongly that what they encounter electronically is a rich and authentic community experience.

The following chapters build on this conceptual material and discuss modern Paganism online from three particular perspectives. It seems clear to me that in terms of their Internet involvement many, perhaps most, religious traditions will continue to cluster at the religion online end of the continuum. Although some adherents may find their way to experiences that incorporate aspects of online religion, for the reasons discussed briefly above, liturgy, worship, prayer, and meditation *in real life* will remain the experience of the vast majority of practitioners and believers worldwide. This is so especially for traditions with substantial off-line histories and institutional structures, and for which the Internet could never be more than a technological adjunct. In terms of religions whose traditional roots are more fluid, however, whether that fluidity occurs by historical accident or evolutionary design, cyberspace does present more interesting opportunities for innovation. In the next chapter, I discuss the "open source" movement in Internet history and apply it by analogy to modern Paganism. In many ways, I believe, this addresses the question of which religious traditions will benefit most from the Internet and, conversely, how those traditions will pay the price for that electronic beneficence. Rather than simply follow the path trod by others, many modern Pagans *are* attempting to use the online environment to experiment with the creation of their own religious traditions—although not to the degree that I initially expected to find when I began this work. Still, while "eclectic Wicca" has been a prominent aspect of modern Paganism since the 1960s, the advent of the Internet has opened up the potential for a considerably expanded repertoire of imagination and invention.

With this in mind, Chapter 4 examines both the creation of online Pagan communities and the ways in which their creation has stretched and challenged more traditional understandings of modern Paganism.

Chapter 5 continues this discussion but locates it in the context of ritual participation in cyberspace. Though, like the concept of community, critics might contest the authenticity of online Pagan ritual—experienced across thousands of miles, mediated through a metatechnology such as the World Wide Web, and occurring principally in the imaginations of the participants—for many of those modern Pagans who do participate, "Cyberhenge" seems a very hospitable ritual environment and no less real for its online character. This chapter explores three particular aspects of the online Pagan ritual experience: (1) the mystery and the reality of the online ritual, (2) the phenomenon of ritual in the electronic environment and the social functions it serves for participants, and (3) the inescapable problem of the body in the midst of rhetoric that often claims the body has ceased to exist. Chapter 6 discusses the World Wide Web as a stage for the performance of modern Pagan identity, various venues of disclosure that allow participants to experiment with an assortment of modern Pagan selves ranging from tentative neophyte to vulgar demagogue.

For the majority of this study, I take most of what is presented online at face value. That is, unless there is a compelling reason *not* to suppose that actors are participating in e-space authentically, I treat their participation as real aspects of dramaturgical performance. *Cyberhenge*, though, is not designed to be an exhaustive compendium of modern Paganism on the Internet. The sheer volume of material, the ephemeral nature of the online world, and the constantly evolving character of its metatechnology render any such attempt self-defeating. Throughout the chapters, however, a number of research directions are implied, and Chapter 7 reprises and makes explicit some of these possibilities, prospects, and problematics.

*Notes and Caveats*

At all points where I have quoted someone directly—either from a Web site or a discussion forum of some kind—I have used his or her chosen Pagan name, rather than use given names. The only exception is where no Pagan name is provided. There are three reasons for this. First, it allows for consistency, because many (in some cases, most) discussion forum members do not list their "real" names, but communicate online using only their Pagan or Craft names. Second, using Pagan names allows for a certain measure of protection for people who perhaps had no idea their online posts would attract the interest of an inquisitive sociologist. Although, as a basic research dictum, I contend that individuals who participate in discussion forums that neither screen potential members nor moderate postings are uploading their comments into a public space and intend them to be viewed by an audience over which they have no control, I also have no wish to embarrass or otherwise expose Pagans who may not have disclosed their religious beliefs to close friends and family. During the research for this book, I certainly read enough online chatter—and talked to enough modern Pagans off-line—to realize how sensitive the issue of "being out of the broom closet" remains. Third, using Pagan names seems to me simply more respectful of the religious path these men, women, and youth have chosen. Taking a new name when one makes a significant religious commitment is common in many traditions, and is an important part of the internal and external identity formation that commitment implies. We would hardly think to insist on calling professed Buddhist monks, Catholic nuns, or Hare Krishna devotees by their former, nonprofessed names. Thus, using mundane, given names instead of chosen, Pagan names—even when the former are available—seems to me both inconsiderate and inaccurate. If no Pagan name is given, but the person is clearly "out of the broom closet," I have used the name as given; if there is any question of whether they have disclosed their modern Pagan identities to friends or family, I have used pseudonyms.

Next, given the rather tenuous nature of the World Wide Web in terms of where individual threads are located and how one goes about finding them, I wrestled with the problem of including Universal Resource Locators (URLs) in the text—especially since a number of the ones for modern Pagan sites changed during the course of research for this book alone! I chose to include them, however, for a couple of reasons. When I noticed that Web addresses had changed, they usually went from free Web space on large commercial providers such as America Online, Geocities, or Tripod to more intentional spaces with dedicated Web domain names. Using the analogy of physical space, they moved from a large apartment complex into either a smaller complex or a single-family dwelling. This suggests to me that these Web site operators are trying to create sites that are more stable and durable. More important, though, it made little sense to write about Web sites that readers had no opportunity to visit and explore for themselves. Thus, if a URL that I have provided is no longer active, I have tried to provide enough information about the site that a search engine should turn up the new domain address fairly quickly.

Finally, few people who spend any time on the Internet will have failed to notice the sometimes appalling degradation of spelling and grammar that occurs when participants unused to communicating in written form send e-mail, upload messages to discussion forums, or create their own Web content. Whenever I quote from electronic communication, then, I have restrained my editorial inclination to correct spelling, grammar, and orthography, and I present the messages precisely as they appeared online.

# CHAPTER 2

# The Road to Cyberhenge
*Conceptualizing Modern Paganism Online and Off-*

> If someone wants to blend pantheons of a couple of trads, if that's what
> feels right to them, then so be it. For example, my husband leans more to
> a Druidic/Welsh area, and I lean more to Scottish. We blend those pan-
> theons together because we have two children, and we want to do this
> together as a family. We can't worship together if we're keeping our pan-
> theons separate.
>
> Erin, e-mail to Celtic-Cauldron

## Conceptualizing Modern Paganism

Scholars from a variety of disciplines have long recognized that the keystone of
social order—whether that order is manifest in table manners, traffic laws, or
the often turbulent nature of the sacred—is *agreement* between social participants. Different cultures have come to different states of agreement, for example, on the propriety of belching after a satisfying meal. Traffic laws have force
in society because we agree to submit ourselves to them—both for our own
good and for the larger good of the traveling public. And the nature of the sacred—including its objects, the myths and narratives in which it is embedded,
and the taboos and rituals by which it is surrounded and approached—is culturally specified according to similar processes of agreement. Whatever technologies are used to facilitate their emergence and evolution, as social and
cultural products, religious beliefs, practices, and traditions exhibit their durability because of the agreement between participants that those things in which
they participate are sacred as opposed to profane, meaningful as opposed to

trivial, and efficacious as opposed to impotent. This is not to say, of course, that agreement in these matters is never coerced; that there are never contesting domains of agreement between different groups of social actors; that, following Berger and Luckmann (1966), those who are in agreement do not lose sight of the constructed nature of the constituents of their agreement; nor, finally, that the objects of agreement in one social setting do not change as they move through time and across space. It is merely to say that in the social construction of religious belief and practice, agreement plays a crucial role, and to suggest the contours of agreement within particular religious communities is a useful place to begin to understand the complexities of those communities.

Made originally to the Yahoo! discussion group Celtic-Cauldron, Erin's comment—"If that's what feels right to them, then so be it"—epitomizes the agreement among modern Pagans that personal gnosis and the intuitive, intentional construction of one's own religious beliefs are the benchmarks by which modern Paganism, both online and off-, is measured. In fact, this is also the *problem* of personal gnosis by which modern Paganism is both blessed and cursed. They may not agree on what constitutes the essential elements of a particular Paganism—honoring Kuan Yin as a Celtic deity might invoke the imprimatur of individualism but would hardly elicit the agreement of many other Celtic Pagans or, indeed, Buddhists—but that individuals have the right, indeed the responsibility, to construct their own ritual practices and mythical pantheons is not in dispute. Before considering in more detail the various cultures of modern Paganism and the ways in which the Internet contributes to or hinders their evolution, a preliminary discussion of what I am calling "open source" versus "closed source" religions will help set the stage. Because it originates with the early technological cultures of the Internet and later the World Wide Web (Castells 2001; DiBona, Ockman, and Stone 1999; Raymond 1999), the term "open source" is particularly appropriate for describing the ways in which different religious traditions are making use of these new communications technologies, and how modern Pagans are, in fact, "hacking religion."

*Hacking Code: The Open Source Revolution*

Colloquially, of course, a hacker is a computer criminal, someone who illegally accesses computer systems, and either steals or modifies the data and programming found there (Badham 1983; Hafner and Markoff 1991; Littman 1997; Slatalla and Quittner 1995; Softley 1995; Sterling 1992; Stoll 1990). The product of real-life criminal activity sensationalized by the entertainment industry and news media, hackers are portrayed as social deviants—either outcasts and loners (Badham 1983; Littman 1997; Sterling 1992) or outcasts who pack together like cybernetic hyenas (Slatalla and Quittner 1995; Softley 1995). The emphasis in these cultural narratives is clear: hackers are reprobate, dangerous, and must be controlled at all costs. Although viruses, worms, and other invasions of protected computer space have done tremendous damage, and will no doubt continue to do so, computer programmers themselves, as well as historians of the Internet and the World Wide Web, insist that the word *hacker* is misused in these cases (Abbate 1999; Castells 2001; DiBona, Ockman, and Stone 1999; Hafner and Lyon 1996; Raymond 1999). Indeed, many credit what has come to be known as "hacker culture" with the creation of both the Internet and the World Wide Web. Rather than criminals, hackers were the first "real programmers" (Raymond 1999: 7–26), the ones who solved the frustrating problems of computer interconnection and the intricate riddles of software compatibility, file sharing, and Web browsing. To these men and women, a "hack" was simply an improvement in computer programming through a modification of the source code, an alteration that rendered the software more functional and the code more elegant. And, in this regard, a primary tenet of the hacker culture is the concept of "open source programming."

Tim Berners-Lee, the man who invented the World Wide Web but who has not chosen to profit from his creation, defines open source programming as software for which the basic building blocks—the source code—is freely available for modification. "Anyone can scoop up the source code—the lines of programming—and edit and rebuild them, for free," he declares (Berners-Lee 2000: 171). In practical terms, this means that software users are no longer limited to the range of performance options provided by those who wrote the program. Since the source code is open and available, users are encouraged to tinker with software, modify it as they see fit, and ideally improve the programming for the benefit of all users. While certainly not the only example, the most celebrated case of cooperative open source programming—which Raymond (1999) has labeled a "movement" and DiBona, Ockman, and Stone (1999) a "revolution"—is Linux, the operating system designed by Linus Torvalds in the early 1990s and distributed free across the Internet. In stark contrast to the various versions of Microsoft® Windows, which exemplify the "closed source" model of software design and marketing in which the programming code is not available to the purchaser and the products must be used as they are supplied by the company, bugs and all, as Castells notes and users around the world attest, "Linux is widely recognized as one of the most reliable operating systems, particularly for computers working on the Internet" (2001: 46).

Freely available software and unlimited license to modify the program code are only two aspects of the open source movement, however. Open source etiquette suggests that, once improvements have been made to a specific piece of software, those changes—complete with their new source code—should be made available on the Internet so that the entire computer culture may benefit. That is, although Linux was the invention of Linus Torvalds, its success— both as an operating system and as a means by which the control of knowledge resources could be taken or kept out of the hands of corporate elites like Microsoft—depended on the participation of thousands of unnamed computer enthusiasts worldwide. "The most important feature of Linux," writes Eric Raymond, whom Castells (2001: 41) describes as "an icon of the [hacker] culture," "was not technical but sociological. Until the Linux development, everyone believed that any software as complex as an operating system had to be developed in a carefully coordinated way by a relatively small, tightly-knit group of people" (1999: 24). This is certainly the model preferred by closed source entities such as Microsoft, and the myth on which their cultural and commercial dominance depends. Raymond, however (1999: 24), continues that "Linux evolved in a completely different way. From nearly the beginning, it was rather casually hacked on by huge numbers of volunteers coordinating only through the Internet. Quality was maintained not by rigid standards or autocracy but by the naively simple strategy of releasing every week and getting feedback from hundreds of users within days, creating sort of a rapid Darwinian selection on the mutations introduced by the developers. To the amazement of almost everyone, this worked quite well."

## Hacking Religion: The Open Source of Modern Paganism

Like open source programmers who freely modify and then just as freely distribute computer software, encouraging its continued alteration and improvement, modern Pagans are "hacking" their own religious traditions out of the "source codes" provided by pantheons, faith practices, liturgies, rituals, and divinatory processes drawn from a variety of cultures worldwide. If in the computer culture the source code defines, delimits, and operationalizes the programming intent of the software designer, in religious cultures it defines, delimits, and operationalizes the beliefs and faith practices of adherents and practitioners. In terms of religious traditions, embedded in the source code are the epistemological assumptions according to which the difference (or similarity) between the sacred and the profane is defined; sacred cosmogonies and mythistorical narratives, from which are derived ethical and moral dicta; ritual and devotional practices; the pantheons of divine and semi-divine beings, together with the myths, rites, and attributes associated with them; and the various "totems and taboos" distinct to different groups within particular traditions (Freud [1913] 1950).

Like religion online and online religion, the distinction between open source and closed source religious traditions is ideal and heuristic rather than typological and absolute. Briefly, though, *open source traditions* are those which encourage (or at least do not discourage) theological and ritual innovation based on either individual intuition or group consensus, and which innovation is not limited to priestly classes, institutional elites, or religious *virtuosi*. This is

similar in some ways to entrepreneurial models of new religious formation (see, for example, Stark and Bainbridge 1979), of which modern Paganism is certainly an example, but it differs in that it restricts itself neither to new religious movements nor to control of the source code material by religious elites. It is also distinct from so-called "cafeteria religion," in which components of different traditions are gathered into an eclectic whole based on the individual tastes of the participants. There are similarities, of course, but the selection and modification of religious components in the open source model occurs at a deeper level, the source code level, as it were. In the cafeteria model, although Christians may incorporate aspects of Buddhist practice, Native American beliefs, or Celtic mythistory in an attempt to augment or tailor individual religious preference, the basic constituents of those incorporations rarely change. Buddha remains Buddha, for example. Buddhist practice may become part of a Christian's life, but the Buddha does not become part of the Christian pantheon. In the open source model, on the other hand, even the nature of deity is potentially open to modification and reinterpretation.

Conversely, *closed source traditions* are those whose source codes are either not open to modification and innovation, or in which the processes that reshape the code are reserved for institutional elites, that is, "a relatively small, tightly-knit group of people" (Raymond 1999: 24). The history of the Roman Catholic Church, for example, from the competing orthodoxies of the first centuries (cf. Bauer 1971; Ehrman 1993; Robinson 1988) to the great ecumenical councils of Nicaea (325 C.E.), Constantinople (381 C.E.), and Chalcedon (451 C.E.), from the immense theological pressure brought to bear by the Protestant Reformation and the Catholic Counter-reformation to the tensions that have emerged as a result of modern church movements such as liberation theology, feminist theology, and creation spirituality, could be written as a history of conflict between open and closed source influences in which the closed source came to dominate. To safeguard the received orthodoxy of the church and maintain control of the knowledge resources according to which the faith is constituted, the source codes of Catholicism are officially regulated by institutional elites, including such curial bodies as the Congregation for the Doctrine of the Faith, which was known until 1908 by its original name, the Sacred Congregation of the Universal Inquisition, and the Congregation for Catholic Education. Though theological innovators such as Hans Küng, Edward Schillebeeckx, and Matthew Fox, liberation theologians such as Gustavo Gutierrez, Leonardo Boff, and José Porfirio Miranda, and feminist theologians such as Rosemary Radford Ruether, Elsa Tamez, Miriam Thérèse Winter, and Mary Daly have issued serious challenges to the closed source nature of Roman Catholic doctrine and practice, and despite the transformations initiated by Vatican II, the source codes of the Church remain firmly in the hands of institutional elites.

Perhaps the most trenchant late modern example of a closed source religious movement, however, and one which has fought a number of Internet battles to maintain the integrity of its more advanced teachings, is the often controversial Church of Scientology, founded by L. Ron Hubbard. In closed source terms, the foundational practice of Scientology—known as "auditing" —is believed by Scientologists to be 100 percent effective only as long as it proceeds in strict accordance with the instructions laid down by Hubbard himself, principally in his book *Dianetics* ([1950] 1990). Invoking the non-falsifiability common to religious beliefs and practices worldwide, lack of success in the auditing process or stunted progress in one's spiritual development is often attributed to deviance from the protocols established by Hubbard and guarded by the Church through an aggressive program of copyright enclosure and infraction surveillance. To ensure uniformity and avoid what the Church's Religious Technology Center regards as "the nemesis of alteration and reinterpretation" (2003b), for instance, during these auditing sessions participants pause frequently to "word clear," that is, to look up the exact meaning of a word in its Scientological context. This precludes the kind of multiple interpretations that are anathema to the closed source tradition. Similarly, during church worship services, sermons are read verbatim from a master text, and neither innovation nor deviation is permitted. Institutionally, on the other hand, Scientology as a closed source religion—one in which the source codes for the religion provided by Hubbard are not open to challenge or modification in any way—is best demonstrated through the Religious Technology Center (www.rtc.org), the organization charged with safeguarding Scientological orthodoxy. "Scientologists across the globe," reads part of the RTC's online mission statement (2003a), "view the maintenance and incorruptibility of their religious technology—in precise accordance with the founder's source writings —to be essential to their very salvation." While this is no doubt due in part to the host of Scientological imitators that have appeared since the 1950s (Stark and Bainbridge 1979; Wallis 1976) and the problem of unauthorized reproduction of Church esoterica, which is only exacerbated by the Internet and the World Wide Web (Cowan 2004; Peckham 1998), it would be hard to imagine a clearer statement of a closed source religious tradition.

There are, however, examples in which the open source nature of one religious tradition inspires innovation and syncretism in particular, exceptional adherents of more closed source traditions. Dom Bede Griffiths, for example, an English Benedictine monk who lived for most of his religious life in India, eventually assimilated aspects of Advaitic Hinduism into his Roman Catholic devotions and monastic practice. In Hinduism, he declared, he had found "the other half of his soul" (cf. Bruteau 1996; Griffiths 1976, 1989). Similarly, the well-known Trappist monk Thomas Merton wrote to D. T. Suzuki in 1959 that although he could not begin to express what Zen was, he knew that he could

not survive without it (Merton 1985: 561–62; cf. 1967, 1968). Similarly, in *One God Clapping*, Rabbi Alan Lew (2001) describes his spiritual journey exploring Judaism and Zen Buddhism. And "Reverend B" (1996; cf. Pittman 2003) writes in "Priestess and Pastor" about her twin callings as both an ordained Christian clergywoman and a Wiccan high priestess. To the alarm of some adherents in both religious camps, the phenomenon of "Christo-Wiccans," though hardly common, is not nearly as oxymoronic as it might once have seemed, and is a topic to which we will return.

Arguably, all traditions exist somewhere along a continuum between the open source, *laissez-faire* individualism of many modern Paganisms and the closed source, tightly controlled regimentation of Scientology. It is also very important to note that the openness of a particular tradition at a certain time should not suggest similar receptivity throughout either its history or its geographic distribution.

Examples of modern Paganism as the open source tradition *par excellence* abound. "I've been a witch since I was about 13," writes Ethereal Soul in her personal introduction to the Yahoo! discussion group, Moonwitch. "I practice a bit of everything I suppose though my main beliefs are in Vodou. However, I'm not yet initiated in it." Similarly, WulfWuman, who also goes by the name Crzy Wolf, has designed an Internet shrine to her patron deity, Sekhmet, the lion-headed Egyptian goddess who was the daughter of Ra. On a visit to an off-line Temple of Sekhmet, a small adobe shrine outside Cactus Springs, Nevada, WulfWuman left a written prayer asking that the goddess would "show me my destiny in helping in your name to cleanse the world in light & love" (1998). Besides the main statue of Sekhmet, however, the Nevada shrine also includes statues of a Native American Earth Mother, Bast (Sekhmet's sister), Kuan Yin, and Mother Mary. And on her "Goddess-a-Day" page, Tarotlaydee, a modern Pagan and all-around diviner from Clearwater, Florida, who promotes herself as a scholar of the Tarot and whose MSN Web site is called "Tarotlaydee's Powergems!" (groups.msn.com/tarotlaydeespowergems), offers an extensive list of female deities from which visitors are encouraged to choose depending on the time of year and their personal needs. Often illustrated by modern Pagan artists and accompanied by brief descriptions (the majority of which are taken verbatim from Telesco 1998 and McCoy 1995), Tarotlaydee has constructed her list of goddesses from pantheons around the world and includes, for example, Sri (Hindu); Awehai, Mother of All Eagles, and White Shell Woman (Native American); Aphrodite, Juno, and Mnemosyne (Greek and Roman); Nemetona, Cerridwen, and Mala Laith (Celtic); Ashtart (Ancient Near Eastern); Maat, Bast, and Seshat (Egyptian); Pele (Hawai'ian); the Holy Spirit and Mary (Christian); as well as goddesses that are claimed to be from places ranging from Borneo (Fire Woman) to the Middle East (Whale Goddess), and Japan (Dainichi-nyorai) to Morocco (Nejma).

However, since Tarotlaydee and Telesco are neither Bornean nor Arab, and neither Japanese nor Moroccan, they also illustrate both the historical and cultural decontextualization that is fundamental to modern Pagan open source appropriation of worldwide spiritual resources, as well as the proliferation of these recontextualized resources through the Internet. Fire Woman's only connection to her original context, for example, is that she is called "Fire Woman of Borneo"; in Tarotlaydee and Telesco's hands (1998: May 15; n.b. this book is not paginated and so references are given by date) she has been turned into the goddess of the barbecue. To honor the Whale Goddess, which Telesco (1998: March 6) and Tarotlaydee claim is the Arabic version of the creature that swallowed Jonah in the ancient Near Eastern narrative, they suggest devotees "send a donation to a whale foundation" or, somewhat incongruously, "visit an aquarium and watch whales there today." Similarly removed from her context, the Japanese goddess Dainichi-nyorai has become simply a patroness of weather magic: "If you need rain in your area, burn a lily; to banish rain, wave the lily in the air to move the clouds away!" (Telesco 1998: June 17). And Nejma, the Moroccan goddess of healing, according to Telesco (1998: May 17) and Tarotlaydee, can be invoked by "eating carrots, turnips, beets, or other vegetables [which] internalizes Nejma's protective qualities for year-round well-being." That "year-round well-being" might reasonably be regarded as one of the more general health benefits of eating vegetables, and not due necessarily to the intervention of a putative Moroccan deity to which practitioners have no other connection, seems not to concern these modern Pagans because the open source nature of their appropriation leads to and encourages a localized adaptation of spiritual resources.

Setting aside the rather crass attempts by some companies to access different markets over the Internet using religious titles, rhetoric, or meta-tags—one mortgage company, for example, has titled its Web page "God's Judgment" (www.mortgages-approved.us/gods_judgment)—Tarotlaydee's online replication of Telesco's material illustrates the manner in which the Internet both serves the open source nature of modern Paganism and presents one of its major conceptual problems. While there are obviously multiple sources available both online and off-line for information on well-known goddesses such as Isis, Cerridwen, and Hecate, less familiar deities replicate on the Internet through discussion forums, often drawing their information ultimately from a single source. According to Telesco (1998: July 5) and Tarotlaydee, for example, "Mala Laith is the ancient Celtic crone goddess." Searching Mala Laith on Google one finds the same information—much of it taken from Telesco's book, some of it obviously via Tarotlaydee's Web site—simply replicated on a number of different sites. More than a dozen modern Pagan discussion groups on Yahoo! quote either all or part of the Tarotlaydee entry; some Web sites simply change a few words, modify the punctuation, and upload the material with no attribution at all. Thus, originating in a single, questionable source and replicating over the Internet, Mala Laith makes her way into the modern Pagan community as a social fact.

## Personal Gnosis: The Cultures of Modern Paganism Online and Off-Line

According to Manuel Castells, a culture is "a set of values and beliefs informing behavior" (2001: 36). This implies that each of us lives not in one culture, as we often think, but in several, moving between and among them according to the demands of our daily lives. The "values and beliefs informing behavior" in one of these cultures—our family, for example—could be quite different (though not entirely divorced) from those which obtain in another culture, say, our college fraternity. However, continues Castells (2001: 37), culture is not individualistic; rather, "it is a collective construction that transcends individual preferences, while influencing the practices of people in the culture." In terms of the open source nature of modern Paganism, however, "individual preference" *is* one of the primary constituents of the interrelated cultures by which the various modern Paganisms are informed and, somewhat paradoxically, held together. Using open source religion as a broad organizing concept, these aspects of modern Paganism can be represented as three sets of paired tensions, each set describing a particular cultural dynamic within the broader movement: (1) a culture of appropriation and innovation, (2) a culture of eclecticism and traditionalism, and (3) a culture of solitude and community. Obviously, this is not the only way to think about either these cultures or modern Paganism, but as heuristic devices, they are useful because, rather than concentrating on (and often going no further than) the intricacies of individual—and individualized—belief systems, these paired cultural tensions elucidate many of the underlying dynamics and dialectics by which modern Paganism is influenced and shaped. It is also important to point out that these cultures are not discrete entities within modern Paganism but are instead part of a mutually interpenetrating and reinforcing array of social processes that help us map the emerging geography of a new religious movement.

Overall, for a religious movement that claims to have no standard sacred text, modern Paganism is a remarkably textual culture. Many modern Pagans see an important connection between the collection of resources related to one's spiritual beliefs and the ritual practice of one's spirituality; indeed, many are inveterate bibliophiles, some amassing substantial libraries on all aspects of the modern Pagan spiritual journey. Much of the online conversation in the discussion lists I followed throughout the research for this book were related to the variety and quality of resources available. In other traditions, and especially in those parts of the world where books are less available and more expensive, believers might own a copy of their sacred text—a Bible or New Testament, a copy of the Qu'ran, a collection of sutras—but it would be unusual to find general adherents who have large collections of commentaries, manuals of ritual and practice, or histories of their faith. Not so in modern Paganism, and at least some of the reasons for this seem clear.

First, because of the social marginalization suffered by many new religious movements, and especially those (such as Wicca) that draw the particular ire of socially dominant religious traditions (such as evangelical Christianity), the ability to learn about one's faith, to develop it in practice, and to deepen one's devotion and understanding through community connection is often limited. Textual resources, then, become one of the primary means by which modern Pagan traditions both expand and contract, especially in what I call below their culture of solitude. Expansion occurs as more and more texts, whether print or electronic, are added to the pool of available resources on which modern Pagans can draw; contraction takes place when the information contained in those resources is simply replicated instead of contributing new material to the pool.

Second, despite constitutional guarantees of religious freedom and practice, and despite the rhetoric of tolerance with which religion in American society is often cloaked, "coming out of the broom closet" and declaring oneself a Wiccan or a Witch remains a very risky act for many people, precisely because of the different cultures in which they reside. Internet discussion forums, for example, routinely contain messages from Pagans—both children and adults—who are certain that their families would not understand their religious beliefs and fearful of the consequences were they to find out. Modern Pagans from a variety of traditions have made a concerted effort over the past two decades to educate the general populace that they are neither Satanists nor devil-worshipers. Some evangelical Christians (e.g., Hawkins 1996, 1998) appear to have gotten this rather straightforward message; others (e.g., Larson 1999; Marrs 1990) clearly have not. As one modern Pagan, a solitary living in a rural community on Vancouver Island, wrote in her review of *Texe Marrs Book of New Age Cults and Religions* (Marrs 1990), "I felt as if all my panic buttons had been punched. I no longer wanted to be out of the broom closet, with the risk of meeting someone like the author of this book. Fear, anger, and anger at being afraid have invaded my life in a way I have never experienced" (Doerksen 1995: 38; cf. Cowan 2003a: 86–93). In situations like these, rather than the risk involved in seeking out a teaching coven or other ritual working group, textual resources offer a much less threatening entrée into what many still consider a significantly deviant religious tradition. And, in the face of these social pressures, textual resources, whether commercially produced or Internet based, as well as the electronic conversation and confirmation provided by the thousands of modern Pagan discussion groups on the World Wide Web, have become very important in the ongoing construction of modern Paganism. It appears that some modern Pagan traditions, or at least some clusters of modern Pagan belief and practice, are collecting as much around the simplified Wicca of Scott Cunningham (1988, 1993) and Silver RavenWolf (e.g., 1993, 1998)—both of whose writings are regularly recommended as resources for inquirers and beginners—as they are the more complex traditionalism of a Gardnerian or Alexandrian coven, and certainly more than the very complicated ceremonial magick traditions in which at least some modern Paganisms find their origins (Hutton 1999). And, where print resources are less available either because of geographic isolation, financial constraints, or off-line risk, Internet discussion groups become for many modern Pagans a primary means by which resources are amassed and religious insights developed.

The open source adaptation and construction of individual belief notwithstanding, however, modern Pagan ritual and devotional practices are more often than not derived from a common set of textual resources, one that has been driven as much by the flood of commercialized Paganism from publishers such as Llewellyn as it has by constraints imposed by traditional Pagan lineages. The liturgical year within which rituals occur, the implements and liturgical elements that modern Pagans consider essential to magickal working, the pantheons and elemental correspondences according to which magick is worked all come from a pool of resources the outlines of which are readily identifiable. Although this derivation is obviously more pronounced in traditional modern Pagan lineages such as the Gardnerian or Alexandrian, even eclectic solitaries participate in this common resource culture. The resources on which modern Paganism draws, therefore—as well as the discussions and debates that go on about the value of different resources—open an important window into the development of the traditions themselves, the ways in which these traditions are bounded by the limited (and often simply replicated) nature of the resources themselves, and how modern Pagan traditions construct themselves dialogically and electronically.

## A Culture of Appropriation and Innovation

Throughout this chapter I have touched on the *culture of appropriation and innovation* by which the behavior of modern Pagans is informed at its most basic level. As Telesco (1998) and Tarotlaydee amply demonstrate, there are few if any spiritual resources that at least some modern Pagans do not regard as potential candidates for both pantheon and practice. Just as WulfWuman found in the Nevada Temple of Sekhmet deity figures drawn from Chinese Buddhism, North American First Nations spirituality, and Roman Catholicism, other examples of appropriation and innovation abound, and the Internet is an important vehicle by which these are communicated to and validated by the modern Pagan community. One particularly important instance of this occurs in the dedicatory process of some modern Pagan traditions, specifically, the search for a personal deity or deities, a pantheon with which the believer will have a special relationship over the course of his or her spiritual journey.

"I feel like I am 'pantheonless,'" writes Sparx to the Yahoo! group, _Wicca. "I don't feel that it would be fair for me to latch onto an Egyptian pantheon or say a Native American pantheon because I'm neither Egyptian nor Native American." This post generated a number of responses that illustrate the tensions inherent in the open source culture of appropriation and innovation, especially when neophytes enter and are unsure of the boundaries of that culture. "You know," replied Tashila, "sometimes a 'pantheon' may choose you! (for example) I have always been drawn to Egypt and anything to do with Egypt, since I was a small child." She goes on to say how, through a series of serendipitous events that she later interpreted as divine action (if not intervention), Anubis and Isis as patron deities "chose" her. Aradia concurs, although she offers a somewhat more sophisticated theological explanation for the process of deity patronage. "Just because you're not Egyptian," she writes, "doesn't mean you can't work with their deities. Maybe there's a past life involved somewhere? Do a bit of digging and listen to those who seem to call out to you . . . whether they're Celtic, Egyptian, or Buddhist, their message is the same. Go with whatever feels right for you." Because reincarnation in various forms is part of many modern Pagan belief systems, Aradia's advice both validates her own appropriation of Egyptian deities and, within the context of the open source tradition, functions as an authoritative voice for the younger seeker. Although this is hardly a situation unique to interaction on the World Wide Web, because Aradia is in northeast England and Sparx in Alabama, it is difficult to imagine this conversation taking place apart from the Internet.

Drawn in by the discussion, Avaloketishvara, who writes that she has "practised wicca about 1 yr.," responded to Sparx that a "few yrs back had terrible stress and wasnt following any faith went to help my stress through meditation at buddhist group Tara deity found me I felt her so inspiring and was drawn to her beauty. now she is my goddess for my wiccan practise." This generated a number of posts from a list member who was confused by Avaloketishvara's appropriation of a Buddhist deity and her claim to be a practicing Wiccan. The exchange is worth quoting at length for the dynamics of open source religion it reveals.

> Craftyjack: Please tell me how Buddhist meditation helped you find the Goddess Tara. Is Tara another name for our Mother Earth? Or a wiccan goddess you feel close too?
> Avaloketishvara: when I went to meditate I knew nothing about tara she is a buddhist deity I now see her as my goddess just lovely easy image to visualise as im poor visualising.

Craftyjack: I'm more confused now. Did you see an actual picture of her or as in a vision? As you accept her as your deity, why say your wiccan and not buddha?

Craftyjack [less than 10 minutes later]: I meant no offence to your deity Tara! But she is not wiccan. If you feel drawn to her then you should learn her ways . . .

Avaloketishvara: im wiccan as I've been thinking that way for yrs without realising it and it makes me stronger person id dreamt of tara B4 I went to buddhist group then saw her statue and photo.

Put on the defensive a bit by Craftyjack's questions, Avaloketishvara invoked the personal gnosis that lies at the heart of the open source tradition of modern Paganism:

Avaloketishvara: frm what I've learnt so far frm websites books ect u go with what ur drawn to for the goddess so whats wrong with tara if I feel I've been lead to her her beleif system is the same as most dieties like giving caring to others with love etc.

Innovation is as much a part of this particular culture as appropriation. As I noted in Chapter 1, in their *Cyber Spellbook*, Knight and Telesco (2002) have decontextualized a wide range of gods and goddesses, and pressed them into service as patron(ness) deities of what they call "Web witching." Thus, Bast, daughter of Ra and the cat-headed Egyptian goddess of the hearth, is the "protectress of your home and car music systems" (Knight and Telesco 2002: 54); Inanna, the "Sumerian Mother Goddess who brought civilization to humankind," is the patroness of "mining, homes built underground, basements, and underground parking lots" (Knight and Telesco 2002: 66); and Ogma, the Irish hero called variously the son of "Elatha the king of Ireland" (Matthews and Matthews 1994: 49) and the son of Brigit (MacCulloch [1911] 1991: 75), but remembered most for his invention of the Celtic ogham script, is best called upon "when you are downloading fonts, e-books, and current events from the Internet" (Knight and Telesco 2002: 72). While this kind of innovation may appear wildly speculative and inappropriate (cf. Aldred 2000; Pike 2001), a blatant example of the decontextualized "cultural strip mining" with which both the larger New Age and modern Pagan religious cultures have been charged, three important aspects need to be considered.

First, there is no "pure" religion. The issues related to cultural appropriation, syncretism, and recontextualization within religious traditions are hardly limited to the modern Pagan context, and the dynamics that inform them are often far more subtle and complex than either their detractors or supporters are willing to admit. Second, in the open source culture of appropriation and innovation within modern Paganism, Knight and Telesco are merely the far end of a continuum that stretches from those modern Pagans who seek to reinvigorate historically accurate pre-Christian religious traditions, to those who attempt syncretisms that are theologically coherent and culturally respectful, to those who feel free simply to invent pantheons, deity correspondences, and ritual practices with no regard for the original context at all. Because creativity is a positive value in open source traditions—indeed, one observer remarked that she was "accepted" as a witch simply by virtue of her creativity (Orion 1995; though, see Cowan 1998)—few at either end of the continuum feel comfortable entirely excluding the other. Third, in the context of modern Pagan epistemology, however frivolous some of their correspondences might appear at first blush, Knight and Telesco at least have a rationale by which their modification and deployment of these recontextualized deities is justified. "This sounds a little silly," they write (Knight and Telesco 2002: 48), "but given some serious thought, there's no reason why we cannot create new mythologies based on the world as it is today and the techno-tools in it." And, silly though it may sound, this raises the very important question of where myths and mythologies actually come from and how they gain power within particular social groups. In his reconceptualization of the problem, Bruce Lincoln categorizes "myth" as "that small class of stories that possess both credibility and *authority*" (1989: 24, emphasis in the original). That is, myths have both a truth value and a motivational value. But neither is universal, indeed neither holds outside the culture within which the myths are embedded and by which their efficacy is granted. As Gary L. Ebersole points out in his discussion of the social function of myth, myths, mythologies, and mythistories are not "timeless and static structures but dynamic agents in the ongoing process of the creation and maintenance of a symbolic world of meaning" (1989: 6). Put simply, just because something sounds "silly" to nonadherents does not diminish its capacity for meaning-making among adherents.

Knight and Telesco, for example, continue: "Over time, 'thought forms' begin to have viable power as long as that form receives proper honors in your life. Thought equals energy. So if you choose to venerate Snap (the God of microwaved foods), Click (the computer mouse Goddess), Popup (the Goddess of toasters and toaster ovens), Ram and Rom (the computer twin Gods), Bit and Byte (the computer twin Goddesses), or Wireless (the spirit of cell phones), go for it! Just remember that such interactions won't be quite the same as traditional deities because they're younger and still gaining power" (2002: 48; cf. Ashcroft-Nowicki and Brennan 2001; Cabot and Cowan 1989; Farrar and Farrar 1984). Here, they also illustrate the tension between two distinct innovative subcultures within modern Paganism, what I have called the research-oriented and the fantasy-oriented. Research-oriented subcultures regard some measure of historical accuracy in both Pagan belief and practice (insofar as these may be determined) as central to the reconceptual or reconstructive religious enterprise; historical accuracy in fantasy-oriented subcultures, on the other hand, is less important and, as Knight and Telesco amply demonstrate, for these the potential canon of belief and practice is expanded considerably. The clearest example of research-oriented subcultures within modern Paganism are the reconstructionist traditions which will be discussed more fully below as part of the tension between eclecticism and traditionalism. Fantasy-oriented subcultures, on the other hand, find exemplars in such modern Pagan groups as the Church of All Worlds, many of whose beliefs and practices (and, indeed, the CAW's name itself) quite self-consciously originated in Robert A. Heinlein's science fiction classic, *Stranger in a Strange Land* (1961; cf. Iacchus 2001). The Church of All Worlds (2001) regards itself as "the first religion to draw as much of its inspiration from the future as from the past, embracing science fiction as mythology with the same enthusiasm as we embrace the classical myths of ancient times." It is, however, hardly the only one. Several prominent works of fantasy have inspired modern Pagans, including J. R. R. Tolkien's *Lord of the Rings*, Marion Zimmer Bradley's *The Mists of Avalon*, the Cthulhu mythos of H. P. Lovecraft, and the *Dragonriders of Pern* series by Anne McCaffrey. This culture of appropriation and innovation would be impossible were it not for an underpinning belief in the primacy of personal gnosticism that lies at the epistemological heart of modern Pagan belief and practice.

## A Culture of Eclecticism and Traditionalism

This is not to say, however, that modern Pagan acceptance of a personal gnosticism is all-encompassing, which is at least implied by Craftyjack's response to Avaloketishvara above. Indeed, a good deal of the tension within the larger open source culture of modern Paganism is between personal gnosticism and an incipient orthodoxy that seeks to establish boundaries between acceptable and unacceptable expressions of modern Paganism. This tension exemplifies the modern Pagan *culture of eclecticism and traditionalism*. If eclecticism recognizes at least theoretically the potential for an all-encompassing appropriation of spiritual and religious resources, traditionalism seeks to impose limits on which of those resources are appropriate for modern Pagans and the manner in which those appropriations are integrated into the tradition. The presence of the Buddhist Tara as a Wiccan deity indicates this tension, but it is seen much more clearly in the cultural conversation generated by the concept of the "Christo-Wiccan."

Despite the inclusion of Mary in a number of modern Pagan pantheons, and a concomitant reinterpretation of her as the Christian version of the Mother Goddess (see, for example, Walker 1983: 602–613), Christianity is the most common tradition rejected by modern Pagans as a candidate for open source appropriation. Whether it is a mythistory of the so-called Burning Times, for which many modern Pagans still quote Matilda Gage's fictional figure of nine million women killed at the hands of the Christian Church ([1893] 1980; cf. Starhawk 1989: 22), a residual (and often not unreasonable) anger at the religious tradition many modern Pagans have left behind, or simply a form of cultural resistance against the dominant religious tradition in the West, many modern Pagans see any attempt to include Christian figures in Pagan pantheons as problematic at best and an outright betrayal of Paganism at worst.

Anne Newkirk Niven edits or publishes a number of popular modern Pagan magazines, including *SageWoman*, *PanGaia*, and *newWitch*. In a 1996 *SageWoman* editorial, she disclosed to her readers that in the midst of some personal life difficulties, "I reached out to an old friend and found a voice and a hand that helped me back to sanity and peace of mind" (Niven 1996: 4). That old friend was Jesus. Though concerned about possible reactions to this, Niven assured her readers that "the Goddess is here with me, as She has been since I was a little girl." One wonders, though, if she was prepared for the emotional and in some cases vitriolic responses her disclosure provoked. One reader, for example, not inappropriately named Autumn Storm (1996), wrote: "I find your little bombshell about reaching out to jesus to be an outrage, a betrayal and a vicious joke. How dare you?! . . . I can think of nothing more tastelessly bizarre or despicably inappropriate than tossing out your reconciliation with christianity to readers who have supported this MATRIFOCAL, PAGAN, GODDESS magazine for ten years!!" Another reader wrote that "I am a Pagan because the story, the worldview, and the teachings of Christianity are incorrect; they are wrong . . . Christianity is destroying this world, and to actively choose to aid and abet this ruin (as you did) rather than to oppose it, is to walk a path of pain and sickness" (Sarah 1997: 86). Still others called for Niven to step down as *SageWoman*'s editor, suggesting that "your choice to do an extremely Christian, patriarchal church type of thing by declaring you have 'accepted Him into your life' and chosen to bear Christian witness to your Pagan sisters in a Pagan format is, in my opinion, outrageous" (Jeanne 1997). Though nowhere in her column does Niven actually do either of the things Jeanne accuses her of, the volatility of the issue for the modern Pagan community is clear. Similar responses appeared over the course of subsequent issues.

A year later, though, Niven (1997: 80) recapped the controversy, indicating that only 10 percent of the letters she received contained this kind of harsh criticism; 70 percent were from readers she placed in "the 'pro-toleration' group," —that is, those for whom the authority of personal gnosis overrides whatever antipathy they may feel towards the particulars of individual religious construction—and 20 percent were from readers "who were already holding these two traditions together [in] their hearts." The range of replies that Niven chose to print in this issue illustrates nicely a number of the vectors along which tensions within a culture of eclecticism and traditionalism proceed. Responding to a reader named Sarah (1997), for example, who has "always made a point of distancing myself and the Goddess from the New Age movement" (much of which she regards as simply "nonsense"), Christie (1997) wondered whether self-admitted New Agers were as unwelcome in the modern Pagan community as Christo-Wiccans. Some readers called for Niven's resignation, but another was frightened by the anger in Autumn Storm's original response (Judy 1997). Finally, one reader argued, somewhat paradoxically in the light of the innovative culture of modern Paganism, that because "historians are still arguing over whether Jesus was an actual historical figure," any debate about his place in a modern Pagan's pantheon is premature at best and moot at worst (Kathi 1997). Adverting to the modern Pagan bedrock of personal gnosis, however, she continued that "if you truly believe in something and make it your Power greater than you are, and believe it can see you through the rough and shadowy places in your life, then it doesn't matter what that thing is." As so often happens in appeals to personal gnosis, the logical extension of these beliefs is either ignored by or lost entirely on adherents. That is, arguing about the historicity of Jesus as a function of whether he can be legitimately included in a modern Pagan pantheon seems a bit strained given the manner in which other deity figures have been appropriated and recontextualized.

The Internet has greatly expanded the opportunity for this particular discussion to take place, and it occurs in a number of different forums. In contrast to the *SageWoman* debate, which took place over a relatively long period of time and whose elements were selected for presentation by Niven, online interaction, although not necessarily in real time, conforms more closely to the immediacy of conversation. Questions, comments, and philippics often generate multiple responses within hours, sometimes even minutes. One lengthy discussion about the place of "Christo-Wiccans" in the modern Pagan community took place on Mystic Wicks, which bills itself as an "Online Pagan Community and Pagan Forum" (www.mysticwicks.com). Again, these various discussion threads illustrate both the tensions that emerge in open source religions as a result of the conflict between eclecticism and traditionalism, and the value of the Internet as a venue for these tensions to surface. "One can surely not be a pagan and a christian," writes Reeny. "The basic beliefs of paganism are quite different from the christian belief system." Here, Reeny uncovers a derivative tension within this particular culture: traditionalism is privileged when modern Pagans want to exclude religious beliefs such as Christianity from legitimate participation in the open source values of modern Paganism, while eclecticism is privileged when religious beliefs are considered viable candidates for open source appropriation. That is, while Tara can be reinterpreted in a Wiccan context, Jesus cannot. Because of the antinomian reinterpretation that informs so much modern Paganism, though, that there are vast differences between many (arguably most) religious traditions brought together under the banner of open source eclecticism is an issue examined considerably less closely by many modern Pagans. Responding to Reeny (and other similar posts), Lilu, a frequent contributor to Mystic Wicks discussions, wrote that "I have several patron gods and goddesses, one of which is Hindu (Ganesh) one Chinese (Quan Yin) one Celtic (Brigit) and the fourth is Jesus, in his true self, not necessarily the way the Church sees him (son of God, Saviour, etc.)." Sylph concurred, indeed epitomized the open source nature of modern Paganism: "one of the very attractive things about Wicca . . . is because it blends very, very well with other belief systems." A bit of a *post hoc* problem for modern Paganism, I think it could be more accurately stated that Wicca (accepting Sylph's terminology for the moment, and many Wiccans would not) does not blend well with other traditions because of anything inherent in Wicca, but because those who have chosen to call themselves Wiccans (or witches) have blended traditions in an open source, antinomian fashion. Finally, though he recognizes the right of modern Pagans to choose their own paths, Eaglewolf, another frequent participant, also challenges the notion that one can be both Christian and Wiccan. In doing so, however, he also criticizes the open source character of much that passes for modern Paganism. "Religions," he writes, "including Wicca, are based on disciplined ideals, regardless of what you may have read in one of those books written for financial gain. The 'make it up as you go along' attitude taken towards Wicca is ignorant at best."

Not only do these examples highlight tensions inherent in the open source culture of eclecticism and traditionalism, but they also point to a more important issue that is obscured somewhat by modern Paganism's frequent adversion to the authority of personal gnosis and the putative egalitarianism of the modern Pagan path. That is, a hierarchy of voices is present in the discussion; these cultural conversations take place within the framework of disparate power relationships; and, however much modern Pagans may militate against it, authority (whether established or emergent) plays a crucial role in the dialectic of open source religious evolution.

In his discussion of how authority is constituted and mediated in different social situations, Bruce Lincoln provides a useful working definition of authority, one that describes the dynamics we find in these cultural tensions very well. For Lincoln (1994: 4), authority "is best understood in relational terms as the effect of a posited, perceived, or institutionally ascribed asymmetry between speaker and audience that permits certain speakers to command not just the attention but the confidence, respect, and trust of their audience, or—an important proviso—to make audiences act *as if* this were so." Institutionally, of course, authority within modern Pagan communities often rests with ritual leaders and teachers—high priestesses and priests, acknowledged adepts, and, as we have seen, those who manage to see their opinions into commercial print and whose views are credenced by their audience. In terms of Lincoln's proviso, for example, whatever actual authority writers such as Knight and Telesco bring to their work, at least part of their readership *acts* as though they are authoritative voices in the modern Pagan community. In terms of online discourse, while the lines of authority may be less distinct, they are no less evident, a discussion to which we will return at several points, not least in Chapter 6.

If we understand authority in Lincoln's terms of asymmetrical relationships, the foundation of the initial asymmetry is laid when modern Pagan seekers such as Sparx or Avaloketishvara ask for advice or direction, and other discussion participants—who may have been practicing Pagans for no more time than those seeking guidance—provide answers and thereby assume the authoritative position in the asymmetry. Despite the often utopian rhetoric about the allegedly egalitarian nature of Internet discourse, several scholars have pointed out the very clear mechanisms by which authority and control are established in such venues as chat rooms, discussion lists, and e-mail groups (cf. Baker 2001; Paolillo 1999; Rheingold 1993; Slevin 2000; Smith, McLaughlin, and Osborne 1997). On the modern Pagan Internet, however, although these dynamics are no less present, they are always in tension with the individualism and antinomianism that characterizes the open source religion.

### A Culture of Solitude and Community

Finally, for a number of reasons already described, the modern Pagan community off-line exists in a basic tension between those who practice often very eclectic brands of Paganism as solitaries (cf. Cunningham 1988, 1993; Green 1991; RavenWolf 2003) and those who choose to work in more organized communal contexts such as covens, groves, nests, and ritual circles (cf. Adler 1986; Berger 1999; Berger, Leach, and Shaffer 2003; Farrar 1991; Greenwood 2000; Greer 1998; Luhrmann 1989; Salomonsen 2002). Because I discuss the online character of the coven or ritual working group in more detail in Chapter 4, I will limit this brief consideration to modern Pagans who either by choice or by circumstance work their magick in solitude. Although the growing acceptance of modern Paganism may lead more and more people to seek out ritual working groups—the "Wicca 101" classes I took, for example, were offered through our local Communiversity—the open source character of modern Paganism, especially in its more eclectic, antinomian forms, almost ensures that many will continue to work alone. A number of solitaries online report that this choice is motivated at least in part by the dominance of conservative Christianity in the areas where they live and their concomitant fear of "coming out of the broom closet." According to Berger, Leach, and Shaffer (2003: 120), however, although many solitaries report that they live in some manner of geographic isolation—

a rural community, small town, or farmstead—most modern Pagans who responded to their survey, *including* solitaries, continue to "live in urban or suburban communities." More importantly, they claim that modern Pagans who choose to work in covens or ritual groups appear to have more formal education than solitaries, though their survey data do not indicate significant or remarkable differences between categories, and in some cases (e.g., having a high school diploma) the numbers dispute their own interpretation. They attempt to explain what differences there are, however, in terms of the ages of their survey respondents, suggesting that those who work as solitaries are younger and "most likely not to have completed their education" (Berger, Leach, and Shaffer 2003: 120). Two of the questions begged here, of course, which are not addressed by Berger, Leach, and Shaffer, are whether and to what degree solitaries who "complete" their education move into more communal modern Pagan environments. They acknowledge that solitary practice serves for many as an entrée into modern Paganism, but conclude rather obviously that some "will ultimately join a group, some will remain solitaries" (Berger, Leach, and Shaffer 2003: 120).

I point out this particular example to highlight one of the very difficult research problems presented by the different cultures of modern Paganism: its open source character, which includes all of the cultural tensions discussed in this chapter, makes for a very messy religious cartography, one that becomes only more complex as it moves onto the World Wide Web. Indeed, as a number of solitaries point out in online discussion, choosing to work as a solitary in no way means that one has not been either trained or initiated in more traditional lineages. Although the open source nature of modern Paganism invites all manner of typological and statistical reduction by scholars and other observers (for example, the theological reductionism found in religious countermovements such as the evangelical Christian countercult; cf. Cowan 2003a, 2004), it ultimately frustrates attempts at static categorization and easy explanation.

All this is not to say, of course, that those who are solitaries now neither want nor require social interaction, and the Internet has provided a venue for these individuals to participate in a form of community that was unimaginable little more than a decade ago. As I write this, for example, the Yahoo! portal lists more than 100 discussion groups for solitary Pagans from a wide variety of traditions. Solitary Witches 13 (groups.yahoo.com/group/SolitaryWitches13), for example, has nearly 200 members and welcomes participants from "all traditions including Faery, Green Witch, Heathen, Asatru, Druid, Celtic, Alexandrian, Garderian [sic], Cabot, Egyptian, Eclectic"; since this is a discussion group designated exclusively for solitaries, however, those who work in covens are not welcome. Solitary Druid Spiritual, on the other hand, (group.yahoo.com/group/SolitaryDruidSpiritual), caters to a much narrower group of modern Pagans, but still numbers nearly 150 members from countries including the United States, Canada, the Netherlands, South Africa, England, and Chile. The largest of the Yahoo! groups of this type that I encountered, Solitary (groups.yahoo.com/group/solitary) has over 1,400 members, with every state in the Union and over 30 other countries represented among those participants who disclosed a location, and more than 45,000 posts in 6 years. While for whatever reasons solitaries choose to work alone, they appear no less gregarious than other modern Pagans, and discussions on forums for solitaries orbit around fairly predictable topics: Pagan resources, qualitative differences between working as a solitary versus a covener, information for beginners on the modern Pagan path, requests for magickal workings in times of trouble and blessings in times of celebration, as well as the more general conversation by which group boundaries are established and tested, and through which in-group ties emerge and strengthen. In terms of the modern Pagan solitary, the importance of this general conversation on the Internet cannot be overstated; it is one example of the "specialized relationships" that some scholars believe are well supported by the relatively "weak ties" established through Internet communications (Wellman and Gulia 1999: 175).

Consider as an example the Solitary Witches 13 forum (groups.yahoo.com/group/SolitaryWitches13). Though it had been in existence since March 2001, Solitary Witches 13 posted only occasional messages for more than a year, with three months showing no message traffic at all. In September 2002, however, traffic jumped considerably and the list has maintained a message volume averaging more than 200 posts per month ever since. The reason for this seems clear. Prior to September 2002, the list was called RI Wiccans 13, and was mainly concerned with modern Pagans in the Rhode Island area. When the list owner dropped the Rhode Island designation and began to include solitaries from other areas, including participants from another solitary discussion group that was closing, membership grew dramatically. As new participants began to greet each other on the list, a number realized they were already acquainted from participation in other solitary discussion forums. In fact, one member characterized the increased traffic as "old home week" for solitaries. Further, when some of the new members posted personal introductions to the list, a number of these were met with requests to get together off-line if members found they were within reasonable geographic proximity. They did not want to meet to form ritual working groups or covens, but to continue the camaraderie and conversations that had begun online. This supports research in other Internet contexts that suggests one of the important functions of online activity is as an entrée and an adjunct to off-line relationships (cf. Birnie and Horvath 2002; Kraut et al. 1998, 2002). That is, in terms of relationship building and maintenance, the World Wide Web provides a different *venue* for conversation, not a different *type* of conversation.

It is obvious, however, that participation in Internet forums also allows for conversations that would never have taken place otherwise. As in the example of Aradia and Sparx above, though few solitaries actually say how important online conversation is to them in terms of their religious practice and, in many cases, their identities as modern Pagans, the World Wide Web is the only venue in which these individuals are likely ever to meet. In this regard, two aspects of this culture of solitude and community are particularly important in terms of the Internet. First is the simple fact of communication that was not possible even a decade ago. As Lorne Dawson and I have noted elsewhere (2004), the speed with which the Internet has penetrated the technologized societies of the world and the readiness with which it has been accepted by those societies often masks the sea change in communications it represents. For those who use them, Internet communications are now so much a part of daily life that we often forget how recent an innovation they are, and take for granted our ability to communicate with people we would not have known existed even a few short years ago. Put in terms of the modern Pagan culture of solitude and community, even if the only thing most solitaries do on the Internet is exchange e-mail on discussion forums, this by now mundane activity brings them into contact with people they would not have met under any other circumstances.

Second, it is clear just from the discussion forums on Yahoo! and MSN—not to mention other portals such as Delphi, discussion board providers like EZBoard, or the myriad of alt.-discussion groups—that while modern Pagan solitaries may prefer to work alone, it is equally important that they know they are not alone in their working. If, as I noted at the beginning of this chapter, agreement among participants is one of the hallmarks of social organization, then validation of the beliefs and behaviors that constitute particular cultures within that social organization is an important function of that agreement—one that is served particularly well in modern Paganism through the Internet. A frequent question, for example, on both solitary lists and discussion lists aimed at ritual working groups concerns coming out of the broom closet—public or family disclosure as a modern Pagan. In a coven setting, obviously, the individual has the support of the group, however well or poorly that support is meted out. Solitaries, by definition, do not. Any support they get for what is, in many cases, a very traumatic process must come from elsewhere. For solitaries online, this support often comes from those with whom one shares some measure of online community. On the Solitary forum alone, for instance (groups.yahoo.com/group/solitary), dozens of discussion threads containing hundreds of posts respond to this issue.

This kind of encouragement, which in many cases would not occur apart from the World Wide Web, also supports, maintains, and reciprocally reinforces the personally gnostic, open source framework of modern Paganism. Ultimately, though, whether the issue is the appropriateness of a pantheon, the proper way to conduct a particular ritual, or the problem of coming out of the broom closet, each person bears the responsibility for identifying, defining, and following his or her own modern Pagan path. This is the Pandora Problem of the open source religion, and it affects all aspects of modern Paganism, from belief to ritual, and from working group organization and development to problem-solving and dispute resolution.

## The Pandora Problem of Open Source Religion

Put simply, the Pandora problem of modern Paganism as an open source religion is that if personal gnosis is the ultimate guarantor of religious authenticity and creative eclecticism one of the hallmarks of modern Pagan religious conviction, then (1) subjective experience at the individual level has been raised to the status of personal ontology and (2), as a result of this, emergent tensions between modern Pagan dreams, desires, and what we might call "the historical facts of the case" cannot but continue. First, as Agehananda Bharati has noted so trenchantly, "conviction is no proof of anything; it is merely an indication of the emotional intensity of the person who feels convinced" (1961: 79). In this, he speaks directly to one aspect of this Pandora problem: the conviction of modern Pagans such as Erin (and many of the others cited in this chapter) that "what feels right" must be right. "'Inner certainty'," he continued elsewhere in *The Ochre Robe* (1961: 108), "is, of course, a very edifying possession but it has nothing whatever to do with fact. All religions and all ideologies suffer from the same prejudice." Recall, for example, Sarah (1997: 85), who wrote to *SageWoman* that "the teachings of Christianity are incorrect; they are wrong," and concluded her letter with an appeal to inner certainty on behalf of modern Paganism. "Real healing and real peace," she writes (1997: 86), "come from the Goddess within, from reconnecting with all life, and realizing your place is 'next-to,' not 'above' others." Certainly no less dogmatic a position than that which she rejects.

Similarly, the eclectic Wiccan appropriation and recontextualization of such culturally and historically specific deity figures as Tara, Inanna, and Dainichi-Nyorai illustrate the problematic tension between what modern Pagans such as Avaloketishvara and Patricia Telesco may want these figures to be, and what the facts of their origin and development suggest that they are. In this regard, the "facts of the case" are important for a number of reasons. First, there is the respect that ought to be due them simply as the facts of history, many of which are often either selectively or completely at odds with modern Pagan interpretations. Telesco and Tarotlaydee's reinterpretation of Inanna, for example, which reduces the Sumerian *prima mater* to little more than a patron goddess of parking lots and crawlspaces, pointedly ignores the more violent aspects of Inanna's mythistory (cf. Thomas 2004). Despite the fact that information on them is limited to the Bible and such extra-Biblical texts as the Nag Hammadi library, explicitly Christian figures such as Mary Magdalene and the Virgin

Mary are regularly reinterpreted by many modern Pagans as crypto-goddess figures ripe for appropriation and use in one's own personal pantheon. Second, there is the respect offered these mythistories by traditionalist Pagans who do not want to participate in a pantheogenic free-for-all. These are the modern Pagans for whom history matters, as it were. Although they would not deny innovators their personally gnostic right to reinterpret and reinvent, they recognize at least implicitly the problems inherent in many such innovations. Modern followers of northern European Paganism, for example, might find Silver RavenWolf's *Teen Witch* characterization of the Norse Frost Giants as *"always* willing to help you" just a wee bit problematic (1998: 211; see Young 1971). That is, the Frost Giants were the enemies of the Norse gods and one of the functions attributed to Bifrost, the rainbow bridge connecting Asgard (the home of the gods) and Midgard (the world of humankind), was to prevent their return to the heavens.

Finally, as many modern Pagans appear to recognize, simply ignoring the facts of history and "making it up as one goes along" often hinders their ability to be taken seriously in late modern society. This is not to say that the mythistories of a culturally dominant religion such as Christianity are necessarily less fanciful than those created by any number of modern Paganisms or other new religious movements. Instead, the fact of Christianity's cultural dominance means that those religious traditions that challenge it with new or different mythistories have to work that much harder to overcome cultural prejudice and marginalization. As a number of the examples cited here indicate, though, the Pandora problem for modern Paganism both online and off-line is that once the lid is removed and the open source jar is open, it appears quite impossible to close.

The open source movement in computing has been a technical success because the potential benefits of each new innovation were submitted to the computing community for peer review and testing. In this environment, the relative usefulness of modifications to a piece of software becomes apparent rather quickly. No such peer review exists within the open source framework of modern Paganism, and this is the point at which the analogy loses some of its analytic utility. The essentially nonfalsifiable nature of religious belief in general, the personally gnostic character of modern Pagan spiritual practice in particular, and the underpinning principle of inner conviction articulated by adherents such as Erin (in the epigraph at the beginning of the chapter) generate considerably different standards of evidence. Thus, we return to the basic premise that religion exists as a function of social agreement, and the nature of that agreement depends entirely on the social group under consideration. For many modern Pagans, the Internet has become an important locus for this process of agreement and for the evolution of their religious beliefs and culture.

CHAPTER 3

# The Mists of Cyberhenge
## *Mapping the Modern Pagan Internet*

> The net of Indra works its real magic by dissolving our habitual tenden-
> cies to divide the world into separate and autonomous zones: inside and
> out, self and other, online and off-, machine and nature.
>
> Erik Davis (1998: 322)

### The Internet: Is It Really Virtual or Is It Merely Online?

Most important in Erik Davis's comment on what we might call the nondual-
izing effect of "the net of Indra," by which he means "the punning leap" between
the infinitely interconnected nature of reality according to the Flower Garland
(Hua-yen) School of Chinese Buddhism and the seemingly infinite number of
interconnections possible on the World Wide Web, is the slip into hyperbole
about the degree to which the separation between human consciousness and
machine language is being dissolved in the information age. Setting aside for a
moment the digital divide by which the world is increasingly and unequally
separated into information "haves" and "have-nots" (Castells 2001; Lenhart
2003; Loader 1998; Mossberger, Tolbert, and Stansbury 2003; Norris 2001;
Wresch 1996), even in the world of those with Internet access, in most respects
what is commonly (and I will argue inaccurately) called "virtual reality" is at
best a cyber-shadow, an electronic reflection of real life. Shopping online may
offer consumers more convenience, for example, but presents them with little
more than catalogues accessed electronically. Personal banking online is more
interactive, perhaps, with more options for managing household finances, but
it offers little that is not available at one's local branch. Even simply browsing

the Web reveals the inescapable connection between off-line interests and on-line searches for information. And, for all this, the Pew Internet & American Life Project (2003) still reports that by far the most common use of the Internet is simply sending and receiving e-mail. Online role-playing games, on the other hand, which in their MMORPG (massive multiplayer online role-playing games) variant present arguably the closest popularly available electronic versions of "virtuality," account for a very small percentage of daily Internet usage, and even these stretch the usefulness of the "virtual reality" concept. While I have certainly been guilty of this in past writings (e.g., Cowan and Hadden 2004b; Hadden and Cowan 2000a), in most instances to speak of virtuality and popular Internet usage both overstates the case for activity that occurs in computer-mediated environments such as the World Wide Web and blurs important technological distinctions between activity that does take place in "virtual reality" versus that which simply comes and goes online. Cinematically posed, this is the difference between Andy and Larry Wachowski's *The Matrix* (1999) and Irwin Winkler's *The Net* (1995).

In *The Matrix* we encounter *virtual reality*—human activity taking place in an illusionary world generated as a function of cosmogonic computer software. Though virtual in essence, it appears entirely real to most of the film's participants because the Matrix program fulfills all the requirements of embodied sensation: direction, time, and dimensionality; the experiences of touch, smell, hearing, sight, and taste; action, reaction, immediacy, and consequence. By convincing participants technologically that they are wholly experiencing particular embodied sensations, virtual reality misleads them into thinking those sensations occur apart from their computer generation (cf. Heim 1993; Negroponte 1995; Schroeder 1996). As Michael Heim points out (1993: 160), the *sine qua non* of virtual reality lies in "convincing the participant that he or she is actually in another place, by substituting the normal sensory input received by the participant with information produced by a computer." When consumers purchase books through Amazon.com, few if any believe they are in an actual bookstore. Paying bills online may be considerably more convenient than going to one's local bank branch, but hardly simulates the experience of waiting in line for a teller or an ATM.

*The Net*, on the other hand, is an example of *online reality*. Though it has obvious real world consequences for the main characters in the story, online reality is encountered on the two-dimensional computer screen, and almost entirely as a world of text, icon, and image. Whereas computer-mediated experience in the Matrix is virtually embodied, but coded according to the conventional precepts of physical sensation, experience on the Net is represented either textually, iconographically, or pictorially, and often requires the use of social codes unique to the online environment in order to fill out the communication process. Acronyms such as TTYL ("Talk to you later"), LOL

("Laughing out loud"), and ROFL ("Rolling on the floor laughing") facilitate faster communication exchanges, while the growing list of emoticons ("smiley faces") seek to bridge the interpretive gap between communication sender and receiver. Both provide some of the often unspoken aspects of communication required for meaningful social interaction, a particular aspect of e-space that has been recognized by researchers for some years (see, for example, Aycock 1996; Danet, Ruedenberg-Wright, and Rosenbaum-Tamari 1997; Donath 1999; Donath, Karahalios, and Viégas 1999; Herring 1999; Turoff et al. 1999).

Directly or indirectly, experience online engages only three of the senses (touch, hearing, and sight) and renders any more complete embodiment of on-line interaction either to the realm of imagination or to real life intervention. In modern Pagan rituals mediated online, for example, these translate into such instructions as "Think of a cool forest glade," "Light a candle now," or "Burn some incense next to your computer altar." In terms of the online real-ity, the presence of a familiar off-line referent is both crucial and ubiquitous. Among other things, it provides an obvious point of reference for visualiza-tions that are central to many modern Pagan ritual practices, and it connects participants to the very basic conceptualization of modern Paganism as a na-ture religion. Given the opportunity to gather for ritual in a cool forest glade, I wonder how many modern Pagans would choose instead the considerably less complete experience mediated by computer screen and keyboard? Contrary to Davis, though, and recognizing that he is overstating the point for the sake of emphasis, I suspect that most modern Pagans *can* tell the difference between nature (a cool forest glade) and machine (a .jpeg picture of that same glade on a 17-inch monitor), and that for them this difference is crucial.

Why, though, is this conceptual distinction between virtual reality and on-line activity important here? The vast majority of Internet users lack access to sophisticated VR hardware and software, so why worry if enthusiasts and in-dustry supporters contend that online activity is virtual reality? First, there is the issue of simple accuracy. Online activity is *not* the same as that which is me-diated by VR technology, and the two should not be confused. Second, and more important, it makes sense to distinguish between virtual reality and on-line interaction because of the very broad, often hyperbolic claims that are reg-ularly made for the Internet by commercial interests and academic observers alike. If industry and enthusiast rhetoric surrounding virtuality is not parsed— and, in essence, demythologized—then important aspects of how computer technology is marketed, how the often hyperbolic claims made for this tech-nology affect its societal penetration and acceptance, and how both the tech-nology and the rhetoric impact the cultures in which they are embedded are left unexamined. As I noted earlier, for example, Brenda Brasher contends "that online religion is crucial to and positive for the future of religion. It is a vital cultural vehicle necessary for the emergence of religious experience and expression relevant to a future society" (2001: 11). In a similar vein, she continues: "As the latest site of cultural challenge and change, online religions (traditional and new) represent a stabilizing influence in the virtual domain" (Brasher 2001: 13), and that "online religion triggers notable changes in religious experience that cannot help but transform the character of religion itself" (Brasher 2001: 13). Finally, she asserts that "online religion is the most portentous development for the future of religion to come out of the twentieth century" (Brasher 2001: 17), and that it "could become the dominant form of religion and religious experience in the next century" (Brasher 2001: 19).

In terms of parsing the relationship between virtual reality and online activity, the problem here is twofold. First, Brasher presents very little evidence that anything even remotely approaching the mildest of her predictions is taking place. Second, because her techno-utopian language so strongly resonates with and reinforces industry rhetoric by which consumers in the "information-have" societies are pummeled on a daily basis, it masks the more difficult task of social scientific research into the actual effects of the Internet and the World Wide Web on religious belief, doctrine, ritual, and practice. Put differently, Russell McCutcheon's (2001) important distinction between the academic as a cheerleader for religious activity and the scholar as a critic of religion as a social phenomenon is all but entirely lost in Brasher's narrative. In order to get some idea of how modern Pagans are actually using the Internet and the World Wide Web to inform their religious practice, and how that usage is modifying the character of modern Paganism, it is important to deflate at least some of the exaggeration surrounding these new technologies. This distinction is important, for example, in our analysis of how online interaction has affected the nature of the modern Pagan coven, the basic unit of Wiccan social organization, and whether in the light of its online expression the notion of a "coven" has lost some of its off-line meaning. Hyperbole and techno-utopian rhetoric aside, what is the character of community online—is it reality, or is it, too, only the illusion of reality?

## Online Community: Reality or the Illusion of Reality?

"I am Astarte Earthwise," writes the owner of Earthwise BOS (i.e., Book of Shadows; groups.yahoo.com/EarthwiseBOS), a Yahoo! group with more than 900 registered members, "and I offer you a warm welcome to our online community." While she asserts somewhat enigmatically that "this community reflects who we are," she concludes her introduction: "THIS IS NOT A DISCUSSION LIST. This list is instead for learning and information exchange only." I suspect what she means here is that she does not want her list to degenerate into the sort of idle chatter that fills up so many online discussion forums and chat rooms. Like other online groups we have encountered to this point, Earthwise BOS considers itself a site for serious modern Pagan discussions, not an online meeting place for dabblers and dilettantes. But is this really a "community," as she suggests?

Similarly, since March 2000, the Bella Luna Cyber Coven has also operated as a discussion group through Yahoo! (groups.yahoo.com/bellalunacybercoven), and, at the time of writing, with 104 registered members, was posting an average of just under 60 messages per month. However, in the member profiles, the vast majority disclose very little personal information. Of those who listed any information at all, 19 members were male, 54 female, the remainder unknown. That is, more than one-quarter of those who have joined Bella Luna —and whose memberships were active at the time of writing—chose not to share with the group even so much as their gender. Even Bella Luna herself, the list owner, discloses very little personal information online. While this may be interpreted as a disincentive for others to disclose, it raises the more important question of whether describing this as a "community" is any more appropriate for the Bella Luna Cyber Coven than for Earthwise BOS. If one aspect of community-building is reciprocal self-disclosure, and trust in the face of the risk such disclosure entails, then what does it say about a community where so few disclose anything and most of the names by which members do go are made up? While Robin ManyWaters, one of the owners of the Prarie Hearth Virtual Coven (http://prarie_hearth. tripod.com), acknowledges on her introductory page that "it is not possible to create an actual coven environment over the Internet"—a claim with which Lisa McSherry, at least, would disagree—she also claims that "we are here to be a source of information and support to the wiccan or other magickal individual." If Prarie Hearth is not a coven, what then is it? Does it constitute some *new* form of modern Pagan community, one that is more uniquely electronic?

Finally, operating both as a Web site (www.fortunecity.com/greenfield/deercreek/248) and as a Yahoo! discussion group (groups.yahoo.com/groups/TheSacredMoonCircle), the Sacred Moon Circle was begun by Rowan EagleMoon, "a solitary eclectic witch from Scotland," a few months after she became a practicing Pagan in 1999. With nearly 150 registered members on the Yahoo! group, she describes the Sacred Moon Circle as "an online community for Pagans and those interested in learning about Paganism." As with each of these other examples, however, a number of important questions are raised by her claims: Is this really a "community?" How do we know if it's a community? And, if it isn't a community, despite the participants' self-description, then what is it?

The theoretical problem of the "online community" has been around at least since the popular advent of the Internet and the World Wide Web in the early 1990s. Rather than reprise the growing scholarly literature on the topic, however, I want to make only a few salient points about the discussion. First, while some scholars have dismissed the possibility that authentic community can ever be mediated electronically (see, for example, Lockard 1997; McLoughlin, Osborne, and Smith 1995; Slouka 1995), others have implied that if the ways in which "community" is conceptualized excludes what is happening on the Internet, then the analytic category itself has become inadequate (Cowan and Hadden 2004b; Dawson 2004; Liu 1999; Watson 1997; Wilbur 1997; Willson 2000). Michele Willson (2000: 656) notes correctly that "the idea of 'community' is experiencing a resurgence in interest among both theorists and society at large," but in terms of computer-mediated community—regardless of the particular form it takes or is alleged to take—as Lorne Dawson (2004: 77) points out, "it is simply assumed too often that 'community' is present, without really specifying why or how (cf. Jones 1998; Rheingold 1993; Smith and Kollock 1999; [to which we could add Willson 2000])." This highlights the central problem of stating categorically just what we mean when we say "community." Given the demise of such well-worn concepts as *Gemeinschaft* ("community") and *Gesellschaft* ("association") as they were articulated over a century ago by the German sociologist Ferdinand Tönnies ([1887] 1955; cf. Brint 2001; McCarthy 1996), Dawson asks what we would expect "community" to look like in the online part of society and whether this demands a more thorough reworking of the community concept. "Condensing, modifying, and adding to [the] analyses" of a number of scholars, he proposes six identifiers of online community that, once again, mirror similar conditions off-line: "(1) interactivity, (2) stability of membership, (3) stability of identity, (4) netizenship and social control, (5) personal concern, and (6) occurrence in a public space" (Dawson 2004: 83). The last of Dawson's characteristics is the most problematic theoretically, especially in terms of such historical cases as secret societies and the off-line emergence of modern Pagan covens as sometimes *very* private communities, but as a whole they indicate a useful analytic framework within which to examine and evaluate online activity. With the exception of a requirement that it occur in some manner of public space, each of Dawson's identifiers characterizes *intentional* versus *accidental* patterns of association—social groups as opposed to social aggregates. This differs from Tönnies's *Gesellschaft* by virtue of the fact that they are not limited to (and may not even include) the contractual and exchange relations that he regarded as central to the concept, but resemble more Georg Simmel's (1906) conditions of disclosure and reciprocity within secret societies, dynamic attributes by which conceptual separation as a primary group is established, social relations within the group are strengthened and extended, and group identity and loyalty is maintained in the face of the social pull of other groups to which participants may belong.

Second, it is important to remember that "community" is hardly a point in conceptual space. It is not the case that something called community either exists or it doesn't, blinking into being when a sufficient number of characteristics are present and disappearing the moment it falls below some theoretical threshold of viability. In many cases, communities that meet characteristic tests such as Dawson's contain nested sets of intentional association that exist within much larger frameworks of potential community. That is to say, a wide variety of institutions provide the social structure within which more intentional communities—whether these take the form of affinitive groups or instrumental alliances—emerge, evolve, and eventually expire. Anyone even moderately familiar with the membership decline in North American mainline Protestantism since the 1960s, for example, will also be familiar with this reality. Although church rolls may list 350 families and nearly 1,000 members for a particular congregation, the concept of "community" in this instance runs the gamut from a small subgroup of very committed church members for whom the congregation is a primary locus of social activity and identity to larger, variously committed subgroups characterized by (ir)regular worship attendance and occasional participation in community activities. On the periphery, a largely uncommitted subgroup, whose constituents know they are Presbyterian, Methodist, or Anglican simply because they know they are *not* Buddhist, Hindu, or Druid, may still consider themselves members of the "community," but their participation is nominal at best and contributes nothing to the intentionality of association that defines the concept. Similarly, while an online discussion forum such as Earthwise BOS may list more than 900 members, a significantly smaller number actually constitute the intentional patterns of association, disclosure, and reciprocity that characterize community in this particular online setting. That is, the Earthwise BOS *community* is an intentional subgroup of its *membership*; the former is realized from the potential framed by the latter.

Finally, and perhaps most important from the perspective of modern Paganism on the Internet, there is the sociological problem of knowledge as it relates to the concept of community and identity, especially the issue of agreement as a key component in any social construction of reality. That is, in terms of modern Paganism both online and off-line, how would those who argue that Paganism is neither an authentic community online nor even an authentic religious tradition off-line answer the hundreds of thousands of participants worldwide who are convinced that Paganism is *both* an authentic, viable religious tradition off-line *and* that the social and ritual experiences they encounter online do constitute examples of authentic and viable community? Here, we are faced as always with the methodological problem of taking seriously the social actors by whom we are confronted. And, while we may not \accept the content of what these actors believe, we must accept (at least *prima facie*) the fact that they believe it. As Berger and Luckmann indicated a generation ago, "the sociology of knowledge must concern itself with whatever passes for 'knowledge' in a society, regardless of the ultimate validity or invalidity (by whatever criteria) of such 'knowledge'" (1966: 15). That is, what is the particular stock of knowledge upon which modern Pagans draw in the construction of both identity and community? How is that stock of knowledge maintained and reinforced in the face of challenge, disconfirmation, and, not infrequently, outright ridicule? And, in terms of our current discussion, what part does (or could) computer technology in general and the Internet in particular play in those dynamics?

## Metaphysical Conversation and the Construction of Magickal Community

As I noted earlier, in many regards the essence of the sacred is agreement between participants in the reality that they deem sacred; the holy is a product of both social and cultural construction. Modern Pagan conceptions of the Internet are no different. Like so many who have either jumped on or thrown stones at the Internet bandwagon, modern Pagans hold conflicting visions about the nature of this new technology and its potential to help or harm society. Some, like Ian Anderson (writing as Ian Lurking Bear [1994]) strike a dystopian note, arguing that the Internet can never approach the character and fullness of real life, that off-line experiences will always infinitely surpass those that take place online (cf. Davis 1998; Stoll 1995, 1999), and that Earth-based religions such as the various modern Paganisms cannot but be diminished when they move online in any substantial way. "There is a sickness at the heart of this whole virtual reality concept," he argues (1994), "that would undermine our efforts at positive, evolutionary magic if it became too mixed up with our spirituality." That is, no matter how beautiful the trees on one's desktop wallpaper, the plain fact remains that those trees provide no shade, shelter no wildlife, and their off-line counterparts still suffer clearcutting at an alarming rate. Life is lived in the *embodied encounter*, critics like Anderson contend, not in the typographic acquaintance of a chat room or the two-dimensional presentation of a computer screen. Another critic, this one a contributor to the *Circle Network News*'s 1996 readers' forum on "Virtual Paganism," both recognizes the problem of the digital divide and insists that this recognition is inseparable from any responsible consideration of the Internet and its effects on society. "Currently," she writes caustically, "the Internet is not much more than a global notice board for the privileged" (Sant 1996).

Others, however, including most of those whose contributions were printed in the *Circle Network News* forum, regard the Internet and the World Wide Web as potentially magickal tools virtually sent by the gods and goddesses to assist humankind's evolution to the next level of spiritual development. Meeting Pagans from around the world online, one contributor rhapsodizes that "this new Pagan group will snowball and a new paradigm of Earth-centered spirituality will displace the Earth-raping, Nature-castrating monotheism which seems an unchangeable part of our society today" (Elder 1996). Another writes that "magickal computers have become the Goddess-send of both rural and city Pagans" (Wilson 1996). As we have noted already, well-known Pagan author Patricia Telesco (1996) weaves almost every aspect of her computer into her craftworking. For her, program passwords become charms that "[reflect] personal attributes or characteristics that you're trying to develop"; when powered down, "the [computer] screen becomes an excellent scrying surface"; and in what we might call "font magic," "**boldface** can be used to engender courage and ~~strikethrough~~ can be used for [ritual] decreasings and banishings." Missouri Pagan Dorothy Morrison concurs, offering a variety of spells, charms, and invocations that she claims have kept her computer equipment functioning properly for years. For example, in addition to a "Fax/Modem Protection Chant," she suggests that modem speed may be increased by putting "a piece of tiger eye on top of your external modem. For internal modems, place the stone on top of the CPU. The results are remarkable" (Morrison 1996). She also recommends using tarot cards and quartz crystals "to keep loaded software running efficiently," and offers chants to keep scanners and CD-ROM drives in good working order.

These different comments indicate the two principal ways in which modern Pagans conceptualize the significance of computer equipment and integrate new technology into what many of them believe to be the most ancient human technology of all: magick and spellworking.

First, obviously, computers are an important means of communicating about the established traditions to which modern Pagans belong and the new traditions that are emerging as a result of modern Paganism's open source character. Second, many modern Pagans now regard computer technology as an integral part of the modern Pagan path, another magickal tool little different from the candle, the cup, and the cauldron.

As a means of communicating about their religion, computers (and more particularly, of course, the Internet and the World Wide Web) both contribute to the open source construction of modern Paganism as a new religious movement, and facilitate the cultural conversation that Berger and Luckmann (1966) argue is central to the ongoing process of reality maintenance in any social group. Since I have already discussed at some length the open source nature of modern Paganism and the part played by the Internet, I would like to focus here on the World Wide Web as a unique mechanism by which the conversation of which Berger and Luckmann write takes place. I would also suggest that, industry and enthusiast hyperbole notwithstanding, this is one of the few singular contributions made by Internet metatechnology. Because once the glitter of the Web has been cleared away and users are faced with the rather mundane realities of equipment cost, connection fees, and the industry-planned obsolescence of both hardware and software, as well as the often fragile nature of Internet service provision, access, and data transfer, an important question becomes: What is so new about this "new technology" in terms of its effects on religious practitioners and the religions of which they are a part?

A number of observers who have attempted to characterize the effects of the Internet have located those effects in online dynamics such as identity play, construction, and confusion, and have concluded that there is something distinctly different from off-line interaction (see, for example, Aycock 1996; Berland 2000; Donath 1999; Miller 1995; Myers 1987; Rutter and Smith 1999; Turkle 1995; Wynn and Katz 1997). The relative anonymity of chat rooms and discussion forums, for example, allow participants to reinvent identity and re-present new identities in an ongoing fashion—and, to a certain extent, of course, this is true. Online, men can pretend to be women, and vice versa. Online romancers can exaggerate their positive attributes in order to attract a love interest. Online ethnographers are faced with the ethical dilemma of disclosure in a research environment where they could easily disguise their academic interest.

However, as more longitudinal data become available and concepts related to identity construction are removed from the technological domain of computer science (e.g., Turkle 1995) and located in the theoretical frameworks of sociology and social psychology (e.g., Wynn and Katz 1997), the postmodern blush comes off the Internet rose. Jody Berland points out, for example, that although "many commentators have claimed that virtual communication would revolutionize gender roles," allowing a postmodern experiment in identity play unequaled in human history, "the simulated persona roaming the Web replicate the most 'stereotypically spectacular' gender stereotypes of the predigital age" (2000: 239). Eleanor Wynn and James Katz (1997) argue that much of the rhetoric surrounding the allegedly infinite multiplicity of selves in the online environment simply ignores social scientific literature on interaction theory and social role presentation. "By contrast," they write in answer to more postmodern interpretations of the Internet experience, "we assert, as the ethnomethodological literature illustrates in painstaking detail, that people are engaged in a constant effort to structure experience together and to establish order in conventions of discourse so that shared meanings are possible" (Wynn and Katz 1997: 302). Which is, of course, precisely the effort that results in social processes ranging from the most rudimentary attempts at language to the most sophisticated theories of symbolic interaction. In terms of the modern Pagan Internet, this points to the larger question of whether they are really doing anything all that different online from off-line. Or are they simply doing the same thing differently? And, if they are, once again, what are the salient effects of the Internet?

## A Web of Potential and Opportunity

The uniqueness of the Internet and the World Wide Web lies not in the creation of an environment in which entirely new identities are constructed and rapidly multiplying discourses frustrate and ultimately prevent meaningful communication, but in the cultural conversation that this metatechnology makes available for participants who might otherwise never interact and the sympathetic reception of culturally specific identities that play out both online and off-line. It makes the potential for community visible, where before perhaps only the vain hope for community existed. According to Berger and Luckmann, the kind of conversation that is crucial to the ongoing project of reality construction and maintenance occurs in two principal domains: the explicit and the implicit. Explicitly, of course, modern Pagans do actually converse on the Internet. They share experiences and concerns, ask questions about rituals and pantheons, swap spells and incense recipes, and often *kvetch* about the lack of seriousness displayed by other modern Pagans, the arrogant dominance of Christianity in North American society, or simply the fact that good dragon's blood is hard to come by these days. Without doubt, these types of interactions constitute the bulk of e-mail and discussion forum postings.

Implicit, however, and Berger and Luckmann are careful to point out that for the process of reality maintenance this is the more important conversational domain, is the cultural background against which this explicit conversation takes place, that is, "the background of a world that is silently taken for granted" (1966: 172). Put somewhat crudely, explicit conversation that is meant to serve the function of reality construction and maintenance for modern Pagans would ordinarily *not* occur on discussion forums at www.Come-to-Jesus.com; background aspects—the epistemological assumptions, theological prejudices, and purposive dynamics—are simply too hostile for such conversation to be successful. Extending the parameters of Berger and Luckmann's implicit background, though, three facets of online interaction work to create an environment in which cultural conversations that appear highly successful in terms of reality construction and maintenance do take place: (1) the simple but important fact that, apart from the Internet, the vast majority of this conversation would not take place; (2) the reality that much of this conversation presents a much lower risk for participants than similar interactions off-line; and (3) the presence of an epistemological backdrop conducive to the maintenance and reinforcement of modern Pagan constructions of reality.

The Yahoo! discussion group Celtic Druids (groups.yahoo.com/group/celticdruids), for example, advertises itself as a discussion forum where participants "can share experiences, ask questions, talk about Druidism and the Celtic Religion," and on which questions "will be answered by experienced, real-life Druids." Even if that description somewhat overstates the reality, the group has nearly 800 members and posts an average of 175 messages per month. On it, Renfestlady from Olathe, Kansas, shares her passion for Renaissance Festivals with Chriscrosscelt, a 60-year-old writer living in Amsterdam; and Solus Laiden, a Druid Hearth Mother from Howell, New Jersey, trades modern Pagan poetry with Meadow Pagan from the southeast of England. Similarly, with nearly 850 members, Beginners Wicca (groups.yahoo. com/group/beginners_wicca) provides a discussion forum for participants from Laquey, Missouri, to Penticton, British Columbia; from Brighton, England, to Fort Knox, Kentucky; and from Johannesburg, South Africa, to Ankara, Turkey. One brief exchange that will be discussed in more detail below brought together three participants from California, Texas, and Mumbai, India. And, finally, of those who disclosed a real location (that is, not "The Halls of Asgard" or "Somewhere in Middle Earth"), among the nearly 400 members of The Witches Cottage (groups.yahoo.com/group/TheWitchesCottage) we find participants from all 50 states and over 15 other countries. Without the World Wide Web, few of the participants in any of these lists would even know that these other modern Pagans existed, let alone have any chance to interact with them. In this way, the Internet provides one of the most basic components of conversation: potential and opportunity.

## Anonymity and Disclosure on the Web

As opposed to face-to-face interaction, however, or the often intimidating prospect of visiting a local modern Pagan gathering when one has no prior history with the community or the tradition, conversation on the World Wide Web entails much lower risk for potential participants. Online, this lower risk threshold occurs in two principal ways: ephemerality and anonymity. In modern Pagan conversation online, what I am calling ephemerality is simply the fragile nature of computer-mediated communication, and the ease with which participants can disengage themselves from online discussion forums, e-mail lists, and chat rooms. Participants can exit chat rooms at the click of a mouse and withdraw from online forums and e-mail lists simply by not logging on to them. On the other hand, because it speaks to larger issues of involvement and risk, anonymity is a more important issue. As I noted briefly above, one indication of anonymity on the modern Pagan Internet is how few participants disclose any personal information. Though some modern Pagan discussion lists have hundreds of members and post hundreds of messages per month, very few of these participants reveal much about themselves. For example, at the time of writing, only 6 percent (30/485) of the members of the Yahoo! group _Wicca (groups.yahoo.com/group/_wicca), and 7 percent (59/836) of Beginners Wicca (groups.yahoo.com/group/beginners_wicca) disclosed what appear to be their real, full names in member profiles. Smaller groups reveal a similar lack of disclosure. Of the nearly 100 members of the Magick Cauldron (groups.yahoo

.com/group/magickcauldron2), only six (three male, three female) disclosed their real names; 44 members, on the other hand, chose not to reveal so much as their e-mail addresses. Keltria-L had a nominal disclosure rate of 28 percent (with 19/152 full names), TechnoPagan 22.5 percent (7/102 full names), and Asatru-TNG, a Yahoo! group designed for those between the ages of 16 and 25 who are interested in "Norse Heathenry," 31 percent, with 8 out of 64 members revealing their full names. And, just like the Bella Luna Cyber Coven, in all of these cases this lack of disclosure extended to the designated moderators of the lists. Though in each case considerably more participants disclosed their first names, still less than one-third of the membership were willing to do even that.

By comparison to these modern Pagan groups, three Christian-oriented discussion groups with similar membership numbers and traffic volume demonstrated significantly higher nominal disclosure rates. With 770 members and message traffic averaging more than 500 posts per month since November 2001, 458 members of Christians for Truth (groups.yahoo.com/group/christians_for_truth) disclosed either their full names (194) or first names (264); that is, nearly 60 percent of the membership provided some kind of personal identification to the group. Online about the same length of time, though with a slightly lower traffic volume, the Christian Leadership Support Center (groups.yahoo.com/group/christianleadershipsupport) numbers more than 500 members, 253 of whom (50 percent) disclose either full or first names. Finally, Reformed Theology (groups.yahoo.com/group/reformedtheology) has only 97 members, but 44 of them (45 percent) disclose their real names. Not surprisingly, it seems clear that conversation taking place against the cultural background of a dominant religious tradition encourages participants to disclose more personal information than conversations that occur in the context of religious traditions that remain culturally marginalized. What is surprising, and what challenges the perception of the Internet as an inherently safer environment to explore alternative beliefs and identities (e.g., Rafaeli and Sudweeks 1997), is the very low rate of online modern Pagan disclosure, and, as we will see, the relatively low rate of discussion group participation.

Two modern Pagan groups that returned disclosure rates closer to (but not exceeding) the Christian discussion forums were Wodenserpent, an Asatru list (groups.yahoo.com/group/wodensperpent), and OBOD Gathering, an online group for members of the Order of Bards, Ovates, and Druids (groups.yahoo.com/group/obodgathering; cf. Carr-Gomm 1996, 2002; Nichols 1975). Forty-five percent of Wodenserpent's members disclosed either a full name or a first name; 57 percent of OBOD Gathering did so. More research is clearly needed in the area of online identity and anonymity, but I suspect that the difference in disclosure rates reflects in part the age of participants on the different lists. Not only does this make sense intuitively, it is suggested by some rough comparisons drawn from a few of the smaller lists. On the Magick Cauldron group, for example, 46 percent of participants listed their age in member profiles, with an average age of 28 years; 69 percent of Wodenserpent's members and 76 percent on OBOD Gathering listed their age, with an average of 33 and 36 years respectively. More important than this difference, however, is the finding that only one member of Wodenserpent (1 percent) and two members of OBOD Gathering (3 percent) listed their ages as younger than 20 years; conversely, ten members (10 percent) of Magick Cauldron did so. Given the inverse relationship between age disclosure and number of members under 20 on Magick Cauldron, at least, it seems reasonable to suggest that willingness to disclose personal information in online environments that are neither age-specific nor age-restricted correlates to the age of participants. Young people are less willing to disclose personal information because they are both less comfortable with personal identity during adolescence and young adulthood, and they often inhabit off-line social environments that preclude sharing potentially risky information online. A number of teen and preteen participants in modern Pagan discussion groups, for example, expressed concern that if their parents ever found out that they were exploring a religious tradition different from the one in which they were raised, there would be dire consequences.

Although these data are clearly impressionistic and drawn from a very small sample of groups from the Yahoo! portal only, they do reflect certain off-line realities about the willingness of modern Pagans to identify themselves in a culture where they are not a dominant religious group, but instead one in which self-identification as a Pagan often carries considerable risk. This reality comes into even sharper focus when we consider some of the questions raised on modern Pagan discussion forums and the real world consequences they either imply or state bluntly. On a number of forums, for example, questions about coming out of the broom closet—especially to one's parents—are common. Fearful of family reaction, teens seek advice from other list members on how to broach the subject of their new religious interests. Often, participants want to know how to manage the gradual disclosure of their modern Pagan beliefs in the overtly Christian contexts they inhabit. On the _Wicca group (groups.yahoo.com/group/_wicca), one member even asked how he should conduct himself responsibly as a modern Pagan at the Southern Baptist school in which his parents had enrolled him. Obviously, these are sensitive issues and the relative anonymity provided by the Internet allows them to be raised in ways that would be impossible off-line.

*The Web as a Common Stock of Knowledge*

Finally, both these implicit aspects of conversation take place in modern Pagan discussion forums against a cultural stock of knowledge that is both common and sympathetic to the beliefs of participants. We have already seen how the open source understanding of different pantheons among modern Pagans is supported by a basic epistemology of subjective appropriation and personally gnostic authorization. Precise interpretations may differ among online participants, but fundamental understandings of modern Paganism—the interconnectedness of life, the sacredness of the earth, the reality of the spiritual realm, and the efficacy of magick—go largely unchallenged in these discussion venues; instead they form an understood part of the background against which more explicit conversation takes place. On the Beginners Wicca list, for example, Hyacinth Apollolover, a gay Indian man from Mumbai whose spiritual path seeks to syncretize Shaktism and Wicca (Apollolover 2003), wrote that he had recently begun spellworking in his parents' home and that small objects had started to go missing. "Is there any ritual I can do," he concludes, "to ensure this happening won't have any magickal component?" Two responses in particular are instructive for the modern Pagan stock of knowledge each assumes, deploys, and implicitly validates. "Your use of magic has probably awakened the spirits in the house," writes Nuada Stormbringer, from Lancaster, California. "These are probably not ghosts but faeries, wights and brownies who like to borrow things. You will most likely need to do some research to find out exactly who they are and talk to them and ask them not to borrow things." Another respondent, Texan Elana Mojica, replied that it "sounds like someone needs to lay out a shiny dime and ask the faeries to give your mother's stuff back."

This brief exchange reveals a number of important aspects of modern Pagan belief that function as background against which more specific information is sought; each aspect validates and reinforces the participants' modern Pagan worldview. First, while Hyacinth does not assume that his spellworking has adversely affected his mother's home necessarily, the modern Pagan aspects of his belief raise this as a distinct possibility; after all, he asked the question on a discussion forum oriented toward those who are just starting out on the Wiccan path. Second, both responses assume the reality of a culturally specific Otherworld inhabited by elemental creatures such as faeries and sprites, and accept that the modern Pagan can both communicate with those beings and affect their behavior. Celtic myth and legend is filled with stories of mischievous magickal folk such as faeries, wights, sprites, and brownies (see, for example, Evans-Wentz [1911] 1966; Jacobs [1892] 1968, [1894] 1968; MacCulloch [1911] 1992; Murray 1931; Wilson 1954), which have, not surprisingly, found their way into modern interpretations of Pagan belief and culture (see, for example, Andrews 1993; Knight 2002; Matthews and Matthews 1994; McCoy 1994, 1995; Stewart 1999). The question, though, is whether the respondents bothered to learn anything about Hyacinth before answering his question. Did they know he is Indian? Did they know he is attempting to fuse Eastern and Western spiritualities in Shaktism and Wicca? Did they wonder whether the

Celtic elementals whom they suggest might be responsible for the thefts actually know the way to Mumbai? Or, would they make a rough (if unwitting) equation between those elementals and such Hindu spiritual beings as daityas, danavas, and yaksas? Finally, would any of these questions even matter to them? I would like to suggest that they would not, because, third, by acting as "significant others" (Berger and Luckmann 1966: 169–72)—authoritative voices who legitimate particular subjective realities—Nuada Stormbringer and Elana Mojica reflexively reinforce their own modern Pagan reality, their own belief in the action of Celtic elementals regardless of whether the spirits themselves know Mumbai from MacGillicuddy's Reeks.

### "Demigods in a Box": Modern Pagan Visions of Hardware and Software

In addition to reality-maintaining conversations that are facilitated by the Internet, many modern Pagans see computer technology as an integral part of their magickal pathworking, little different from the metallurgy that produces cauldrons and athames, or the written language that allows for the existence of grimoires, magickal journals, and books of shadows. "Computers are like demigods in a box," write Patricia Telesco and Sirona Knight almost epigrammatically (2001: xiii). "They run on energy, store vast amounts of knowledge, and seem to have persnickety tendencies all their own. This demigod has a quintessential servant: the Internet." Conceptualizing the World Wide Web theomorphically, Telesco and Knight indulge utopian language that, on the surface, rivals the crassest of commercial advertisements. It is "a community support system, a spiritual lifeline," they continue, that "holds tremendous potential for magic" and "provides virtually unlimited possibilities for Wiccans with access to it" (Telesco and Knight 2001: xiii). In their introduction, they continue that "the Internet is a mirror of the universe, showing us that we are all connected together, and it is our connections to one another that make us whole" (Telesco and Knight 2001: xiv). How these utopian visions are realized through the World Wide Web, though, the authors do not say. They conclude that Web Witching is here to stay, however, and that "personal and planetary transformation starts here and now by simply turning the page" of their book (Telesco and Knight 2001: xv).

Echoing Telesco and Knight, in *newWitch*, a magazine aimed at teenaged and young adult modern Pagans, Galina Krasskova (2003: 15) writes of the computer: "It's ALIVE!" "Because the physical hard drive is a conduit for a unique type of energy," she continues, though she does not disclose precisely what is unique about it, "it is possible for nature spirits (called *Vaettir*) to take up residence within it." Since *vaettir* are, apparently, "extremely sensitive to emotions," Krasskova offers her readers the "Golden Rule" of computer operation: "No one likes to be yelled at. The same holds true for *vaettir* who may inhabit your computer. Do not curse, yell, smack, or otherwise vent your anger on your computer." And, since failure to observe this rule can result in "the dreaded 'blue screen of death,'" she suggests that Web witches treat their computer equipment with the respect due all magickal tools.

> Do what you can to make the computer feel welcome in your home. This includes talking to it (and you may receive a distinct impression of gender), naming it and even offering words of encouragement. (I went through an extended period where my computer simply would not boot unless he was verbally encouraged to do so). At times, it may also include sending healing and soothing energy to it. I have found that Reiki works extremely well on computers (and other electronic equipment). (Krasskova 2003: 15)

Krasskova (2003: 16) also encourages users to cleanse the "psychic gunk" she believes can accumulate around computers and slow them down. However, because the smoke from traditional smudging can damage delicate electronics, she suggests a process called "sound-smudging": "Either clap your hands around the computer or use a rattle. A handful of coins in an old coffee can works just as well—the object is to break up stagnant energy. Shake your rattle or coffee can around the computer." Somewhat paradoxically, though, Krasskova differs from other modern Pagan authors we have encountered to this point in her interpretation of "the most basic magical survival technique of all":

> TURN THE COMPUTER OFF COMPLETELY WHEN YOU ARE WORKING MAGIC. I cannot emphasize this enough. I've had friends who have had their computers completely crash due to simple energy overload when they inadvertently left them on while doing spellwork. The same goes for rituals. You raise energy during rituals and Deity presence can be extremely powerful. It can easily overload a computer. (Krasskova 2003: 16; emphasis in the original)

Although these accounts may seem just a wee bit silly to some non-Pagan observers, they are important here for three principal reasons. First, sociologically, they constitute "what passes for 'knowledge'" (Berger and Luckmann 1966: 15) in at least some domains of modern Paganism, and in this they function little differently than more culturally dominant spiritual practices such as prayers for healing, anointing with oil, and laying on hands. Second, whatever the reaction of the modern Pagan community to them (recall Shanks 2003), there is no reason to suspect that all three of these authors do not expect to be taken seriously by their readers. Although sincerity in no way guarantees veracity, it does disclose aspects of both identity and epistemology. And third, modern Pagan epistemology—specifically the rationale for the efficacy of magick that is underpinned by this epistemology—not only allows for but encourages precisely the kind of understandings demonstrated by Krasskova, Knight, and Telesco.

For modern Pagans such as these—and here we could include Lisa McSherry, Macha NightMare, and many others who have established an online Pagan presence—incorporating computer technology into, for example, the Wiccan worldview makes eminent good sense. Indeed, making a computer workstation part and parcel of one's magickal lifestyle, choosing appropriate herbs, incense, essential oils, and minerals to bring out the best in your hardware, software, and the computing experience that exists in the interface between them is no more problematic than the use Wiccans make of any other technology. For example, Telesco and Knight recommend placing iris flowers in the vicinity of one's computer because, according to them, irises are "sacred to the cyber Goddess" and work to ensure the "longevity of hard drive, printer, scanner, and software" (2001: 41). Similarly, nutmeg, which they call "a maintenance herb," "keeps things running smoothly," and sage is good "to extend the life of disks and drives" (Telesco and Knight 2001: 43). When used as an essential oil, sage "protects your system from crashes and viruses," and is "great to use when dumping your e-mail trash" (Telesco and Knight 2001: 47). Mineralogically speaking—because "what's a good witch to do without a few good rocks?" (Telesco and Knight 2001: 25)—the authors suggest using jade because it "increases the longevity of your disks and drives," while serpentine "debugs your machine" (Telesco and Knight 2001: 48). They offer spells written specifically for operations such as defragmentation and loading new software, a "techno-thaw" spell to protect one's system from freezing, an "Antitheft Talisman for Laptops" (which, calling on the Wiccan law of the threefold return, includes the chant, "*Magic here shine, this computer is mine. All thieves beware of this magical snare. Your intent, you will see, returns three by three*" [Telesco and Knight 2001: 54; italics in the original]), and the "Recovery Spell," which "is designed to work in conjunction with the Undelete or Recover function of your system whereby a deleted file or file portion can be rescued" (Telesco and Knight 2001: 55). In terms of online computing itself, "Web Witching means getting online and extending your magical energy through the lines of force represented by the Internet" (Telesco and Knight 2001: 4).

How, though, did modern Pagans such as these establish this elaborate system of correspondences? What makes them think any of these actions will have the slightest effect on computer hardware and software? Just as Tanya Luhrmann wondered in *Persuasions of the Witch's Craft* (1989) how reasonably bright, rational, otherwise socially well-integrated people could devote themselves to such pursuits as ceremonial magick, a similar question obtains here:

what can explain the seriousness with which authors such as Krasskova, Knight, Morrison, and Telesco can suggest spells to keep computer viruses from attacking one's machines or ensuring the successful transfer of files from one computer to another? And how do they explain the billions of times daily that these same operations are performed successfully without "high magic's aid" (Gardner [1949] 1996)?

*An Epistemology of Modern Paganism*

"Witches are neither fools, escapists nor superstitious," contend well-known Wiccan authors Janet and Stewart Farrar (1984: 105), who continue that "if witchcraft did not have a coherent rationale, such people could only keep going by a kind of deliberate schizophrenia." In order to understand more fully the incorporation of computer technology into spellworking, ritual, and magick, a brief excursus into the epistemology of modern Paganism is in order. Broadly speaking, at the macroscopic level modern Paganism regards all aspects of the universe—visible and invisible—as interrelated, interdependent, and interactive. Any appearance of separation between phenomena, whether between humans and other animals, trees and rocks, or the gas clouds of the Crab Nebula and the plasma streams of the Auroras Borealis and Australis, occurs at the level of perception and illusion. Although this view is held in tension with an almost unavoidable anthropocentrism—both the Farrars (1984: 106) and McSherry (2002: 6), for example, regard personal consciousness as the *sine qua non* of *homo sapiens*—that the myriad elements of the universe are intimately connected is not in dispute among modern Pagans. At the microscopic level, this interrelatedness means that, just as touching one strand on a spider's web causes the entire web to vibrate, no action in one part of the universe is without consequence in all parts of the universe—a kind of modern Pagan chaos theory. "The rationale of Wicca, as we see it," the Farrars continue (1984: 106), "rests upon two fundamental principles: the Theory of Levels, and the Theory of Polarity." Though the theory of levels, or planes of existence, can be expressed in a number of different ways—"physical, etheric, astral, mental, spiritual, to give a simplified but generally accepted list" (Farrar and Farrar 1984: 107)—the Farrars are careful to point out that prior to the scientific revolution this was the accepted interpretation of reality for many different cultures. Pythagoreans had their "harmony of the spheres," Roman Catholics their varied levels of heaven and hell, Buddhism and Hinduism the multiple domains of *samsaric* existence. For the Farrars, the rather dubious triumph of the scientific revolution lay in convincing much of the Western world that the physical plane of existence was the only level of reality—an understanding modern Pagans deny. The theory of polarities, on the other hand, which they characterize as "the interaction of pairs and complementary opposites" (1984: 107), we recognize easily in such principles as the Taoist *yin* and *yang*. According to the Farrars, "the Theory of Levels describes the *structure* of the universe; the Theory of Polarity describes its *activity*; and structure and activity are inseparable" (1984: 107; cf. 105–34).

Practically speaking, and challenging Stephen Jay Gould's dictum that science and religion are "nonoverlapping magisteria" (Gould 1997), Laurie Cabot, the well-known "official witch of Salem" (Cabot and Cowan 1989: inside back cover), claims that "Witchcraft is a science based on cause and effect" (1989: 143). Indeed, she has taken the philosophical interface between modern Paganism and modern science one step further and named her own lineage of Witchcraft the "Science Tradition" (1989: 149). Integrating magickal philosophy with particular streams of modern physics—notably the works of Itzhak Bentov (1977), Fritjof Capra (1975), and F. David Peat (Briggs and Peat 1984; Peat 1987, 1988), to which we might conceivably add David Bohm (1980), Brian Greene (1999), Michael Talbot (1991), and Fred Alan Wolf (1988)—Cabot argues that "the physical universe as described by contemporary physicists and the spiritual universe as described by mystics and sages in every century are shown to be remarkably similar" (1989: 145). "At last," she concludes (1989: 147), "physicists support and confirm an understanding of the universe that Witches have always had, and in so doing they make it immensely easier for us to explain our magic." Lisa McSherry concurs wholeheartedly. "All that is seen and unseen is energy," she writes (2002: 7), "science has taught us this. But the Vedic sages of India, the European Druids, and, after them, the witches, recognized this fact as well."

Thus, if everything in the universe is connected, then to modern Pagans it only makes sense that there ought to be mechanisms by which these connections can be accessed and influenced. Indeed, "each plane is affecting the others all the time," declare the Farrars, "but there seem to be what may be called *points of inter-resonance* where this effect is particularly striking and clearly enough defined to be made use of in practice" (1984: 109; emphasis in the original). According to them, training in Witchcraft involves acknowledging the various levels of existence, recognizing and sensitizing oneself to the "points of inter-resonance" by which these levels can be affected, and operationalizing those effects through ritual practices and magickal techniques. On the other hand, in one of a number of often confusing interpretations she offers, McSherry defines magick somewhat less precisely as "the art of consciously directing energy through focused will and effort to affect the things around us" (2002: 7). Cabot's explanation of the practical aspects of modern Paganism, however, is worth quoting at length for the insights it provides into the rationalization of modern Pagan religious practice as an empirical science—not to mention the forthright nature of her claims.

When I speak of Witchcraft as a science I use the word *science* in its strictest form. Witchcraft is a system based on hypotheses that can be tested under controlled conditions. Magical spells are step-by-step experiments that produce statistical results from which we can derive our success rates. The physical sciences maintain that a 32 percent success rate establishes the validity of a hypothesis. When I teach the science of Witchcraft based on the Hermetic laws, my students' experiments show a 50 percent and often a 75 to 90 percent success rate. In other words, we can verify how often and under what conditions psychic diagnosis can be performed, how often a love potion works, what effect a wand or crystal has on the outcome of a spell or ritual. (Cabot and Cowan 1989: 150–51; emphasis in the original)

Once again, it is important to bear in mind that, whatever criticism hard scientists may level at these characterizations of witchcraft as science, whatever umbrage they may take at their deployment by one half of Gould's "nonoverlapping magisteria," and whatever logical problems Popperian philosophers of science may have with Cabot's notion of "verification," for many modern Pagans this is, once again, precisely what "passes for 'knowledge'" both ontologically and practically. Epistemologically, we have entered the arena of differing burdens of proof. Standards of evidence vary across social domains, and what may be considered sufficient in one venue is often decidedly insufficient in another. For example, in U.S. criminal court proceedings, decisions are rendered based on evidence that is presented "beyond a reasonable doubt." In civil proceedings, on the other hand, there is a reduced burden of proof. A case must be proven only "by a preponderance of the evidence," which means, simply, that a thing is more likely than not. In terms of the rationale of modern Paganism, especially the rhetoric of science in which authors like Cabot and McSherry couch it, the standard of evidence required to convince someone who either already believes or is already predisposed to believe in the efficacy of magick is significantly different than that required to convince someone who is not so disposed. Once again, in this modern Pagans are no different than other religious adherents who believe wholeheartedly in the efficacy of prayer, spiritual healing, or the supernatural power of particular scriptures and ritual objects.

In terms of the multivariate gods and goddesses deployed within the open source culture of modern Paganism, and once again speaking rather broadly, there are two principal ways of conceptualizing deity. On the one hand, the "god" and "goddess," when known by their myriad names are merely aspects of an all-pervasive divinity, and the particular god or goddess invoked represents only a facet of that divinity. Based on need, desire, or purpose, for example,

Wiccans call on one or more specific facets during particular rituals. In a more Jungian manner, these aspects function as archetypes, providing both a ritual and a meditative focus for the participants. To creatively misspeak with Paul Tillich, for a moment, "God[dess] is a symbol for God[dess]" (1957: 47; cf. Salomonsen 2002: 182)—that is, the names, descriptions, and images used to invoke a deity are merely the symbols by which we make comprehensible the much larger and undifferentiated reality of divinity. On the other hand, for some Wiccans each named or invoked deity exists as a separate and distinct entity, independent of every other. If, in the first instance, the names of gods and goddesses are facets of a single divine diamond, in this second understanding each deity represents a different, unique jewel.

In choosing "cyber-gods" and "cyber-goddesses," Telesco and Knight suggest that modern Pagans "look to beings who are patrons or patronesses of the magical arts, since yesterday's magic has become today's technology! You could call upon a god or goddess from your tradition's magical pantheon, or one suited to the magic at hand. A lot here depends on your outlook" (2001: 100). This short passage highlights an important point about the way in which many modern Pagans conceptualize magick, technology, and the historical relationship between the two. Throughout their two books on modern Paganism on the Internet, Telesco and Knight offer variations on the theme: "yesterday's magic has become today's technology," and rather blithely equate "magic" with "that which is not popularly understood." In so doing, however, they actually detract from the overall epistemology of modern Paganism I noted above. The problem is that although they may not understand how computers work, someone does. There is no mystery involved. Indeed, millions of people understand them precisely because they are human inventions. There is nothing supernatural or occult about them. To the electrical engineer, the software designer, or the network architect, there is nothing mysterious about computers at all. In fact, for all its breadth and seemingly limitless avenues of exploration, even the Internet (in its most recognizable form as the World Wide Web) is a thoroughly mapped territory. Users may explore that territory in different ways and discover aspects hitherto unknown *to them*, but the Web itself exists as a function of its indexicality (see Shields 2000). Simply because particular users have not explored various strands of the Web does not mean that they have not been explored. How could they not be, since they are human constructs, products of human ingenuity and labor placed in particular locations for specific purposes and indexed with designated, singular addresses? Despite enthusiast rhetoric, it is not exactly the case that there are vast undiscovered territories in cyberspace just waiting for intrepid travelers to explore. Everything in the online world is a human product. Every Web site, every home page, every link, drop-down menu, and .jpeg file has been chosen, placed, inserted, uploaded, and indexed. It is not undiscovered, it is simply waiting to be found.

The telephone may have "seemed" like magic to those who first used it, but for Bell and Watson there was no mystery, no supernature, no magic. An intriguing aspect of Telesco and Knight's presentation is the equation of magic with ignorance. That is, if one doesn't understand how something works, it must be magic.

### "Magick" or "Like Magic?": Conceptualizing Pagan Computing Space

Technologically speaking, when all is said and done, the Internet is little more than trillions of digital switches, opening and closing in response to the commands and requests of millions of users around the world, storing and transferring the relevant (and sometimes not-so-relevant data) between networks, nodes, ISPs, and eventually personal computers, PDAs, cell phones, and, perhaps someday, wireless contact lenses and subcutaneous audio systems. Whatever the shape and size of the terminal, though, at the end of the day, whether it's the newest generation of wireless phone, fully equipped to take digital snapshots and send them over the Web, or the latest supercomputer fresh out of the R&D clean room, the key is that it is still a "terminal." It is still a means by which switches are opened and closed in very precise arrangement and according to very precise timing. It is still a mechanism by which communications of various kinds are broken down into standardized information packets (see Abbate 1999), transferred by the best available route (which may mean that not all packets in a particular communication follow the same path), and then, stripped of their address headers and authentication codes, reassembled in the correct order at their various destinations. The fact that all these events happen in the chronological domain of milliseconds means that they appear to the user as though they are happening in real time (Abbate 1999: 14). This is not unlike the cinema, in which the standard 24 frames-per-second of a movie take a series of still photographs and project them in a way that creates the very convincing illusion of seamless movement. In terms of the Internet and from a technological point of view, all that has changed in recent years is the speed with which data can be uploaded, stored, rerouted, and downloaded by the average user (i.e., *not* those with access to the research and development labs at Microsoft, Intel, IBM, or Macintosh), the amount and type of information that can be sent and received at a commercially viable rate (e.g., it was the introduction of high-speed Internet connections such as Digital Subscriber Lines, local area networks, and cable modem connections that really made MP3 technology viable; until the advent of (seemingly) hyperfast connections, the files were simply too big to download quickly), and the type of machine from which one can call upon and manipulate the data. Thus, while the intricacies of its technology might be fascinating to some, and the history of the development of both the Internet and the World Wide Web a fascinating subject of study (including, for example, the urban myth that the first Internet, the ARPANet, was designed and built during the early decades of the Cold War specifically with the possibility of nuclear war in mind; cf. Abbate 1999; Castells 2001; Hafner and Lyon 1996), and however utopian the visions of its most ardent supporters, the Internet as a technology remains a store-and-forward system for information—considerably faster, more complex, and self-referentially mutable than anything humankind has developed heretofore, but no different in principle than the Pony Express, Deutsche BundesPoste, or FedEx.

### Technological Magic or Magickal Technology?

The point here is that it is not *magic*, it is *technology*, though in the context of modern Paganism the demarcation between the two is often slippery at best. "I am thoroughly convinced," writes Galina Krasskova (2003: 15), for example, "that computer programming is a very specific form of magic (and I've spoken with more than one programmer who would agree!)." In addition to her definition I noted above, Lisa McSherry also describes "magick" as "the study and application of psychic forces, using mental training, concentration, and a system of symbols to program the mind" (2002: 6), and, somewhat more confusingly, as the process of "building community, teaching others, expressing the art that comes through your individual perspective, speaking truth, and sharing human existence" (2002: 8). Storm Mist, the list owner of the Beginners Wicca Yahoo! group, an ordained minister in the Universal Life Church (which will be discussed further in the next chapter), and the "Priestess of Sacred Mists," defines it as "the harnessing focussing and directing of energy/power to affect change," while Branwen, another member of that group, defines it in terms of traditional Witchcraft (which she differentiates from Wicca) as "any attempt to affect the outcome of a given situation by supernatural means."

On Unreal Magic, a Yahoo! list originally founded by well-known modern Druid Isaac Bonewits (1989), one participant, Hommel, defines magick idealistically: "like sex, [magick] happens in the brain of those practicing it. Magick is a way of transforming the world by transforming yourself." Flidais Silverthorn, another contributor to the Unreal Magic list, declares simply (and tautologically) that "magic is magic." While some modern Pagans conceptualize magick in terms of the supernatural (or "hypernatural"; cf. Skelton 1997: 22–24), others insist that the energies involved in magickal practice are entirely natural, but marginalized and occulted by late modern society (Fisher 2002). In *The Spiral Dance*, one of the most popular introductions to modern Paganism, Starhawk defines "magic" as "the art of sensing and shaping the subtle, unseen forces that flow through the world, [and] of awakening deeper levels of consciousness beyond the rational" (1989: 27). And, finally, Scott Cunningham, among the most recommended authors for beginning Wiccans, wrote that "magic is the projection of natural energies to produce needed effects" (1988: 19). While this may sound at least tautological and at most nonsensical—if I use the natural energy contained in my arms and upper back to chop wood, is that a magickal act?—Cunningham qualifies what he means by "natural energies" to include "divine power," that is, "the energy that exists within the Goddess and God—the life force, the source of universal power which created everything in existence" (1988: 20).

The problem, of course, is that if magick is everything then, ultimately, magick is nothing.

Indeed, just like the appropriation and construction of personal pantheons, ritual practices, and spiritual beliefs, definitions of "magick" within modern Paganism are guided by the movement's open source character and its use of personal gnosis as the touchstone of religious authenticity. For more than a century, since the rise of the academic study of religion late in the nineteenth century, scholars have struggled to define "magic," usually with the intent to differentiate it from "religion"—a pursuit that seems less and less realistic in the context of modern Paganism. (See, for example, Brooke 1991; Durkheim [1912] 1995; Eliade 1958; Evans-Pritchard 1965; Evans-Wentz [1911] 1966; Greenwood 2000; Lévi-Strauss 1962; Luhrmann 1989; Malinowski 1948; Mauss [1902] 1972; Stark 2001; Thomas 1971; Winkelman 1982, 1992.) In a recent attempt to delimit more precisely the terms of the discussion, for example, Rodney Stark states that "*Magic refers to all efforts to manipulate supernatural forces to gain rewards (or avoid costs)* **without reference to a God or Gods** *or to* **general explanations** *of existence*," whereas "**Religion** *consists of* **explanations** *of existence based on supernatural assumptions*" (2001: 111, emphases in the original; cf. Stark and Bainbridge 1987). Although Stark continues the functionalist distinction between magick as an attempt to manipulate reality and religion as an attempt to explain reality, and maintains an essential difference between the two, in the end definitions such as these do not take into account either the manipulative aspects of religions such as Christianity (e.g., prayer and ritual) or the explanatory aspects (e.g., cosmologies and cosmogonies) of many modern Paganisms. If we accept Stark's definition—which many modern Pagans, obviously, would not—we are left with the problem that although many modern Pagans do seek "to manipulate supernatural forces," they do so with direct and explicit reference to gods and goddesses. Indeed, this is part of modern Witchcraft's legacy from nineteenth-century ceremonial magick (cf. Hutton 1999). Further, as modern Paganism evolves, this magick is performed within increasingly complex and sophisticated cosmologies—"general explanations of existence"—that attempt, as we have noted with modern Pagans such as Laurie Cabot, the Farrars, and Lisa McSherry, to wed religion and science. While I suspect that few hard scientists would credence Cabot's claims to the empiricality of magick, that does not explain either the attraction of modern Paganism for hundreds of thousands of people in late modern society or modern Pagans' attempts to locate explanations for their beliefs within culturally accepted epistemologies.

We return, then, to the question of how to treat the claims of such adherents and practitioners. Are they deluded? Misguided or misinformed? In the name of an etic precision, do we sacrifice the emic reality? Or, rather, should we concede, at least as a working hypothesis and recognizing the socially constructed nature of all religious traditions, that there is no less "evidence" for the reality and efficacy of modern Pagan magick than there is for a Roman Catholic novena, and no less reason to take it seriously as an authentic aspect of deep religious commitment?

Part of the rationale of witchcraft, especially as it is used in the programmatic fashion of authors such as Cabot, Knight, and Telesco—Cabot's claims to empirical verification notwithstanding—is that it is essentially nonfalsifiable. Statements of faith and practices based on statements of faith are believed to operate with the power of fact, and are not open to falsification. For those who believe, the fact that one's disk drives have lasted as long as they have has everything to do with the sage kept by one's computer station. When challenged about the efficacy of crystals, herbs, essential oils, and incense, the rejoinder could well be: "OK, prove that it wasn't the quartz crystals that kept the computer functioning." If the machine does break down, crash, or freeze, the various magickal elements can be interpreted as having lost their potency (witness the number of charms or spells that Telesco and Knight insist must be replaced at specific intervals or reinvested with power over time). The underlying rationale behind Web Witching, including the very complex correlations made by Telesco and Knight between computer hardware, software, and operating procedures, and various herbs, minerals, essential oils, and deity figures, is precisely the monistic interconnectedness of all things that lies at the heart of Wiccan philosophy.

This is not to say, of course, that modern Pagans understand what they mean by magick any more clearly than scholars. Many often confuse—whether willingly, for the creatively anachronistic and not unromantic effect it elicits, or unwittingly, because they simply know no better—the notion of *magick* as the communication with and control of arcane forces of nature, spirits, demons, gods and demigods, and the concept of being *like magic*, that is, merely something whose operative processes are not understood by the participant. How many grade-school science classes have asked variations on the theme, "Surely the lightbulb (Bunsen burner, crystal radio, television, Polaroid camera, insert-appropriate-technological-reference-here) would have seemed *like magic* to a Neanderthal man or woman." How many quote Arthur C. Clarke's venerable Third Law, "Any sufficiently advanced technology is indistinguishable from magic" (Clarke 1977; cf. McSherry 2002: 6; Telesco and Knight 2001), which

Christopher Dewdney (1999) suggests ought to have read: "Any sufficiently advanced technology is indistinguishable from magic to those unfamiliar with that technology." The point being, of course, that magic and science are matters of perception and chronology. Yet, quite unselfconsciously, some modern Pagans make extraordinary claims for the Internet, the World Wide Web, and their ability to partipate in it.

"How is it that your computer understands that a particular keystroke is equivalent to a specific symbol?" asks Lisa McSherry (2002: 6), echoing Galina Krasskova's claim to the magickal nature of computer programming. "This lack of direct knowledge makes writing a letter on your computer a magickal experience. The loci of technology has become invisible—literally, occult. Then again, these glorious technologies are also magickal because, with their aid, we now can impress our will upon the stuff of the world, reshaping it, at least in part, according to our imagination." Here it appears that "magick" is merely a function of ignorance; if we don't know how something works it must be magickal, or at least we can understand it as magickal, or we can call it magickal. In this instance, any difference between "it's magick" and "it's like magic" is lost. Similarly, it is magickal if it can be used to "reshape" the world "according to our imagination"—criteria which would apply equally, it would seem, to hoes, trowels, house paint, and those rocks that "magically" appear in one's garden every spring.

Invoking the spirit of Arthur C. Clarke, techno-pagan Erik Davis begins his discussion of new technology by declaring romantically that "the velocity and mutability of the times invokes a certain supernatural quality" (1998: 1; cf. Vale and Sulak 2001, also Drury 2002). But . . . does it really? The well-known "God Hypothesis" invokes various dimensions of the supernatural in situations of ignorance and inadequate comprehension. Thunder in the mountains is God rearranging heaven's furniture, hosting a celestial barn dance, or forging the next generation of supernatural weaponry. Natural disasters—floods, earthquakes, volcanoes, tornadoes and hurricanes, hailstorms, forest fires, mudslides, and plagues of frogs—are interpreted through religious eyes as clear evidence of Divine displeasure and the indisputable result of God's judgment called down upon humanity. Sacrifice became one of the mechanisms by which the tripartite relationship between deity, humanity, and either calamity or blessing could be managed, if not necessarily understood. In recent decades, despite the answers to many questions heretofore relegated to the God Hypothesis, modern versions—e.g., what we might call the "Gods from Outer Space" Hypothesis (for a variety of perspectives on this, see Collins 2002; Harrold and Eve 1995; Picknett and Prince 1999; Raël 1986; Sitchin 1976, 1985, 1990, 1995; Temple 1998; von Däniken 1969, 1970)—have been similarly invoked to bridge the gaps between our understanding of certain ancient civilizations, particularly their technological sophistication and capabilities, and the feats of architecture and engineering left to us by these cultures: Nazca, Giza, Machu Piccu, Stonehenge, and Easter Island. And there remains a mystique about each of these, for we do not know, precisely, how their construction was accomplished. There are theories, some more plausible than others, but we do not *know*.

## Transparency and Hyperbole

Computer technology, however, is of an entirely different order, despite the supernaturalist rhetoric by which it is often surrounded and the air of mystery its capabilities convey to the average user. In fact, it strains language about the supernatural precisely because there is no mystery; there is no *cultural gap in understanding*. For the most part, the builders of everything from machine language and source code to routers, servers, and cable modems, and from those who debugged the code for software such as DreamWeaver and Frontpage to those who use that software to design cyber-temples for themselves are still among us—a fact whose importance cannot be overstated. The "mysteries of the Internet" are manifestly *not* mysteries to them. We may not know exactly how the enormous blocks of limestone and granite were quarried, transported, cut, dressed, and set in place to build Khufu's great pyramid at Giza; we may not know who carved and erected the massive stone heads on Easter Island—or why; we may not know who designed and carved the Nazca lines, or what purpose they served. But we do know who wrote the first Unix code; we do know how dissatisfaction with Microsoft® Windows led to the creation of Linux and the open source revolution; we do know how Pentium chips work down to the last component. We know how modems and routers work, and we know how e-mail functions. Because if we didn't know those things, they wouldn't work. It's really not any more complicated than that. Indeed, through such social movements as the "open source revolution," which has continued to produce not simply more robust versions of Linux, but a wide range of software to run on it, those for whom the arcana of computer programming and software design are patently opaque are invited to participate in the open source culture and achieve technological transparency—if not necessarily enlightenment (see especially Raymond 1999: 231–50). Yet, in much of modern Pagan e-space, supernatural language persists, and it betrays in certain instances a willing embrace of ignorance as evidence of or validation for the supernaturalism (or occulted naturalism) by which the modern Pagan worldview is underpinned.

"Cyberspace is a technological doorway to the astral plane," writes Lisa McSherry (2002: 5), though once again, technologically speaking, it is no such thing. It is the communication space created by trillions of digital switches, opening and closing in response to the commands and requests of millions of users around the world. The High Priestess of JaguarMoon continues, however, that "once we enter Cyberspace, we are no longer in the physical plane; we literally stand in a place between the worlds, one with heightened potential to be as sacred as any circle cast on the ground" (McSherry 2002: 5). This very brief passage embodies much of the modern Pagan response to technology that we have discussed in this chapter—and points to many of the discussions that follow. One might be tempted to take McSherry for a lyricist, trying to explain metaphorically (and, again, somewhat romantically) what she experiences through her faith—were it not for her use of the word "literally," as in "we *literally* stand." Not we *metaphorically* stand, or we *mythologically* stand, but we *literally* stand. Similarly, "we are no longer in the physical plane"—never mind that we connected to Cyberspace through a physical machine using our physical fingers to type in the relevant commands or move the ever-obedient mouse (the cyber-witch's true familiar!); never mind that, if we are AOL customers and we have e-mail waiting, it is our physical ears that register the cheery (or annoying, depending on your perspective) "You've got mail!" message; never mind that everything that appears on the screen, everything to which we respond—from text messages to .jpeg files, from command icons to streaming video—is part of a physical system that includes the coherent pixels on the screen, our eyeballs, optic nerves, and brains. All of which tell the fingers to do something else—something physical, something ineluctably embodied. According to McSherry's partner, however, "'Cyberspace is just a techno-term for the astral plane or any other nonphysical reality'" (McSherry 2002: 5).

And this is the key, because, technology notwithstanding, ultimately the World Wide Web, the Internet, Cyberspace, whatever label one gives to the communication that is mapped out, quilted together, and ongoing in those trillions of digital interstices, is an environment of the mind—and the mind has the power to shape things in ways far removed from those intended by their creators.

CHAPTER **4**

# Online Solitaries and Cybercovens
## *(Re-)Inventing the Modern Pagan Path*

> Never feel inferior because you're not working under the guidance of a teacher or an established coven. Don't worry that you won't be recognized as a true Wiccan. Such recognition is important only in the eyes of those giving or withholding it, otherwise it is meaningless. You need only worry about pleasing yourself and developing a rapport with the Goddess and God.
>
> Scott Cunningham (1988: 53–54)

### Alone and in Community: Modern Pagan Working Practice

"Isn't the Internet the greatest thing?" asks the unnamed Web mistress of Solitary Wicca (www.angelfire.com/ar2/solitarywicca/aboutus.htm). "Back in 1987 when I first began to study Wicca, not only was the written material limited, but the places to obtain it were even more restricted . . . Now with the internet, you can get all the information and products you could want or need and then some. Perhaps one of the best things though, is that we get to meet one another and share our knowledge and experiences." According to another online biography, Selina Silver, a Canadian "Eclectic Solitary Witch," initially wanted to join a coven. However, "I live in a small rural town in Ontario with an almost non-existing Wiccan community. Those that do live here have learned as I have to be a Solitary Practitioner. My purpose in creating this web site is to assist any Solitary Practitioner in their journey with some of the knowledge I have gained throughout the years" (www.geocities.com/selina_silver). Like many solitaries, the works of modern Pagan authors such as Scott

Cunningham have been very influential, and much of the information Silver provides for visitors to her site is taken from two of his books (1988, 1993). In addition to information and online shopping, some modern Pagan solitaries use the Internet in attempts to foster community among those who practice their path alone. The somewhat oxymoronically named Circle of One (www.geocities.com/azalins_circle) and Circle of the Solitary (www.circle-ofthesolitary.org) both exist to provide community opportunities for modern Pagan solitaries.

On the other hand, Lady Gueneva, a 30-year-old mother of two from Pennsylvania, is the High Priestess of the Blue Moonlight Coven (www.blue-moonlightcoven.com), which operates both online and off-line, and the founder of the online Blue Moonlight Coven Seminary of Living Earth Religions, Inc., which she claims is the teaching center for her legally recognized Pagan church (www.bluemoonlightcovenseminary.com). Indeed, her elaborate Web sites appear to provide everything the online Pagan could want. In addition to online classes and off-line correspondence courses in both basic and advanced Wicca, Lady Gueneva offers instruction in Reiki, as well as a "Priest-ess Ordination Program." Like Lisa McSherry's JaguarMoon Cyber Coven, fully committed participants may take first-, second-, and third-degree Wiccan initiation and training through the Blue Moonlight Coven. Online rituals are conducted in chat rooms and are open for public observation, as long as observers maintain an appropriate attitude of respect for the proceedings. At the other end of the modern Pagan spectrum from Selina Silver and the Web mistress of Solitary Wicca, however, Lady Gueneva makes explicit reference to the authority of lineage in Wicca, declaring that "it takes a witch to make a witch" (www.ladygueneva.com), a claim that finds its origins in the British Wicca of Gerald Gardner, Alex and Maxine Sanders, Raymond Buckland, and the Farrars, Janet and Stewart. Lady Gueneva and her partner, Lord Gawaine, also operate an online occult supply company (www.moonlitmagickonline-store.com).

Perhaps the most basic organizational distinction among modern Pagans, one which often both precedes and proceeds from diversities in tradition, path, or lineage, is the difference between the solitary practitioner and the ritual group worker. The tension between those who are initiated and trained by a coven or other ritual working group and those who are self-initiated and auto-didactic exemplifies an important aspect of emergent orthodoxies within the larger orbit of modern Paganism, and it is a topic to which we will return at several points. As I noted in Chapter 2, solitaries are those modern Pagans who, for a variety of reasons, choose to work either primarily or exclusively alone; group practitioners, on the other hand, locate their religious practice and ritual either primarily or exclusively in a communal context. Because many solitaries feel that coveners (or those who practice in other kinds of ritual working group) consider them "second-class Pagans," as though they are somehow less authentic or less committed to the modern Pagan path if they are not part of a working lineage (even though many solitaries have been initiated in one or several traditions), I would like to suggest that solitaries are among those who benefit most from online presence and interaction.

*Solitaries Uniting Online*

Solitary Witches 13, for example, the Yahoo! discussion group we first encountered in Chapter 2, is very clear that the list is for solitary practitioners only; because of the very different perspective they bring, coveners are simply not welcome to participate in its discussions. Several months after the list began, however, and the first tentative online contacts had given way to more significant and extended interactions, a number of messages began to appear inviting members to various Pagan functions in the Rhode Island area. "Do you feel born to or drawn to the Craft?" asked Lady Rhiannon in one post/advertisement. "Have you had your fill of pop-wicca books? Learn the basics of the Old Religion from a Traditionalist High Priestess and Priest. We are seeking serious students only." Though other members quickly reminded Lady Rhiannon that the list was for solitaries only, this posting drew the particular ire of the list owner, Hemptress, whose response is worth quoting at length for some of the tensions within modern Paganism—both online and off—that it reveals.

> I created this list to be a safe haven for RI solitaries, who, for the most part, get little or no respect from coveners, HP [High Priests] and HPS [High Priestesses]. I refuse to allow this list to be used as a trolling ground for coven recruiters. I choose to be Solitary, it is part of my tradition, handed down to me from my grandmother. I have no need of followers, I care not if anyone shares my beliefs, I need no one's help to raise power or celebrate my religion. I am Solitary and Proud. I hope to one day create a legal 'church' for solitaries, a safe haven where we can teach our children, socialize, gather for circle if we so choose, teach and learn from each other. Where we will all be equals. I am on at least 7 other pagan/witch related lists and know firsthand the bias against solitaries and the outright recruiting that goes on from covens.

The message index for the discussion group indicates that Lady Rhiannon did not return to Solitary Witches 13.

In this example, though, notwithstanding the somewhat paradoxical notion of a "legal 'church' for solitaries," for Hemptress the issue of "a safe haven" reveals a number of separate, but interrelated aspects in the current evolution of modern Paganism. Fundamental to the problem is the general lack of respect she contends solitaries receive from coveners, as well as the more specific problem of online discussion groups as a new coven recruiting space. A number of list members quickly supported Hemptress's declaration, offering their own stories of rejection and aloofness encountered at the hands of more "legitimate" modern Pagans, often when they tried to participate in public rituals. One aspect of this particular problem, however, which passes unnoticed in these discussions, could have less to do with the fact that these people are solitary practitioners than that they were simply new participants in an established group. In at least one case, the subsequently snubbed solitary loudly proclaimed the differences in ritual procedure during the ritual itself. In this instance, by establishing clear conceptual and hierarchical distance between herself and the other members of the working group, it appears that the solitary ensured she would not be welcomed. Thus, masked by an a priori (and not entirely unreasonable) feeling of marginalization and exclusion, larger issues of group dynamics—insiders and outsiders, established members versus newcomers, and accepted patterns of behavior occasionally interrupted by outspoken visitors—are often interpreted by solitaries as clear evidence of disrespect for their chosen method of pathworking.

*Legitimating the Solitary Path*

Legitimation and validation of the solitary path are ongoing issues within modern Paganism and likely to remain so, largely because the open source nature and personally gnostic authorization of modern Pagan belief and practice encourages levels of experimentation and syncretization that some modern Pagans will simply find unacceptable—all claims to the contrary notwithstanding. As important as the bounding of solitary discussion space online and the assertion of legitimacy for those who choose to practice alone, however, is the larger issue of authority within modern Paganism more generally. How do those who create their own belief system and program of practice assert not only their right to do so, but the appropriateness of their choice? Briefly, in terms of the modern Pagan solitary, this authority is instantiated in three ways: (1) a belief in the rapid growth of modern Paganism as a new religious movement; (2) the location of one's solitary practice within the context of a family lineage or esoteric tradition; and (3) the appropriation of culturally significant symbols of religious power and privilege.

First, many participants—both solitaries and coveners—believe that modern Paganism is one of the fastest growing religious movements in the Western world, and infer from this a certain measure of authority and legitimacy. Having just returned from the Heartland Pagan Festival, for example, an annual gathering of modern Pagans held in Leavenworth County, Kansas, a modern Pagan solitary named Windwalker pointed out to the Solitary

Witches 13 group what is becoming a common refrain among many modern Pagans. At the festival, Windwalker writes, "it was discussed that Neo-Paganism/Wicca/Asatru/Shamanism . . . etc. is the fastest growing 'belief system' (trying to avoid that Religion word) in the United States, England, Canada, and Australia. Supposedly doubling in size every (there's debate on this figure) 18 months." Although she does not disclose who made this claim or on what basis, because a number of her other comments mention Phyllis Curott, a New York entertainment lawyer, modern Pagan author (1998, 2002), and guest speaker at the 2003 Heartland festival, and because Curott does make similar claims in her Wiccan autobiography, *Book of Shadows* (1998: xiv), she was likely Windwalker's immediate source. Whether she is or not, though, a number of other modern Pagan authors have made these claims explicitly. In the foreword to the third edition of *Witchcraft from the Inside*, for example, Raymond Buckland states that, despite Gerald Gardner's fears that Wicca was "a dying religion," "the Craft has grown at an unprecedented rate" (1995: xii); indeed, he subtitled this edition, *Origins of the Fastest Growing Religious Movement in America*. Likewise, in *Teen Witch*, Silver RavenWolf states that "recent statistics tell us that Witchcraft is the fastest growing religion in the United States today" (1998: 22). Like Buckland, however, RavenWolf declines to disclose the source of her "statistics" or the research on which they were based. Finally, at the beginning of her ethnography of Wicca, *Never Again the Burning Times*, modern Pagan scholar Loretta Orion implies a similar growth rate, claiming that "conservative estimates suggest that approximately a few hundred thousand individuals participate in Neopaganism" (1995: 1). In her endnote, however, she states that "this estimate is based on readership of books published on related subjects" (1995: 279 n.2)—though she does not say how that "readership" was determined, how readership constitutes "participation," nor how broadly she cast the net of "related subjects" (for a critical review of Orion's work, which has been lionized by many modern Pagans, see Cowan 1998). Although I will have more to say about the influence of the World Wide Web on the perception of modern Pagan growth (for which there is some statistical evidence; cf. ARIS 2001) in Chapter 7, there are three brief but important points to be made here in terms of the social construction of modern Pagan reality: the source of the "statistics" on which Orion and Windwalker base their claims, the implications of the growth rate modern Pagans such as Windwalker claim for modern Paganism, and the sociological fact that the veracity of neither matters in the construction of modern Pagan reality.

First, echoing Orion, Windwalker writes that "this figure [i.e., the growth rate of modern Paganism] was determined by book sales in these groups. Book sales representing about 10% of actual group size." The rather dubious nature of her latter claim notwithstanding, as I have noted elsewhere with particular reference to Orion, "surely not everyone who reads material associated with a given movement or phenomenon could be categorized as a participant. If that were true, then every researcher in every field would be, almost by definition, a participant in that field" (Cowan 1998: 399). My personal library of modern Pagan literature, for example, is extensive, to say the least, and includes among other things complete back sets of a number of modern Pagan newsletters and magazines. The same is true for the collection of fundamentalist Christian material on which I based research for *Bearing False Witness?*, an introduction to the evangelical countercult movement (Cowan 2003a). Yet I am neither a modern Pagan nor a fundamentalist Christian. It should be obvious that simply reading, even purchasing, the *Baghavad Gita* no more makes one a member of the International Society for Krishna Consciousness than reading or receiving a copy of the *Doctrine and Covenants* makes one a Latter-day Saint. Yet, modern Pagans like Windwalker and Orion appear ready to credence this kind of flawed demographic methodology if it supports their claims to religious authority and cultural legitimacy.

Next, even if we give credence to Windwalker's statistics for the sake of discussion, their implications are fantastic. Using the lowest possible base figure argued by Orion—i.e., that there were about 300,000 modern Pagans in the United States during the time she was conducting her research in the late 1980s and early 1990s, but going back only to the year of *Never Again the Burning Times*'s publication in 1995—if the modern Pagan population is doubling every 18 months as Windwalker claims, there should be nearly 20 million modern Pagans in the United States by now. While this is clearly an absurd figure—both Berger (1999: 6) and Pike (2001: xii) put the American modern Pagan population between 150,000 and 200,000, ARIS (2001) at 134,000, though modern Pagans such as Macha NightMare believe there are more than one million (2003)—it is, nonetheless, instructive for the social construction of reality it illustrates and the often uncritical manner in which modern Pagans such as Windwalker willingly accept such problematic statistics. In terms of legitimating modern Paganism, the underlying logic seems clear: a growing movement is one that has (or ought to have) more cultural authority than one that is in decline, and the faster it grows, the more authority it accrues.

Those familiar with the taxonomy of logical fallacies will recognize this easily as an *argumentum ad populum*, the "bandwagon fallacy"—concluding that something is true, authoritative, or credible simply because large groups of people believe it. To reiterate our earlier discussion about relative domains of evidence and authority, however, these sorts of arguments are far more important for the maintenance and reinforcement of modern Pagan reality than they are as indicators of any increase in the social or cultural influence of modern Paganism as a result of its undeniable growth over the past two decades. That is, arguments from growth are more compelling for those who are already disposed to believe them, or who have a vested interest in believing them, than for those who are not so disposed; whether they carry any freight in terms of conversion to modern Paganism, and the place of the Internet on that particular train, is a topic I will take up in the last chapter.

Finally, in the social construction of modern Pagan belief and practice it cannot be overstated that the empirical reality of the statistics really matters very little. If those who deploy these statistics in support of their belief that modern Paganism is the fastest growing religious tradition in North America and Australiabase their behavior on that belief, then whether modern Paganism is or isn't growing faster than other traditions ceases to be of importance. In this, it passes almost into the realm of theology: a statement of faith on which behavior is based as opposed to a statement of fact that is empirically demonstrable. As I have noted elsewhere, with particular reference to the evangelical Christian countercult but which is equally applicable to modern Paganism, "one of the fundamental premises of a sociology of knowledge . . . is that *perceived* reality is not inevitably congruent with *actual* reality. It may well be, but it is not necessarily so. However, because individuals and groups operate within the constraints of perceived reality, it is this dynamic that governs behavior. Social action is predicated on the perception of reality, not necessarily the accuracy of that perception" (Cowan 2003a: 5).

The second mechanism by which the solitary Pagan path is legitimated and validated is the location of one's solitary practice within an established family tradition or esoteric lineage—whether that lineage is hereditary or metempsychotic. "I choose to be Solitary," writes Hemptress (2002), "it is part of my tradition, handed down to me from my grandmother." Though rejected by some modern Pagans, adverting to a hereditary tradition is a not-uncommon method of instantiating religious authority for both solitaries and coveners. A number of modern Pagans from a wide variety of traditions, both the prominent (for example, Raymond Buckland, Z Budapest, Marguerite Elspeth, Raven Grimassi, Lady Sheba, and deTraci Regula) and the less well-known claim similar genetic authority. While Ondine, a middle-aged solitary from Utah, declares on Solitary Witches 13 that "ancestral ties to witchcraft are [not] necessary for one to become a Witch," but she does regard them as crucial for her own sense of modern Pagan self. She continues, "My ancestral witch links make me, personally, feel wonderfully connected to the past—it now feels like it's in my DNA." "I am sure that all of us have Witches/herbalists/faith healers/folk medicine practitioners in our ancestral lines," she concludes. "The odds are each of us has at least one ancestor who practiced village magick." Her logic for hereditary authority—personally gnostic and empirically nonfalsifiable—resonated very strongly with a number of other group members. One of those, Diana, agreed that "it does give one a warm feeling to know that it is in the blood line," but also invoked modern Pagan belief in reincarnation (metempsychosis) to explain the pull she feels toward modern Paganism: "I know I lived as a Celtic priestess many lives ago."

Third, many modern Pagans, including Hemptress, have chosen to declare their legitimacy through the appropriation of culturally significant symbols of religious power and prestige—most obviously, ordination. While there are emerging modern Pagan training centers such as Cherry Hill Seminary (www.cherryhillseminary.org) and online "colleges of Witchcraft and Wizardry" such as the Esoteric Theological Seminary (also known as the University of Esoterica; www.northernway.org) and the College of the Sacred Mists Online School of Wicca (www.workingwitches.com) that offer ordination and/or initiation after a suitable period of study, a number of modern Pagans have had themselves ordained online through such organizations as the Universal Life Church of Modesto, California (www.ulc.org) and the Church of Seven Planes (www.sevenplanes.org), which is headquartered in the small town of Cooper, Texas. "I just received my certification today!" wrote Heather Johnston, for example, to the Yahoo! group, Solitary (groups.yahoo.com/groups/solitary). "I am now 'Angelic Minister' Heather True Johnston as ordained by the Universal Life Church. I am so happy!" Luna Nokomis, who introduced herself to the same discussion list as "a Wiccan High Priestess of a family passed down Scandinavian tradition," is "also an ordained minister of the universal life church." Two list participants who were seeking information on handfasting—the ceremony in which modern Pagans, whether monogamous or polyamorous, are committed to one another—were told: "If you already have an HP have them get credentials; from Universal Life Church; fast and free unless you get other things."

The most famous of the mail-order churches, the Universal Life Church (ULC) claims to have ordained more than 20 million persons since it first began advertising in 1959 (cf. Ashmore 1977; Miller 1995). Offering a wide variety of religious commodities and services, the ULC's most common product remains ordination-on-request. What used to be facilitated through the postal service, however, has gone online through the Church's extensive Web site (www.ulc.org; other versions of the site are at www.ulchq.com and www.ulc.net). Once a prospective ordinand has filled in his or her "TRUE Legal Name," as well as a valid e-mail address, an "official certificate" of ordination in the ULC arrives about three minutes later. Other e-mails follow, advertising the various products available for purchase by the newly ordained minister. Among other things, for example, "Ministry in a Box," at $129 the ULC's "finest product," contains Marriage and Renewal of Vows certificates, a Wedding Business video, wall and wallet credentials, as well as a ULC Clergy badge and "Laminated Parking Placard." For $105 and a score of 15 out of 20 on the final examination (for which the answers are available free on request), "serious students" can receive a "PhD in Religion"; a "Masters Degree" is available for $65, as well as "Doctor of

Immortality" and "Doctor of Motivation" degrees. All degrees are accredited by the "International Accrediting Association," the "accrediting arm of the church" which is located at the same Modesto address (www.ulc.net/shop). Finally, for $10 each, the church offers a profusion of "Universal Life Church Religious Titles," including Druid, Goddess (no God!), High Priest and High Priestess, Wizard, Shaman, and (my personal favorite) Universal Philosopher of Absolute Reality. Instead of charging extra for some of these titles, however, the Church of Seven Planes advertises: "NEW with every ordination a free Doctor of Divinity at the time of your ordination issued *Honoris Causa*" (www.sevenplanes.org/ordination_request.htm; emphasis in the original).

It would be easy for readers to dismiss both the ULC and the CSP as transparent and rather pathetic religious scams, "gone from the classified ads at the back of *Fate* magazine to the Java-script and Flash graphics of the World Wide Web" (Cowan and Hadden 2004b: 128). However, although there are a number of obviously spurious ordinations meant either to ridicule the entire process or entered into at the far end of too much beer, and although anyone who has been through the rigor of real life seminary training might cast a jaundiced eye over those whose ordination credentials arrive via e-mail, if only one percent of the 20 million ordinations the ULC claims to have performed are taken seriously by participants, that still constitutes 200,000 persons in the past half-century. And, in terms of our current discussion, there is little to suggest that many of the modern Pagans who have taken advantage of the ULC's service are not entirely serious about their claims, their commitment to their spiritual paths, or their belief that the ULC has conferred upon them some measure of legitimate authority.

The Rev. Edward D. Allen, D.D., for example, who also goes by the Pagan name Medicine Hawk, is part of an eclectic working circle of Wiccans some of whom have chosen ULC or CSP ordination because they believe it "adds a 'legitimacy' to what we are doing as far as the community at large is concerned." In this case, members of Allen's circle serve as Wiccan or Pagan chaplains at a number of area hospitals. And SeaMaiden, a modern Pagan solitary from Long Island, told the Yahoo! group Solitary that she had planned a two-and-a-half hour "commitment ceremony" to mark her ordination in the Universal Life Church. In a different message, she wrote that the ULC seemed "to have a very nice philosophy," and that "it was also very neat receiving my welcome letter to 'Rev. Karel,'" her mundane name. Finally, although many who have worked as ordained clergy might dispute the alleged "high regard" with which late modern society views them—which the ULC refers to as "respect, honor, dignity and yes, some fear because you represent God" (http://ulcmonastery.safeshopper.com)—there is little doubt that the title of "Reverend" still carries a certain cultural cachet and functions as a culturally significant symbol of religious power and prestige.

Obviously, though, use of these three markers of legitimacy and authority are hardly limited to the modern Pagan solitary. Indeed, all are claimed by a variety of ritual group workers as well. Few coveners seeking to establish the credibility of modern Paganism do not point to its recent growth as an implicit indicator of legitimacy. Many modern Pagan working groups invoke the authority of lineal transmission. And a number are ordained through one online mechanism or another. Storm Mist, the "Priestess of Sacred Mists" and list owner of Beginners Wicca (groups.yahoo.com/group/beginners_wicca), is also ordained by the Universal Life Church, as are other Yahoo!-group luminaries: Bella Luna and WulfWuman (Bella Luna Cyber Coven), Piper Silverwing (Druid Celtic-Sidhe), Dan Silverstorm and Lavender Dawn (Temple of Duality). Katia, moderator of the Yahoo! discussion group, Goddess Christians, and director of the online Esoteric Theological Seminary (www.northern-way.org), also offers ordination credentials through her Web site, although the prices are significantly higher than either the ULC or CSP.

### From Gardner to Gigabytes: The Evolution of the Wiccan Coven

In order to understand the effects of the Internet and the World Wide Web on modern Pagan working groups, a brief consideration of their development is in order. Because there are such a wide variety of groups, however, and because few operate under identical principles and charters, as a working exemplar I have chosen the coven as it occurs in Wicca and non-Wiccan Witchcraft. Because Wicca and Witchcraft together constitute the largest "denomination" of modern Paganism, they offer the most useful opportunity for an analysis of the historical development of the coven. As a basic caveat, though, it must be remembered that the community of Wiccans and Witches as a whole is no more agreed on how a coven must (or even should) operate than it is on many other aspects of modern Pagan belief and practice. That is, not all covens are the same, nor do participants consider what it means to be a coven in similar ways. Who, then, gets to decide what constitutes an authentic modern Pagan working group? What are the constituents of authenticity and legitimacy? Are there identifiable attributes that distinguish bona fide covens from discussion groups, chat sessions, and sewing circles? Given that any attempt to enforce or codify the social structure of a coven would be in immediate tension with the open source character of modern Paganism and the highly individualistic sentiments of many participants, these are not unimportant questions.

Fortunately, there is something of a social and conceptual history to the coven that we can sketch from its modern Pagan origins in the 1950s through to the emergence of cybercovens, e-groves, and online ritual groups. Once sketched, we can ask what sort of working groups have appeared online, and how that appearance has affected their structure, function, and the consequent conceptualization of these groups among modern Pagans. While popular, non-Pagan conceptions of modern Wiccan covens find influences as wide ranging as the engravings of Albrecht Dürer ("Four Witches," 1497) and the chiaroscuro woodcuts of his student, Hans Baldung Grien ("Witches' Sabbath," 1510), the often maudlin or sensationalized portrayals in late modern cinema, television, and journalism (e.g., *Charmed*, *The Craft*, *Practical Magic*), as well as the blatant propagandizing of some fundamentalist Christian apologists (e.g., Abanes 2001, 2002; Larson 1999; Matrisciana 1994), the actual beginnings of the modern Wiccan coven are somewhat more prosaic than even the mildest of these portrayals. They are, however, much more important, I think, for the ways in which they demonstrate the appropriation, mythologization, and creative synthesis that marks so much of today's modern Paganisms.

*Gerald Gardner and the Modern Wiccan Coven*

As is well established now, modern Wicca as a new religious movement traces its origins to Gerald Brousseau Gardner (1884–1964), a retired British civil servant who claimed to have been initiated into a secret witches' coven in the New Forest region of southeast England just as the Second World War began (see, for example, Adler 1986; Farrar 1991; Farrar and Farrar 1981, 1984; Frew 1998; Guiley 1999; Hutton 1999; Kelly 1991; Luhrmann 1989; Orion 1995). Whether this initiation actually took place, however, whether the old woman who allegedly initiated Gardner—and who is now firmly ensconced in modern Pagan mythistory as "Dorothy Clutterbuck" or "Old Dorothy"—ever really existed, or whether, as modern Pagans such as Aidan Kelly contend, Gardner and his friends simply decided one evening to create the religion of Wicca is, for our purposes, quite beside the point. As Raymond Buckland correctly points out, even *"if Gardner had made up the whole thing, basic idea and all, from scratch, it would not negate Wica [sic] as a viable religion today. Its rapid growth around the world attests to its 'rightness' in terms of people's religious needs"* (1995: 148; emphasis in the original). Here, Buckland echoes both modern Paganism's foundation of personal gnosticism, as well as one of Emile Durkheim's most important "rules for the explanation of social facts," that is, "the utility of a fact does not explain its origins" ([1895] 1982: 119). *"When one undertakes to explain a social phenomenon,"* Durkheim wrote, *"the efficient cause which produces it and the function it fulfills must be investigated separately"* ([1895] 1982: 123; emphasis in the original). Although *The Rules of Sociological Method* may not be regarded as Durkheim's most theoretically sophisticated work (Lukes 1982: 23), the importance of this particular *règle* in terms of modern Paganism is clear. Explaining the fanciful origins of a social fact such as modern Wiccan covens—even if those origins are found to be *entirely* fabricated or drawn from distinctly questionable sources—

does nothing to diminish the cultural force those facts carry for modern Pagan participants today. Covens exist as instantiations of meaningful modern Pagan community regardless of their origin. Additionally, even if Kelly is correct and modern Wicca is Gardner's proximate invention, it still did not come into being *ex nihilo*; there are sources that reveal the conceptual substrata upon which Gardner constructed the practicalities of his vision. First and foremost of these is the work of Margaret Alice Murray (1863–1963).

Though trained as an Egyptologist by Flinders Petrie (Simpson 1994: 89), Murray is best remembered for her theories of fertility cult survival in western Europe, particularly Great Britain. Indeed, as some commentators have suggested, her books "are ground zero for the modern pagan revival" (Hare 2001; cf. Hutton 1991, 1999; Murray 1921, 1931, 1954; Simpson 1994). Beyond this basic notion of pagan survival, however, whose participants became the "witches" of the Middle Ages, the Renaissance, and the modern period, the most obvious of Gardner's borrowings from Murray is the idea of the Witches' coven. Indeed, the modern coven concept is intimately connected to this mythistory of Wiccan origins. In both *The Witch-cult in Western Europe* (1921) and *The God of the Witches* (1931), Murray posited a vast network of small groups—covens—in which pre-Christian fertility beliefs, ritual, and folk practices survived despite the persecution of the Christian church, whose own members "ransacked their vocabularies for invectives and abusive epithets" to use against those they labeled "witches" (1931: 66). One aspect of Murray's narrative, however, has influenced the social structure of modern Paganism arguably more than any other. Basing her argument on the coerced testimony from only one Scottish witch trial and a rather tortured interpretation of the prevalence of the number 13 in myth and history, she concluded that "the number in a coven never varied, there were always thirteen, i.e., twelve members and the god" (1931: 68). Once again, whether Gerald Gardner actually believed that Murray had uncovered the remains of a prehistoric fertility cult, and the evidence that he did is no more compelling than that he did not, is unimportant for our purposes. What is important is that for many modern Pagan writers and authorities, and for a variety of reasons, 13 has become the "traditional" number for a witches' coven.

Janet and Stewart Farrar, initiates of the second major tradition of British Wicca, the Alexandrian (see Farrar and Farrar 1991), though following the Gardnerian Book of Shadows, concur that "the traditional full membership of a coven is thirteen," but suggest that the number "is probably Zodiacal in origin" (1984: 180). Raymond Buckland, considered by many the person responsible for bringing British Wicca to North America (Adler 1986; Guiley 1999; Kelly 1992), acknowledges that "the 'traditional' size is thirteen, though there is absolutely no reason why that particular number should be adhered to" (1987: 53; cf. Skelton 1997: 34). Laurie Cabot contends that 13 is traditional because it reflects the number of lunar months in a year. Invoking the matrifocal epistemology common to many modern Paganisms, she writes that covens "are living vestiges of the old lunar calendars that measured time and events around the twenty-eight day menstrual cycle" (Cabot and Cowan 1989: 102). Whatever the origin, 13 members became "traditional" through repetition and social agreement among modern Pagans.

*The Coven Evolves*

As Wicca evolved in North America apart from its Gardnerian and Alexandrian traditionalism, the concept of the coven expanded further. In *Drawing Down the Moon*, a book regarded by many modern Pagans as the closest thing to an official history currently available, Margot Adler offers what is, perhaps, the most expansive definition: "A coven simply means a group of people who convene for religious or magical or psychic purposes" (1986: 108). For Starhawk, one of the most popular modern Witches and whose major work, *The Spiral Dance*, has influenced countless modern Pagans since its initial publication in 1979, "the coven is a Witch's support group, consciousness-raising group, psychic study center, clergy-training program, College of Mysteries, surrogate clan, and religious congregation all rolled into one" (1989: 49). Indeed, "College of Mysteries" is hardly inappropriate for describing the structure and practice of the modern coven because Gardner's second major source for Wicca was the Western occult tradition of the nineteenth century, the ceremonial magick of adepts such as Eliphas Lévi (whose real name was Alphonse Louis Constant; 1810–1875), Samuel MacGregor Mathers (1854–1918), and Aleister Crowley (1875–1947), and groups such as the Rosicrucians, the Hermetic Order of the Golden Dawn, and the Ordo Templi Orientis (on the relationship between Gardner and Crowley, see Kaczynski 2002; Sutin 2000). This connection is clear from a comparison of the language of his Book of Shadows, which has been available in an edited format since the mid-1980s (Farrar and Farrar 1984) and on the World Wide Web since the mid-1990s (Gardner 1961), and that used by Witches and Wiccans who have developed their ritual and practice both from within the Gardnerian tradition and apart from it (Hutton 1999). In the ceremony of first degree initiation, for example, the ritual is presided over by a "Magus"—not a High Priestess or High Priest—and the initiate is called the "Postulant"; in terms of origins, the nomenclature is not unimportant. As well, after bringing the postulant into the ritual space the circle is closed by invoking the names "Agla, Azoth, Adonai," all of which are mentioned by Lévi in his venerable *Transcendental Magic* ([1855] 1923), and the first of which goes back at least to the Renaissance Hermeticism of Cornelius Agrippa (1486–1534/5) and John Dee (1527–1608/9; cf. Peterson 2003: 10 n.31).

Regardless of its origins, however, and in contrast to the claims of many modern Pagans who point to the growth of modern Paganism as a primary indicator of its (re)emerging religious legitimacy and implicit cultural authority, Starhawk is more temperate in her assessment of the ease with which coven membership is gained. "To become a member of a coven," she writes, in a passage worth quoting at length (1989: 49–50), "a Witch must be initiated, must undergo a ritual of commitment, in which the inner teachings and secrets of the group are revealed." She continues:

> Initiation follows a long training period, during which trust and group security are slowly built. When properly timed, the ritual also becomes a rite of passage that marks a new stage in personal growth. Witchcraft grows slowly; it can never be a mass-market religion, peddled on street-corners or between flights at the airport. Witches do not proselytize. Prospective members are expected to seek out covens and demonstrate a deep level of interest. The strength of the Craft is felt to be in quality, not quantity.

While Starhawk may be forgiven for not wanting Wicca confused with other new religious movements (most obviously Hare Krishna or the Unification Church in this example), modern Paganism *has* become something of a mass market religious movement, and *The Spiral Dance* has played no small role in this. Be that as it may, she identifies the three basic components of the Wiccan coven that have remained constant since Gardner: initiation into a lineal tradition; training in the particular rituals, practices, and beliefs of that tradition; and transmission of traditional esoterica to those who have demonstrated sufficient commitment and progress in training to warrant the trust implied by that information. As Starhawk notes, each of these functions interdependently to construct an intentional religious community marked by quality and depth, as opposed to quantity and breadth. Canadian Witch and poet Robin Skelton concurred. "Covens do not advertise their meetings," he wrote, just before his death in 1997. "Witchcraft is a 'mystery religion,' and the public are not invited. Witches do not proselytise . . . Nevertheless, sometimes one does find groups of people who call themselves witches inviting the public to attend and take part in rituals, usually for a fee. There have even been public invitations to join covens. I find it difficult to believe that those who organize such things are true members of the Old Religion" (Skelton 1997: 36).

## Cyberhenge: A Typology of Modern Pagan Working Groups

Although those who make public appeals for people to join their coven may not be members of the "Old Religion" as Robin Skelton understood it, modern

Paganism is changing rapidly and the Internet has provided a platform for precisely these appeals to be made regularly and frequently.

"Blessings everyone," writes Moon Wiccan in a message to the Yahoo! group, Moonwitch. "I have decided to start my own online interactive coven. anyone interested in becoming a member, contact me at . . ." No one responded on list to her proposal and that was the last time Moon Wiccan posted to the group; nor is there is any indication that a coven was formed. All Teen Witches Coven, which announces itself as "a cyber coven for ages 14 to 19" (groups.yahoo.com/group/AllTeenWitchesCoven), has had only marginally better success. Its Yahoo! description states, "this is just the beginning of a cyber coven. Once there are enough members we will choose an official name, etc. To join just subscribe and you will be sent a small questionnaire as well as a quizlet. You will be accepted when those are looked over." Though the group lists nearly 30 members, message traffic has been almost nonexistent; online since March 2000, only seven messages have been posted since March 2001. In similar straits, the list owner of Illinois Teen Witches (groups.yahoo.com/group/IllinoisTeenWitches) began her discussion forum in December 2000, posting: "I am 16 and want to start a coven in the chicago area. Any teens interested are welcome to join the list and get to know each other. Then maybe in time we can start a teen coven. It's very difficult to find a coven willing to accept teens"— which explains in part the enormous popularity among adolescents of books such as *Teen Witch* (RavenWolf 1998)—"so why not start our own?" This forum has seen only two messages since its inception.

On the other hand, Witches of the World Coven, the online discussion group started by modern Pagan author and fledgling publisher, Starrfire Price (2002; groups.yahoo.com/group/witchesoftheworldcoven) has nearly 500 members and has posted nearly 19,000 messages in a little more than a year. A review of several hundred messages, however, indicates little more than normal online chatter: birthday greetings, what I did on my summer holidays, general questions about spells, pantheons, or Craft names, and other tidbits of information participants find interesting or meaningful. Its purpose *as a coven*, however, seems no more clear for some participants than for those in other online groups that call themselves "covens." "Is our coven name Witches of the World?" writes one member. "Or is it a coven that actually combines all the witches of the world?" Finally, and once again at the other end of the participation continuum, consider the introductory message for Coven of Golden Star (groups.yahoo.com/group/Coven_of_Golden_Star), which has a sister group in Teen Golden Star (groups.yahoo.com/group/teen-golden-star) and which has been online for nearly three years (but posted only six messages total). "wellcome to Golden Star," writes Isis_6, the otherwise unnamed list owner. "the coven was fand on June 3 2000. I'm the HPs of this group. This pay is for anyone intersed in join her little coven. If you are well and chose to conint in are coven, you will be invite to come to Coven of golden star for Deicos. This group is open all yaer be you 1 or 1001 you wellcome here. BB your HPs." In terms of the rather obvious problems with her use of English, since there is so little information available it is impossible to determine whether the author is unskilled at writing (due either to her age or to a lack of education), is writing in a language that is not native for her, or is simply careless and unconcerned about the dreadful condition of her prose. However, some of what she wrote becomes clearer when placed in the context of other messages posted to the group. By "Deicos," for example, she means a "dedicant" in her online coven, a position that will only be granted, apparently, after vetting and approval by all coven members.

Based on the hosting and communication platform chosen, groups that consider themselves "online covens" tend to operate in two ways: as part of a discussion forum through a portal such as Yahoo! or MSN, and/or through a dedicated Web site and Internet chat facilities. At the time I was writing this particular section, Yahoo! listed more than 650 discussion groups under the category of "coven"; MSN groups, which allow for more sophisticated and per-sonalized pages than Yahoo!, listed more than 1,000. On Yahoo!, however, only 17 of these groups had more than 100 members, and more than 300 groups had less than 5; on MSN, out of 100 groups I surveyed in detail, one-quarter had posted less than 10 messages total, and another one-third were no longer active at all. Once again, it appears, online reality reflects off-line social dynamics; namely, it is much easier to start a group than it is to sustain one. A closer look at both types of hosting platform reveals clearly just how far the concept of a coven has traveled from Gardner's New Forest and raises significant questions about the ongoing usefulness of the term both online and off-.

*The Discussion Group as Coven*

Because the discussion forums on both Yahoo! and MSN are numbered—Yahoo! ranks its groups according to membership, whereas there is no clear cri-terion for MSN—generating a sample is relatively easy. Using a random integer generator (www.random.org), I examined closely 100 groups on Yahoo! (15 percent) and 100 on MSN (9.8 percent). I looked at membership and message traffic data (the participative dynamics of the group), the description posted by the list owner or owners (the group's initial public presentation), and the mes-sage contents (the "emic state" of the group). From this, five categories of on-line discussion forums emerged: (1) those groups that claimed to be online covens; (2) online discussion groups for off-line covens; (3) online study, dis-cussion, or chat groups (which may be called "covens" by the members); (4) other groups (e.g., fan sites for television shows such as *Charmed* and *Buffy the Vampire Slayer*, or RPG sites that have called themselves "covens"); and (5) sites for which the available data made a useful determination impossible. Although there is some crossover between categories, especially between online covens and online study groups, these data serve as a snapshot of modern Pagan usage of the Yahoo! and MSN discussion portals. For a number of reasons, I chose not to consider open discussion forums such as the numerous alt.-groups. First, no one is claiming that the purpose of alt.-groups is anything other than open discussion. Second, the organization of the Yahoo! and MSN portals makes for more useful comparisons in terms of message traffic, membership, and group conceptualization. And, three, based on a review of several hundred alt.-messages in a dozen different forums there is no compelling reason to think that modern Pagans are saying anything substantially different on these discussion boards than in the more organized Yahoo! or MSN venues.

On Yahoo!, despite the portal categorization and the names chosen by many of the list owners—e.g., Black Scarlet Coven, Moonlight Coven, Black Rainbow Coven, Coven of the Licorice Unicorn—only 15 groups actually claimed to be online covens; 33 were online discussion forums and announcement boards that were either related or restricted to particular off-line ritual working groups; 34 were designated for study, discussion, or modern Pagan conversation; and 27 groups yielded too little information to make a useful categorization, usually due to a paucity of message traffic. Membership in all these groups ranged from 511 (Witches of the World Coven) to zero (Sacred Circle Coven of Wicca), time online from 63 months to groups that were brand new, and the number of posts per month from nearly 1,000 to zero. While it seems that groups with more members would post higher traffic numbers, this is only the case in terms of gross message traffic, and high traffic numbers are not always an indicator of online conversation that is either persistent or in-depth. For example, while Pagan E-Coven (groups.msn.com/PaganE-Coven) has been on MSN since November 2001 and has posted more than 800 messages, all but a few of them are from the list owner; similarly, online since October 2003, Divine Coven (groups.msn.com/divinecoven) has posted nearly 230 messages, *all* of them from the list owner.

A more useful indicator of online participation and interaction is message traffic factored against group membership and list duration. That is, over the course of its online career, how many posts does a particular group receive per month per member? On Yahoo!, fully 60 percent of the groups surveyed posted less than one message per month per member, including, for example, Mystickal Magick Witches (groups.yahoo.com/group/mysticalmagickwitches) and the Ancient Cauldron Coven (groups.yahoo.com/group/AncientCauldron Coven), both of which have around 400 members each and have been online since August 2000 and October 1998 respectively. On MSN the numbers are similar. Including groups that are no longer active, 64 percent of the sample posted less than one message per month per member.

Thus, at first blush, though it seems that there is an enormous amount of modern Pagan conversation on the Internet—by the time this was written, Yahoo! listed nearly 5,000 groups under its various "Pagan" categories. If the trends revealed by these data hold, few groups have more than 100 members, most have fewer than 10, and most receive less than one message per month per member. This problem is compounded by multiple membership; because enrolment is often no more involved than clicking a button, many participants belong to a number of different lists. The raw number of groups also reveals the fluidity and ephemerality of the World Wide Web. When I first looked for the category "Coven" in the MSN directory, it returned 1,020 results with "coven" in either the group name or its online description. When I searched the term again the next day, it returned only 956. In less than 24 hours, 64 groups had disappeared from the directory; a week later, however, there were 1,034 listed.

On both Yahoo! and MSN, the groups that posted the highest number of messages per month per member were those I have designated "online groups for off-line covens." On Yahoo!, this accounted for 18 out of 35 groups that posted more than one message per month per member. If we include "online study, discussion, or chat groups" as a crossover category, because message content indicates many modern Pagans who interact in these groups also know each other off-line, all but seven groups are represented. Though these data are impressionistic and hardly definitive, this pattern of message traffic accords well with other research into online interaction (cf. Kraut et al. 1998, 2002; Parks 1996). Sankofa Pride, for example (groups.yahoo.com/group/sanko-faprode), is the "virtual covenstead" of an off-line coven in the Los Angeles area. Visitors to the online group are warned (in red font), "***Membership in this Yahoo! Group is limited to members of the physical coven***." Online for nearly two years with only six members, however, it has generated more than eight messages per month per member. Not surprisingly, people appear far more likely to interact online with those they know off-line than they are with strangers, no matter how welcoming a stranger's message may be.

If these represent some of the participative dynamics of modern Pagan conversation online, what then is the public face of that conversation? That is, how do groups present themselves in order to attract potential members? How do they initially conceptualize what it is they are doing online? How does that conceptualization accord both with group performance and with similar groups off-line? While it is axiomatic that not all discussion groups that call themselves "covens" are, what issues do their presentation of themselves as covens raise for the concept in the context of the larger modern Pagan community?

Of the 15 Yahoo! groups that claim to be working online covens, only two posted more than one message per month per member. One, Penumbra Veritas, is a crossover between the two types of online venues, operating as both a public discussion group (groups.yahoo.com/PenumbraVeritasPublicForum) and a dedicated Web site (http://members.cox.net/penumbraveritas). Penumbra Veritas' High Priestess describes it as "a cybercoven, founded in 2003 by three dedicated Priestess of the Lord and Lady . . . While we are not specifically a learning coven, we do offer a strong calendar of classes, discussion, and various other learning opprtunities for those who are Wiccan and who gain access to information about Wicca and alternative religions comes from the internet" (Tarryn 2003).

The other group, Coven Scions of Aradia (groups.yahoo.com/coven_scions_of_aradia), has been online since October 2002 and describes itself as "an online coven that discusses Magick and Witchcraft in the Midland/Odessa, Texas, area. We also have an active live coven of various Pagans and Witches who practice an ecclectic form of The Craft." Off-line, it appears that most of the members have known each other for some time, perhaps years. This continues to support the hypothesis that off-line relations that are carried online tend to be more durable than relationships that form and exist only over the Internet. While a relatively high number of posts to this group relate directly to modern Paganism and the group's practice as an off-line coven—invitations to get together for Sabbat rituals, dedication of new coven members, and exchange of information of spellworking, meditation, and visualization practices—it is clear that the online group's most important function is simply to keep members in touch with each other when, as some put it, their mundane lives interfere and overwhelm. And, despite the fact that per member message traffic on this group is considerably higher than on many other groups, some members at least feel it could be higher still. If there is a lull in the message traffic, for example, plaintive posts such as "Hello????" and "Is anyone out there . . . ?" are not infrequent. Even here, however, looking more closely at the message pattern reveals important details about the dynamics of online conversation, whether modern Pagan or not. On the Coven Scions of Aradia group, one member frequently posts what might be called "CQ" messages. In the technical language of amateur radio, CQ is the code broadcast to indicate that one is transmitting and open to receiving; it has been modified online as the well-known ICQ ("I seek you"). When an exchange occurs with this member, messages are usually of the one-line, "Good morning," "Hi, I'm on," or "Couldn't sleep, is anyone else on?" variety. That is, this member treats the Coven message board—which requires that all posts be vetted by the group administrators before general transmission—as though it were an instant messaging service instead of a temporally dislocated store-and-forward system. When one considers the cost of computer equipment and access, the physical time it takes to compose, type, and upload a message, this is hardly the most efficient means of communication. As well, the intentionality required by Internet communications does not allow for the multitasking that has become a dubious hallmark of late modern society. That is, although it is not a practice I recommend to my students, one *can* talk on the telephone while watching television and working on one's homework. If one is responding to e-mail, however, instant messaging, or engaging in some other form of Internet communication, this kind of split-attention multitasking is more difficult, if not impossible. Computer-mediated communication requires a much higher level of intentionality than many other forms of human interaction; reading and keyboarding comes to most of us less easily than listening and speaking. That said, though, it is equally clear that if the expectations of discussion group members are not met in terms of list traffic and message volume, a number of things happen: dissatisfied list members stop posting and/or leave the list, which leads to even less message traffic, which leads to larger gaps in the fabric of the putative online community. Although these dynamics are hardly limited to online social interaction, the fact that messages are archived and available for scrutiny at a later date provides an important window for research into the way participants are—and are not—using the World Wide Web.

Of the MSN groups that explicitly call themselves covens and are still active, only six had posted more than 10 messages over the course of their online career. Consider the following three examples. The Spiral Phoenix Coven (groups.msn.com/SpiralPhoenixCoven) has been online since April 2002 and has posted nearly 200 messages in that time. The majority of the traffic, however, has taken place between the three list managers; there is very little participation from the other group members. Though it has only seven members (three of whom are list managers), the Black Sanctuary Coven (groups .msn.com/TheBlackSanctuaryCoven) has posted more than 150 messages since August 2003. Despite the list description that the group is "a place where people from all walks of life can come together and discuss about WICCA!" (emphasis in the original), none of the posts have anything remotely to do with modern Paganism. All participants obviously know each other off-line and message traffic is restricted to rather predictable teen chatter: boredom with life, school, or parents; who's popular at school and who isn't, and did you see *Charmed* last night? Most of the site pages that purport to deal with modern Pagan topics are little more than shovelware cut-pasted-and-reloaded from Web sites such as the Ontario Consultants on Religious Tolerance (www.ocrt .org; cf. Robinson 2000). Online since February 2002, Calendula's Garden Coven (groups.msn.com/calendulasgardencoven) also posts basic Net chatter, though some brief discussions have taken place around gardening, the magickal and non-magickal use of herbs, and astrology. At one point, the list owner, Calendula Goth (*calendula* is a small genus of herbs), offered to teach "Beginner's Wicca" online. Five members responded that they would like to participate, but there is no indication from subsequent message traffic that such classes ever took place.

Finally, back on Yahoo!, Avladphoenix's Universal Coven (groups.yahoo. com/group/avladphoenixsuniversalcoven) provides a brief example that all is *perhaps* not what it seems on the road to Cyberhenge. Though the group has posted only 30 messages in 50 months, the "Founder's Message" on the main page reads in part: "This coven is the culmination of 2-1/2 yrs of planning & meditations . . . This is to be a teaching and learning coven where research, study into the origins, & tales of the Craft are both welcomed & encouraged." Only two messages, however, could be even remotely construed as dealing with Wicca or Witchcraft. And although most of the hyperlinks provided for members do navigate to Wiccan or modern Pagan Web sites, fewer than half of them work. The one file that Avladphoenix has uploaded, though, which he lists as "Alternative Dating," links to a Web service advertising "BDSM/Alternative lifestyle personals" and offering subscribers a "Free online Fetish Magazine, and sexy member photos!" Describing himself as "single and looking," Avladphoenix's Yahoo! profile lists him as a 51-year-old male, whose address is "Tartaras, Hades," and whose interests include bondage and BDSM. In addition to the "coven," he claims to operate another group, "Master K. I.'s Kidnap Inc.," a "bondage club" (which is no longer operational on the Yahoo! portal). Though Avladphoenix's intentions for his "online coven" may be entirely aboveboard, the various components he includes on the group site give the impression at least that he has ulterior motives and raises the serious issue of safety in the online environment. It is hardly inconceivable that sites like this are precisely the reason so few participants in online discussion forums are willing to disclose much in the way of personal information.

Compared to a stand-alone Web site, especially one that carries its own domain name, creating a discussion platform on an Internet portal such as Yahoo! or MSN is a very simple process and requires little in terms of creativity or commitment. The design software, organizational templates, and Web hosting architecture are already in place; separate Internet domain support is not required; and decisions about access, membership, and group moderation are dealt with as menu options in the set-up software. Indeed, establishing a new group on Yahoo! can take less than a minute. And, judging by the haste with which some "online coven" descriptions were obviously written, their moderators did not take much more time than that. Despite their description as "online covens," though, it seems clear that very few groups on either portal consider themselves covens in the off-line sense of the term. On the one hand, they are simply discussion groups, asynchronous computer-mediated communication forums, the content of which is frequently banal, uneven, and decidedly mundane; in fact, even to call them *discussion* groups often stretches the boundaries of that concept. For a number of the teen-oriented groups, these forums have the feel of the clubs many of us formed as children and used as preadolescent and adolescent mechanisms of identity formation and boundary making. On some groups, "coven" and "club" are used interchangeably, and it seems that the hand-lettered sign on the tree fort marked "No gurlls!" has simply been replaced online with "Muggles by permission only" and "No Christians allowed." ("Muggles," of course, is the term used for non-magickal people in the enormously popular *Harry Potter* series [cf. Rowling 1998; Von Adams 2003]; discussion list and chat room proselytization by evangelical Christians is a not-infrequent problem for modern Pagans.)

On the other hand, though teens and young adults may think of a coven as cool, without necessarily understanding precisely what it is, the individuals who have created these online groups have chosen this very particular cultural form—a form that is not infrequently marginalized—to express those mechanisms of identity formation. Whether they are practicing Wiccans or Witches, interested in modern Paganism because of personal spiritual or intellectual resonance, or participating in an "online coven" merely for the clandestine thrill and rebellion of it, these groups do contribute to the construction of identity that is crucial to successful social engagement, interaction, and integration. Although it could be argued that they represent little more than religious creativity responding to cultural fashion—a charge which for some is no doubt accurate—as I will discuss more fully in Chapter 6, participation in these groups represents an important component of the social presentation and representation of the modern Pagan self, both online and off-. That is, whether they are successful as "real" covens or not, the creation of online, Yahoo!- or MSN-based "covens" is an important extension of modern Pagan creativity.

As a final example in this category, consider CrystalRock Coven (groups .yahoo.com/group/crystalrockcoven), created in 2002 by a 27-year-old Wiccan who goes by the Craft name "Storm," and who remains one of only two members. In addition to the few messages she has received, Storm has uploaded a collection of modern Pagan graphics collected from other Web sites and some basic shovelware files about the Wiccan religion. Her introductory message to the group reads in part: "I have spent a lot of time this past week thinking about my place in WICCA. There comes a time when we all need to reup our commintment to the craft. I came to that place and I knew it was time for me to do so. I have go and found a place where I can get my licens to be ordainted as a minister. As of July 13, 2002 I am full pleaged High Prestiest. I have now tacken this to a newer high for me, and I am still leering what I can." Her problematic spelling and grammar notwithstanding, I bring this example up because, like those who have availed themselves of ordination through the Universal Life Church, there is little reason to think that Storm does not see CrystalRock Coven as an important part of her identity as a modern Pagan, nor herself as a "full pleaged High Prestiest." Like many others I have considered in this chapter, it appears as though she has created this discussion group as much for herself as for anyone else who might stumble upon it and join.

*The Web Site as Coven*

Though stand-alone Web sites that claim to host online covens are considerably less numerous than those based in Yahoo! or MSN, not least because they require considerably more work than their discussion group cousins, dozens, perhaps even hundreds, still lay claim to the title. At one end of the spectrum, in addition to working groups such as Lisa McSherry's JaguarMoon, is the Blue Moonlight Coven, a very extensive set of interrelated Web sites that we encountered first in Chapter 1 and that will be considered in more detail below. Even a brief visit reveals the enormous investment of time and energy that has been made planning and executing the site. At the other end of the spectrum is a group such as Cyber Coven of the Midnight Moon (members.tripod.com/,MidnightMoonCoven), which appears to be little more than a front page and some outdated member profiles. None of the hyperlinks to the coven's Book of Shadows, "minutes" (presumably from coven meetings), or online newsletter work, and the impression from the service provider's error messages is that these pages were never uploaded. And although nearly 25 members have posted profile pages, only three of the links to their personal sites are active. There is no e-mail link to contact the "coven," a fact that has not gone unnoticed by many of the visitors who have signed the site's online guestbook.

Not surprisingly, site-based covens are no less subject to the ephemerality of the Internet and the short attention span of online participants that we saw demonstrated in many of the discussion groups located on the Yahoo! or MSN portals. Silver Twilight Coven (www.geocities.com/Athens/Marble/2268), for example, claims to be a "Branch of Many Moons' Circle"—a group that is never defined further than that. Though their front page states that "we have classes, plus we have a Community Book of Shadows," it also declares that "we will unfortunetly be soon closing down this section of Many moons. But we will still provided starter packets, which will help you on your way in the Craft." Many Moons Circle no longer exists either. Similar to the Cyber Coven of the Midnight Moon, there are no links to other sites, no e-mail link, and Silver Twilight's guestbook is filled with advertisements for low-rate mortgages, online prescription medication, and pop-ups for offshore pornography.

The conceptual problem of the online coven is only compounded by mixed messages from sites such as Wicca Coven (www.geocities.com/wicca_coven), several pages of which state, in various forms and not a little paradoxically, "Wicca Coven is an on line study group open to all interested in the Craft and paganism. Wicca Coven is a non-profit on line study group (NOT a coven) that discusses Wicca and other such related topics." The enrollment page for online

Witchcraft classes puts this problem even more clearly: ***"Wicca Coven is not a coven"*** (www.geocities.com/wicca_coven/join.htm; all emphases in the original). Curious visitors, I think, could be forgiven for wondering, "Then, what the heck is it, and why call it a coven if it isn't?"

Looking closely at more than 50 different Web sites that claimed in one way or another to be covens, and bearing in mind some of the distinctions that became apparent in our consideration of "online covens" conducted through discussion groups on Yahoo! or MSN, I developed a similar typology as a way of parsing the different site-based attempts at online modern Pagan working groups. Broadly construed, and as we recognize yet again that these divisions are permeable and heuristic rather than discrete and definitive, five categories emerge: (1) exclusively online covens, whether oriented around ritual practice, pedagogy, or both; (2) covens that exist both online and off-line; (3) the online presence of off-line covens; (4) information or discussion sites (which may also be called "covens" online); and (5) sites for which there was too little information to make a useful determination. Not surprisingly, when one considers the data gathered on Yahoo! and MSN, the two most prominent categories are the online presence of off-line covens and information sites that identify themselves as covens online—the first because there is a pool of participants already in place, the second because they require the least amount of interaction and dedication on the part of both site designers and online participants.

Guided by what it appears Web site designers and group members have attempted to do, though, I have organized this typology with no regard for the apparent success of the group. Because, in the real world, if they make it off the drawing board at all, modern Pagan working groups regularly emerge, flare, and fade away half-formed, there seems no compelling reason to impose stricter durability criteria for groups that attempt to form online. In order to do any of this, however, it is useful to come to some decision about what constitutes a "coven," an ideal type on the basis of which other groups may be categorized. As should be obvious by now, the Internet has affected and redefined each of the principal components of the Wiccan coven as Starhawk articulates them in *The Spiral Dance*. In many cases, membership (if not necessarily initiation) is now simply a matter of acknowledging oneself as a Wiccan and clicking on an appropriate hyperlink; some online groups require the disclosure of personal Pagan information, but others do not. In addition to its personally gnostic character, in many cases such training as does take place online is haphazard and taught by people whose credentials and preparation for the task are questionable at best. Similarly, with online Books of Shadows, grimoires, and spell exchanges now a standard component of modern Pagan shovelware, the concept of esoterica is rapidly losing any meaning (not to say mystery) it might once have had. Finally, as I have demonstrated, there is the not insignificant problem that many perhaps even the majority of online groups that call themselves covens bear little or no resemblance to their off-line counterparts, a fact that has not gone unnoticed by at least some modern Pagans. Archer (2003), for example, a Canadian solitary inspired by Starhawk's vision of the coven, had based her solitary practice on reading books and surfing the Internet, but felt that though she often practiced with a couple of friends, "I was still waiting for more. In my mind we weren't *really* a coven; we were too few and too casual." And that is the central question: what attributes constitute the modern Wiccan coven, and do these differ online and off-?

Writing in the teen-oriented magazine, *newWitch*, Ivy (2003), who is among other things the High Priestess of the Coven of the Whispering Brook (see Chapter 1), advises readers on how to "Start Your Own Online Coven." She points out some of the advantages of the Internet for modern Pagans that I have also noted—it is a reasonably risk-free environment for those who lack resources or access to off-line groups, or who "are deeply hidden in the broom closet"—and she identifies what many regard as the *sine qua non* of the Wiccan coven, whether on the Web or off-. "The aspect that sets an online coven apart from other online groups is ritual." She does not dispute the value of mailing lists, discussion forums, or information sites, "but neither constitutes a cybercoven unless they make online ritual part of their activities" (Ivy 2003). Macha NightMare concurs, writing that the coven is "a small congregation of Witches who meet regularly to perform ritual, worship, and/or do magical workings" (2001: 209). NightMare wonders about the efficacy and authenticity of online covens as opposed to off-line, and for her as well what sets the coven apart from other forms of modern Pagan community is ritual practice. This raises an important issue which will be discussed more fully in the following chapter. That is, compared to the thousands of modern Pagan Web sites, discussion groups, chat rooms, and home pages, successful online ritual is comparatively rare.

When I initially proposed this typology, I had in mind a restricted definition of an online coven based on two key attributes, one structural and the other practical. Structurally, although members may meet off-line in the serendipitous course of events, as a *working group* it exists all but entirely online and all substantive coven activities occur over the Internet. Practically speaking, as Ivy and NightMare indicate, online interactive ritual was to be the defining constituent of the group. While other activities such as teaching, discussion, or group chatter may also take place, ritual, even if only the eight sabbats, was to be a necessary component of online group activity. Off-line, many groups identify themselves as teaching covens, but it is precisely ritual that they are teaching to inquirers and neophytes, and encouraging dedicants and initiates to develop further. It would be difficult to imagine an off-line teaching coven instructing students in their particular method of casting a circle, calling the quarters, or performing a banishing pentagram, and then telling them, "Right, then, off you go. Find a coven where you can practice these." If that were the case, I suspect the life cycle of the teaching coven would be measured in hours and days, rather than months and years.

What became evident rather quickly during the research for this book, however, was how few groups that identify themselves as online covens actually meet what we might call the ritual requirement. Some do. However well or poorly it may work out in practice, for groups such as the Coven of the Whispering Brook ritual *is* an important component of group process. Others, such as the Coven of the Far Flung Net, consider themselves "teaching covens," and though they offer very detailed programs of study, online ritual may or may not be a priority. This, then, is one of the ways in which the Internet is affecting the functional concept of the coven. Because successful ritual is difficult to achieve online, for many groups education has become the emphasis. The online environment, it appears, at least at this rather primitive stage of its development, is much better suited to interactive pedagogy than interactive liturgy. Thus, I included in the "online coven" category groups that fit both the more restricted and the more expansive definitions.

*Online Covens*

Because we encountered the Coven of the Whispering Brook (www.whisperingbrook.org) and JaguarMoon Cybercoven (www.jaguarmoon.org) in Chapter 1, I would like to use other examples here to illustrate this category. First, the Coven of the Far Flung Net (home.att.net/ ,ladykaat/coven) claims to be "one of the first, if not *THE* first virtual coven, and is still providing free education in the Wiccan religion into the 21st century." Wholly a teaching coven, which operates on the "group of solitaries" structure, "this goal is accomplished through online lessons, carefully designed to strengthen your skills and knowledge of the Wiccan Faith. CFFN is a fully chartered teaching coven of The Church of Universal Eclectic Wicca with the ability to convey certification up to the completion of the second circle" (home.att.net/ ,ladykaat/ coven). The front page provides visitors with three rather extensive lists of "people who will do poorly in CFFN," "people who should wait to join," and "people who are prohibited from joining." If site visitors are still interested, prospective members of the Coven of the Far Flung Net must be accepted by one of several clans, subgroups of the larger coven with 20 to 24 members each, each of which maintains its own Web site. Initially, applicants to the CFFN submit a short essay using the "Five Points of Wiccan Belief" (home.att.net/ ,ladykaat/coven) to analyze a current event. This paper is then forwarded to one of the clans for review and either acceptance or rejection. Each of the clans has its own particular character. The "main objective of the Sacred Moon Clan," for example, "is to celebrate the spirituality of Wicca. Anyone who does not feel that they are mostly drawn to the spiritual aspects of Wicca, or anyone who is extremely interested in ritual or ceremonial magick, would probably not feel comfortable in this clan" (www.freewebz.com/sacredmoonclan). Clan Willow Branch, on the other hand, is "committed to the study of Wicca from a rational, adult perspective" (www.geocities.com/clanwillowbranch). And Athame's Edge, at the time of writing the only one of the seven clans accepting applications for membership, suggests that "shiftless, shallow, ignorant, unconversant, unintellectual, unreasoning, mindless, witless, reasoningless, brainless, half-baked, smattering bookless sciolists, with no access to a Thesaurus," will not do well in their clan (www.faesgarden.com/ae/athame.html). Once accepted, however, and supported by interactive discussion lists maintained by the individual clans, new members embark on a detailed series of lessons designed to take them through two of the three "circles" of the Universal Eclectic Wiccan Tradition (www.cuew.org).

Though she admits that she is "no where close to being qualified enough to label myself 'High Priestess'" and prefers to be called simply the "Founder and Manager," 21-year old-Lily Galangal "decided to create" the Saahira Moon cybercoven after having been "involved in several online groups who never seemed to meet the expectations I had for a group" (Galangal n.d. [b]). Unfortunately, she doesn't say what dissatisfied her. Saahira Moon, she claims, is an online coven, "a community of witches that share information, educate it's members in it's particular tradition, and celebrate sabbats and esbats together" (Galangal n.d. [a]). "In an attempt at allowing our membership to be as broad as possible," she continues, but "without losing the intimacy of a coven, we require our coven members to agree to the following ordains" (Galangal n.d. [d]). What follows are simply author and title references to rather standard statements of Wiccan belief laid down in the works of Scott Cunningham (1988) and Silver RavenWolf (1993, 1998). Like so many groups that call themselves online covens, however, before being accepted a questionnaire must be filled out by prospective members and approved, in this case by Lily Galangal. "All answers must be in your own words," she writes, "please do not cut and paste from websites or copy out of books" (Galangal n.d. [c]). Her own blatant cutting-and-pasting of Saahira Moon's "Witchcraft 101" page notwithstanding, she appears to recognize the problem of information replication among the growing modern Pagan communities online. Further, "it is required that you have a webpage dedicated to Saahira Moon Coven, this does not mean you need an entire website, just one page!" (Galangal n.d. [c]). By all appearances, however, this is a good example of an attempt at an online coven that has not gone anywhere. She has devised her own degree system, which she terms "houses," though as merely the "founder and manager" and not the High Priestess it remains unclear how she would determine who would be allowed into the "House of Avalon," which equates to the third degree in modern Wicca. Potential members are told, "if you are accepted you will receive invitation to our group mailing list, online community on MSN, and Saahira Moon newsletter. You will also be given information on the house you are in. If you are denied, you will be given a full explanation" (Galangal n.d. [c]). None of the links to the "houses" work, though the page indicates it was uploaded sometime in 2002; and, despite e-mail addresses for both, neither Yahoo! nor MSN have a Saahira Moon discussion group. All attempts to e-mail the addresses provided were returned as undeliverable. The accounts no longer exist, and the only Google reference to "Lily Galangal" is the Saahira Moon site.

Why spend so much time on a Web site (and online group, whether it calls itself a coven or not) that has not been updated in at least two years, for which none of the links work, and the e-mail addresses are no longer operational? This experience appears far more common online than groups that are successful, and a number of reasons militate against success. First, beyond the significant investment of time required to maintain even a reasonably simple Web site, there is the inherent difficulty of forming communities online, especially an intimate, intentional community like a coven. For the most part, successful, durable groups are either based on or supported by significant off-line relationships. Second, the open source, personally gnostic nature of modern Paganism encourages participants to upload shovelware sites and claim to speak with a measure of authority, when in fact they are simply cutting, pasting, and reloading from other Web pages (or off-line resources). As I noted earlier, there is actually very little creativity involved here, in the sense of original thought or original presentation; instead, a tremendous number of these sites simply replicate a fairly limited pool of material. In many cases, the same modern Pagan content is loaded onto pages that are often tediously hard to read (e.g., red font on a black background—potential Web masters, please take note!), graphics files taken (with or without permission) from the same sources, and the same idealistic claims for what the Web site is or will become. Third, many of those who create such pages are quite young and in the midst of fluctuating life situations —going to school, moving out from the family home, perhaps starting a family of their own, beginning a career path, all of which take time and energy away from a project such as an online coven. Fourth, given the personally gnostic character of modern Paganism and the encouragement of modern Pagans like Ivy (2003), why join someone else's coven when you can start your own? And, fifth, despite the fact that a number of groups put up testimonials to the interest they have received in their nascent covens, given the plethora of groups available, but considering the relative homogeneity of information, purpose, and potential for participation, it is easy to imagine that many modern Pagan Web sites are created in an initial rush of enthusiasm—which quickly fades when little or no interest is shown by others in the project.

So, the salient question becomes: What purpose do they serve? This is a question that I will take up in more detail in Chapter 6; briefly put, I consider these attempts at online Web covens important components of the modern Pagan process of identity construction, experimentation, and reinforcement. Crossing the boundaries of what James Coleman calls concentric "circles of involvement" (2001: 186–91), they provide a venue and a mechanism for interested parties to try on the identity of a modern Pagan. For some, the persona fits and participants become more and more identified, both internally and externally, as modern Pagans; in the language of Rodney Stark and William Bainbridge (1985: 26–30), for them modern Paganism shifts from an audience cult in which their participation is superficial and limited, to a cult movement, which provides for them the entirety of their religious identity. Not surprisingly, for others the relative costs of modern Paganism are too high and they drop away, testing other paths and trying on other identities.

Finally in this category, though scripted, interactive ritual does not appear to have been a part of its online activity, I include MoonFire Coven (www.geocities.com/moonfirecoven) because of their "Virtual Altar" and "Light a Candle" pages, as well as the insight their online history provides into the genesis of such groups and the ability of some to bridge the online and off-line worlds. Both "Virtual Altar" and "Light a Candle" are pages to which members of the coven and site visitors are encouraged to contribute. Though composed of readily available Web graphics and located on pages replete (read: cluttered) with Web banners and other graphics, each can be interpreted as an attempt at ritual identity-making. Visitors submit prayer requests to the "Light a Candle" page, which are then uploaded to the site. There is little in these requests that suggests participants are not serious about the nature of their requests, nor their belief that their prayers are efficacious. On the "Virtual Altar" page, visitors are told, "we keep our special tools & devotions"—though it is unclear how either functions in this setting. The "altar" is simply a set of .gif graphics—an athame, candles, a chalice and pentacle, a censer, and images of the goddess (Artemis) and the god (Apollo Belvedere)—uploaded in a static, fairly standard altar arrangement. Although coven members are encouraged to contribute to the altar page, there is no indication of how this might happen; indeed there is no provision for interactivity at all. Equally important in the case of MoonFire Coven, however, is the online history provided by one of the cofounders, Firesilk:

> In June 1998 Moonsong e-mailed me (Firesilk) an Award for my site and then I e-mailed her one for hers, next thing you know we are carrying on a regular e-mail correspondence. Then when Chrissy started the Merry Meeting Place Assembly, my on-line apprentice Moonchild got into the act and we three decided it would be a cool idea to start an on-line coven. A place for solitary 'net' witches to get together and share information and support one another in our paths. After all that's what a coven is for right?" (Firesilk n.d.)

Perhaps, in the online environment, this is indeed another mission of the evolving coven. In this case, its conceptualization and practice are not governed by the *sine qua non* of ritual, but of mutual support and community. Firesilk continues that she and the other founders of the group have never met in person, but know each other only through their online interactions. In terms of at least some of the constituents of online community discussed in the previous chapter, MoonFire Coven seems to have been able to transcend its initial formation and evolve. None of its original members, for example, is part of the elder council now, but are remembered on the site as honorary elders. New members have taken their place, but retained a measure of continuity and group memory. And, presaging the next category in the typology, though most members of the coven remain real life "strangers," their online interactions have moved off-line in some other rather significant ways. In 1999, nearly 20 members decided to participate in an adopt-a-wolf program and became part of a Timber Wolf recovery and repopulation program in Michigan's Isle Royale National Park. The following year, they regarded this project as successful enough to begin participation as a coven in the Nature Conservancy's "Adopt an Acre®" program.

*Online/Off-Line Covens*

As the name suggests, online/off-line working groups are those whose constituent coven activities occur in both environments. Not surprisingly, this is the least populated category. If an established off-line coven gathers regularly to celebrate the sabbats and esbats, for study and training, and for mutual support and community, what reason would they have to meet online for any purpose other than sharing group housekeeping information and general communication? However, if there is a separate group that meets online—with members of the off-line coven perhaps facilitating teaching and ritual—then this would constitute a different type of online coven. As I noted at the beginning of this chapter, one of the most extensive sets of interconnected Web sites I came across during the research for this book is the Blue Moonlight Coven, which includes an off-line coven in the Harrisburg, Pennsylvania, area; an online coven with a regular schedule of rituals, discussion groups, and chat sessions; an assortment of classes in Lady Gueneva's degree system (which are conducted both in chat format and through member-restricted Yahoo! discussion groups); fund-raising for the off-line "Blue Moonlight Coven Seminary Pagan Sanctuary"; and an online occult supply shop.

As open as the Blue Moonlight Coven is to prospective members, however, some groups are either closed entirely to outsiders or affect an exaggerated air of secrecy about their activities in order to entice or discourage potential applicants. Consider, in this regard, the Trad of the Sacred Cauldron, whose front page declares it "a body of, and under the protection of the Universal Life Church" (trad_sacredcauldron.tripod.com/info.html). In addition to the Web site, the Sacred Cauldron exists as both a Yahoo! discussion group and an off-line coven in southern Orange County, California. Of particular interest here are the many requirements for joining and being a part of the group. In terms of the discussion forum, "Anyone can join the online group located at Yahoo! There is a $30.00 annual fee to be part of the group" (trad_sacredcauldron. tripod.com/member.html). Online since February 2003, this Yahoo! group (groups.yahoo.com/group/sacredcauldron) advertises "newsletter courses and online rituals," but has only four members and has posted only three messages in all that time. Joining the local off-line group is no less difficult. "We are not a cybercoven," they state somewhat confusingly, given their Yahoo! description. "To be elgible for potential membership you must start by filling out an online application. From there we will hold several meetings with you over coffee at a local establishment. If we feel comforatble with you, your mental and magickal outlook, then we will submit your application and our findings to the board, as well as other group members for a vote . . . You will be required to provide no less than three character references, preferrably in the Pagan community" (trad_sacredcauldron.tripod.com/member.html). Through this air of secrecy and the rather extensive vetting process, Sacred Cauldron invokes the aura of the mystery school, the guardians of powerful and potentially dangerous arcana. This is compounded by their equally confusing instructions with regard to the coven reading list.

> If you are not a beginner, and you have been practicing less than 30 years, there is a reading list requirement before we will accept you to the group. These books may not be available through sources such as Amazon, Barnes & Noble, etc. We will supply you with the names and URL of a Pagan Merchant who provides a search service for rare books that you cannot through standard sources. You may also order the books through the Trad itself for a discount. In short, you are required to know the history and background of the craft and celtic traditions from the founders themselves, not the modern day authors who are untruthful or ignorant of the origins themselves. You will receive a list of the books after we have received your application. **WE WILL NOT SEND A READING LIST TO ANYONE WHO HAS 'NOT' BEEN ACCEPTED TO OUR GROUP."** (trad_sacredcauldron.tripod.com/member.html; emphases in the original)

Not surprisingly, I have not seen the reading list, but the effect created is not dissimilar to that of H. P. Lovecraft's venerable and entirely fictitious *Necronomicon* (cf. Harms and Gonce 2003), a now famous example of the literary "lost manuscript" conceit finding its way into real life (cf. Greenwood 2003: 89–91). Reference to powerful esoteric information too dangerous for mere neophytes has been the stock-in-trade of the occult community for centuries. Although potential members of the Trad of the Sacred Cauldron may initially provide a post office box for correspondence, when one advances in the application stage "you must give us your home address once you are conditionally accepted into the group for the safety of our members." An admonition to potential detractors reinforces this exaggerated air of secrecy, mystery, and, at times, peril. "WARNING!!! If you are an Xtian intent on infiltrating our group, show up with evangelists for a scheduled meeting, or attempt to serve up a 'hate propelled propaganda campaign' to the management of our chosen establishment we WILL call the police, demand to have you arrested and press charges against you for 'hate crimes'. In addition, you are liable for civil damages resulting from slander, assault, and violation of the anti-hate crime statutes!" (trad_sacredcauldron.tripod.com/app.html; on countercult evangelism as a potential hate crime, see Cowan 2003a).

## Online Presence of Off-Line Covens

Rather than try to operate in both the online and off-line worlds, dozens of covens and other ritual working groups have simply uploaded information sites that tell Web visitors who they are and what they are about. This is what I am calling "Web presence," as opposed to simply an information page about modern Paganism in general that happens to have been put online by an off-line coven. Practically speaking, if there is information for Web visitors who might also be prospective coven members—whether to encourage or to discourage them—then I considered this the online presence of an off-line coven. If the site simply replicates an assortment of modern Pagan shovelware, then it is an information site despite the fact that the site represents itself as a coven. For the five-state, Midwest catchment area served by the doctoral program in which I teach, for example, The Witches' Voice (www.witchvox.com), without doubt the most extensive modern Pagan information site on the World Wide Web, lists more than 90 different working groups. Of these, 40 percent have no Web presence at all beyond their WitchVox listing; nearly 25 percent have discussion lists—whether open or closed—on Yahoo! or MSN; and 27 percent have an online presence as I have defined it here. Mystic Moon Coven, which in 2000 was "officially recognized in the State of Kansas as Church of the Mystic Moon" (www.mysticmoon.org/mmc.htm), is both the coven's online presence and a source of general information on modern Wicca. Part of the "Sasquatchian tradition" (founded by one of the coven elders), Mystic Moon provides extensive information for potential members, from "Dedicate" to "Dedicate Seeker," and from Initiate through first, second, and third degrees.

Classes or rituals are held weekly at the group's covenstead, and Mystic Moon has been successful enough to have hived off both a daughter coven (in Rhode Island) and a granddaughter coven (in Ohio). "It is important to note that we are a *teaching and working coven*," their introduction continues, "not merely a social outlet. If you are looking for a place to learn about the many facets of Wiccan Spirituality, then this may be the place for you." Potential dedicants attend weekly classes until both they and the coven are willing to formalize a seeker relationship. Yarrow Coven, on the other hand (www.yarrowcoven.org), was "formed on Samhain 1989 as a St. Louis neighborhood Coven," but now claims membership from across the state. Though Yarrow Coven considers itself a public group, potential members are screened before being invited to attend a ritual. "As a rule," they state, "a person must attend our activities for a year and a day before being considered for initiation." More restricted yet is the Coven of Celestial Tides, which meets in the Athens, Ohio, area (www.celestialtides.com/Coven/howto.html). Formed in 1990, this coven consists of the High Priest and Priestess, three initiates, and one probationer, and is closed to membership applications from anywhere outside its geographic area. Moonstone Circle, a non-Wiccan, Celtic Reconstructionist group whose members have been together in various forms for nearly 20 years, long before the popular advent of the Internet and the World Wide Web, is not looking for members at all. Their online presence is purely for the enjoyment of its creators. The group is not interested in recruiting hordes of new, but often entirely impersonal members, providing Paganism 101 classes, or answering a flood of electronic correspondence.

> The reason we have a website is to put out the information we currently feel like sharing. Right now, it's one of our main ways of interacting with the public . . . What we don't have is a ***Moonstone/Nigheanan na Cailleachan*** online study plan, formal meetings or public rituals for seekers to attend, or the resources to send out piles of information for free. We're a small circle of friends and chosen family, living our lives and sometimes inspired to write stuff down about what we're doing . . . please don't ask us for spells or info on Wicca." (bandia.net/moonstone/MoreInfo.html)

Though the Ord Brighideach (Order of Brighid; www.ordbrighideach.org) is not strictly a coven, it is worthy of mention here for the use it makes of the Internet as a way of inviting potential members to participate and organizing them into dedicated working units. Divided into 22 cells (*cilli*) around the world, the members of Ord Brighideach are devoted to keeping an eternal flame burning among them in honor of the goddess Brighid. According to Celtic legend, Brighid was the goddess of poetry, fire, learning, and smithcraft. Although many modern Pagans (and others) believe she was Christianized as the Irish St. Brigit of Kildare (Scot. Bride; d. ca. 523), the Roman Catholic Church has steadfastly resisted this correlation (cf. Matthews 1995; Matthews and Matthews 1994; McCoy 1995; Raeburn 2001; Sutton and Mann 2002; Toulson 1993). In the Ord Brighideach, however, the myth of both the Celtic goddess and the Christian saint is kept alive in what are known as "flamebearers." For centuries, nuns of the religious order founded by St. Brigit of Kildare were said to have kept a perpetual flame burning in her name (Raeburn 2001: 45; Toulson 1993: 80–81), a tradition that was rekindled in 1993 by Irish and Norwegian Brigidine sisters. Members of the Ord Brighideach, whether drawn by the mythology of the pre-Christian goddess or the memory of the Christian saint, have reinstituted the practice on a more personal, almost diasporic basis. Wherever they are, whether they use a candle, an oil lamp, or something else, members of the order tend an actual flame on a rotating 20-day cycle—19 days for the Flamekeepers, one for the goddess/saint herself. "One of our basic tenants," reads the Ord Brighideach's FAQ (repeating a very common modern Pagan confusion of "tenet" with "tenant"), "is that you are welcome to join us as a Flamekeeper no matter what side of the mountain you have climbed to find Brighid . . . We currently have both Christian and Pagan Flamekeepers and those who have found a way to fit both paths into their religious tradition" (www.ordbrighideach.org/qa.htm). When I was researching this section, 22 cells, with more than 350 members (flamekeepers), existed in 15 countries. Because few of these members are in geographic proximity to one another, they share information and often emotional "tending stories" through the mother site and individual cell sites. In addition to such off-line relationships as do exist, a clear and unambiguous off-line purpose contributes to the durability of these online groups.

### The Information Site as "Coven"

In this sample, modern Pagan information sites (which may be called "covens" online) differ from the online presence of off-line working groups in that membership information for the off-line group is secondary, if it is available on the site at all. Often organized around a desire to "dispel the lies about Wicca," or whatever path the off-line group follows, this was the most populous group in the sample and contains a wide range of attempts. At one end of the continuum sits a bare-bones shovelware site like the Coven of the Waking Dragon (www.virtualavalon.com/wakingdragon). Though operational since June 1998, it does not appear to have been updated in years. A number of the hyperlinks navigate to empty pages, and the most recent community event listed is a modern Pagan camping trip from 1999. Coven Moonshae, on the other hand, was originally an off-line, teen coven in Belize; indeed, it claims to have been "the first of its kind in the country." The group "decided to go cyber after some its members went to study & live abroad . . . [and] Coven Moonshae is now an online coven, a source for learning and sharing . . . The website is a compilation of information obtained by Moonshae, which is now being posted for the viewing pleasure of all" (www.dreamwater.com/moonshae/intro.htm). Anyone can "click-to-join" the group, though it's unclear what membership means, because anyone, whether member or not, can post modern Pagan information to its various Web pages. The site includes dozens of spells, chants, and rituals, many of which have simply been cut-pasted-and-reloaded on the Moonshae site. Few have any attestation, including a lengthy page on "Astral Projection," which is written in the first person as though it is the original work of the person who posted it, yet which is taken verbatim from reclusive Australian mystic and author Robert Bruce's "Treatise on Astral Projection" (1994; cf. Bruce 1999, 2002).

Like Coven Moonshae, we also met the Prarie Hearth Virtual Coven in Chapter 1. At first glance, with 352 members, a message archive that extends back to November 2000, and a Web site as well as an MSN discussion group, it seems that there is significant interest in the group, especially for online classes. Indeed, a common refrain in the PHVC's message archive is "Wicca 101 classes are coming along slowly, but surely . . . stay tuned for them in the future!" (prarie_hearth.tripod.com/heart.html). By all indications, though, they have yet to take place, a circumstance that has not gone unnoticed by other list members. "I've seen posts on here from back in Nov of 2000, about online Wicca classes," writes Morrigan early in 2002. "It doesn't appear that this ever happened." She had posted a similar message a week earlier, but received no reply from group managers or members to that either. A few months later, Gaia Wulfman-Silvercrow posted a similar message, but received no response online. In fact, very few of the new members who posted initial greetings received any response. While they may have been contacted privately, this situation does nothing to encourage group cohesion, and a number of them posted only once —further indication that they received no replies whatsoever. Consider the effect of walking into an event at the invitation of the organizers, greeting the people, but being completely ignored by those already in the room. If this would have a negative effect on one's willingness to participate off-line, its effect online is only magnified by the ease with which potential participants can disengage. As well, on the Prarie Hearth Web site, very few of the other links go anywhere, including those in the online Book of Shadows. Although the MSN group is currently active, as indicated there is very little interactive traffic. Again, although there may be an active chat community, nothing on the public message boards indicates this is the case, and we would expect some communicative spillover between chat rooms and discussion forums if either is active.

Finally, for some sites, there is simply too little information for an accurate categorization. Some, like Coven Arcadia (www.geocities.com/thetemenos)

appear to be the online presence of an off-line coven. With only two members, however, and most of the hyperlinks either inactive or to off-site shovelware, it is impossible to determine. According to its Web site, the Shadows Scythe (www.geocities.com/theshadows_scythe/origin.html) is a cybercoven, "the phoenix of a coven that was disbanded, the former 'The Shadows.'" Yet despite some rather interesting graphics, like Coven Arcadia there is very little information on what the group is or does. All of the membership pages are "Under Construction," and the site appears not to have been updated in some months.

It is important to remember that the typologies I have discussed in this chapter are based on the claims site designers themselves have made that their creations in some way constitute online modern Pagan working groups—whether cybercovens, e-groves, or Web-circles. There are also thousands of modern Pagan sites that do not claim to be working groups, but whose information is often far superior in both presentation and substance to those that attempt to create the conditions for modern Pagan community online. As noted, for example, The Witches' Voice (www.witchvox.com) is a massive site that is accessible, well organized, and extremely useful. At www.neopagan.net, well known Druid author Isaac Bonewits (1999) welcomes visitors to his "cybernetic grove and virtual stone circle," and includes on his site hundreds of pages of his own work. While the claim of the operators of The Celtic Connection (www.wicca.com) to be "one of the largest Wicca, Pagan and Witchcraft sites on the internet" may be a wee bit overstated, the site still has an assortment of useful links to information about gemstones and minerals, modern Pagan shamanism, astral projection (which includes a recipe for two types of "Nontoxic Flying Ointment"), as well as an online "Magickal Shop."

### Durability and Decline: Explaining Online Success and Failure

As I have indicated throughout this chapter, whether "cybercovens" exist as modern Pagan discussion groups on Yahoo! and MSN or as stand-alone Web sites such as Celtic Moon Coven or Cyber Coven of the Midnight Moon, there is the appearance of far more activity online than the substance of that activity warrants. Many groups begin, but only a few seem to succeed. The reasons for this are related to Internet structure and group dynamics. Structurally, the ease with which groups may be called into being means that more and more groups will emerge in the various modern Pagan information spaces. As I noted above, Yahoo! groups take little more than a minute to create, and many seem to have emerged in the heat of a moment's enthusiasm. Although comparatively few advance beyond that initial state, every new group is listed as part of the Yahoo! index. Newcomers to the portal, then, are met with a plethora of groups from which to choose, all with varying agendas, membership requirements, and message volumes. The market floods, as it were, and consumers are awash in a sea of possible choices. Given these hundreds of choices, which group(s) to join becomes an important question for potential participants. Some join far more groups than they can possibly maintain contact with; others set their membership accounts so that they will not receive individual e-mails from the group but must check the Web site themselves to participate in discussions. As we have seen, membership is hardly an indicator of participation, and some members simply forget which lists they have joined. And, as we will see in Chapter 6, some are put off by the nature of the discussion or the traffic patterns on the list, and far fewer make the transition from newcomer to active participant.

In terms of group dynamics, two principal reasons suggest why some online working groups have such a low success rate: lack of clear purpose and lack of response and accountability.

When off-line working groups lack purpose or their purpose is not clearly articulated, their chance of survival as a group diminishes but does not necessarily disappear. Members still have the opportunity to meet, to plan, and to correct the problem. Online, however, because group contact is considerably more tenuous, especially in terms of newcomers who are trying to decide which group to join, if there is not a clear purpose to which potential participants can commit, then the chances of group success decrease. Nightfeare's_ Coven, for example, a Yahoo! group that describes itself as "a list for witches and all thoses curious about witchcraft," has just 13 members and less than 500 messages total—despite being online for nearly five years. The first discussion thread (and one of the longest to date) set the tone in terms of the group's lack of clear purpose. Darlene, one of the first participants, offered to post a "revenge spell," although she said she would only do so if the group agreed. Erin, another member, objected, and a rather predictable round of misunderstanding, hurt feelings, and computer-mediated backpedaling occurred. At one point, both Darlene and Erin declared they were going to leave the list; Darlene left after a few months, and though Erin remains subscribed she has not posted in more than four years. Threads appeared sporadically after that, but brought no clear focus to the group. After 18 months, one member, Pamela, wrote: "Hello!!?? I had forgotten i was part of this list! its been so long since I recieved anything! How is everyone!!???" Though a few members responded, their replies simply confirmed the silence on the list and its lack of purpose. The list owner, Lady NightFeare, indicated that for a while financial constraints had forced her off the Internet altogether. No clear direction for the group emerged, and Lady NightFeare took to forwarding messages from other groups as a way of maintaining list traffic and provoking discussion. Two rather lengthy threads developed, one around "Christian bashing" on the list (a practice to which Erin also vehemently objected) and the other concerning problems with Christian evangelism in Pagan chat rooms. After that, message traffic disappeared until Lady NightFeare came back some months later. "I have to figure out what I want to accomplish with this list now," she wrote, nearly four years after starting the group. "I had plans, but like I said I am not sure that they are still necessary." In fact, nothing in the message traffic over the course of the list's existence reveals what those plans were. Thus, if the list owner admits "I don't know what this list is for," list participants and visitors are left asking, "We don't know what this list is for either, and therefore we don't know why we should participate."

A correlative of low-risk participation, the second contributing factor to low success rates among online "covens" derives from the first: lack of accountability by site operators and administrators, whether they call themselves high priestesses, priests, or universal philosophers of ultimate reality. Because there is no practical online sanction for not responding to questions, comments, or introductions posted to discussion groups, there is not the compulsion to reply that one encounters off-line. Telephone calls and personal encounters in the coffee shop or bookstore are much more difficult to ignore than questions and comments posted in online chat rooms and discussion lists. In discussion groups, however, a major part of the obligation to ensure list durability rests with site operators and owners—especially those who are regarded as modern Pagan authorities by list members. Recall the young woman discussed above who asked the Witches of the World Coven what the purpose of the group was. Despite nearly 500 members, only one person responded on list and that was a spam message about chakras. Neither the list owner nor moderator replied, and the inquirer never posted again. A number of the MSN groups display a similar lack of response, especially to newcomers' questions. In terms of discussion group durability, the online calculus here seems reasonably clear. Lack of response means lack of posts; lack of posts means both participants and site operators lose interest; loss of interest among participants and site operators means lack of response to new members—all of which results in a decreasing spiral of participation occasionally interrupted by brief spasms of activity. One of the major issues in terms of discussion list durability concerns the all-important transition from casual inquirer to group stakeholder, a process that will be discussed in much greater detail under the rubric of modern Pagan identity in Chapter 6.

# CHAPTER 5

# Among the Stones of Cyberhenge
## *Modern Pagan Ritual on the World Wide Web*

~~(1 minute pause)~~
HP: North?
NORTH: Sorry, I had to reboot.
HPS: Ok, we are all here. Initiate, are you skyclad and ready?
INITIATE: Not yet—hold on, I need to get a pillow.
HP: Pillow?
INITIATE: Yes, I have a metal chair here at my desk. OK—BRB
~~(2 minute pause)~~
INITIATE: Ok, I am ready and skyclad.
HPS: Good, now do you have the cord?
INITIATE: Yes, I have an orange one I got on sale at the fabric store today, is that OK?
HP: It will have to do. OK, now, tie your hands behind your back, then bring the cord up around your neck . . .

Raven Gilmartin (2001)

### The Mystery of the Online Ritual: In Which We Almost Catch a Coven

When I initially planned this book, I expected the chapter devoted to online ritual to look quite different. I envisioned it as a detailed analysis of the interactive weaving of magick and power on the World Wide Web that would draw on dozens of examples and reveal significant differences that realized the imaginative potential of the online environment. Put bluntly, I expected to find much more online ritual than I did. In part at least, this expectation was due to some of the early (in the sense of premature) claims for ritual presence and efficacy online that I and others had made. Though he winds up uncertain of the answer at the end, for example, Erik Davis's famous *Wired* article on "Technopagans" contains the seeds of the problem in its subtitle—"May the Astral Plane Be Reborn in Cyberspace" (1995). And, with particular reference to the presence and use of ritual objects online, Stephen O'Leary's now classic essay, "Cyberspace as Sacred Space," proposes among other things that "the textual reality of a candle as described on the screen is sufficient to ensure ritual efficacy, while the cyber-flame raised in the electronic conference room has no embodiment except in text" (1996: 799). Here, though, the obvious questions raised by the assertions of both authors are: *Is* it? *Is* "the astral plane reborn in cyberspace?" *Is* the word "candle," when typed on a screen in a particular Internet chat venue, "sufficient to ensure ritual efficacy?" And *is* such efficacy as there is sufficient to overcome the inherent difficulties of performing and participating in ritual practice through computer networks? Certainly, for some the answer to all these questions will be an unqualified "Yes." Davis's report on technopagans such as Mark Pesce and Tyagi Nagasiva makes that clear, at the very least. But will online ritual become anything more than the province of a very small group of technologically advantaged and, more important, technologically *oriented* modern Pagans?

While I have already discussed Brenda Brasher's overreaching suggestion that computer-mediated communications "could become the dominant form of religion and religious experience in the next century" (2001: 19), because ritual is a crucial part of that life for modern Pagans a similar question obtains. That is, if these are all accurate assessments of the development of online religion and, in Brasher's case, the predicted migration of religious practice from the real world to the World Wide Web, given the cultural value placed on creativity and innovation by modern Paganism, we should expect to find numerous examples of computer-mediated ritual activity on the modern Pagan Internet. At least, this is what I thought when Jeffrey Hadden and I wrote "Virtually Religious" (2004b). There, with particular reference to the chat log of a ritual and its ensuing online discussion that were archived as public examples at Online Wiccan Rituals (http://go.to/OnlineWiccanRituals), we proposed that "though critics might contest the authenticity of a ritual like this, experienced across thousands of miles, mediated through a metatechnology such as the Internet, and occurring principally in the imaginations of the participants, for these [modern Pagans], at least, 'cyber-henge' seems a very hospitable environment and the experience no less real for its essential virtuality" (Cowan and Hadden 2004b: 130). Although careful readers will note the conceptual shift between "virtual" and "online" that has occurred since that essay was written, we suggested two reasons for the "hospitality" of the World Wide

Web to online ritual: "the imaginative nature of [modern Pagan] ritual itself, and the dramaturgical character of the e-space environment" (Cowan and Hadden 2004b: 130).

Though I stand by the basic substance of our claim, once one starts to investigate the problem more carefully, the empirical reality of online ritual is rather different. Indeed, much like the mysterious and elusive Woozle in A. A. Milne's classic children's story, *Winnie the Pooh*, successful online rituals are notoriously difficult to find. There are numerous signs that they exist—long, discursive ritual texts posted on any number of Web sites, discussion board suggestions that participants meet in a certain chat or conference room to celebrate a particular sabbat, and, almost inevitably, *post facto* questions about where or whether the proposed ritual actually occurred. Spoor, as it were, is everywhere. Some online rituals clearly occur in private, using chat rooms known only to the few participants and disappearing at their conclusion like mist on the moors, but for the broad population of online modern Pagans there is little evidence that cyber-rituals take place either often or successfully. The snippet of Rachel Gilmartin's parody of an online initiation that serves as an epigraph for this chapter is humorous precisely because it so accurately reveals some of the difficulties with the performance of modern Pagan ritual online. Part of that parody continues:

> HP: How do you enter the circle?
> INITIATE: In perfect love and perfect trust.
> HPS: Good, now I need to whisper the sacred words to you.
> INITIATE: Whisper?
> HPS: Yes, do you have two phone lines? I can call you with them.
> INITIATE: No, only one.
> HPS: OK, I'll e-mail them to you BRB [Be right back]
> **HPS has left the chat room**
> ~~(1 minute pause)~~
> **HPS has joined the chat room**
> HPS: OK, I mailed them.
> INITIATE: OK, I'll go look.
> **INITIATE has left the chat room**
> ~~(1 minute pause)~~
> **INITIATE has joined the chat room**
> INITIATE: I can't get into my hotmail—I keep getting a message that the servers are down.
> HPS: OK, you can get them later. Now imagine that I am pushing you from behind into the circle.
> INITIATE: From behind? (Gilmartin 2001; gloss added)

As the cases I will discuss in this chapter demonstrate, none of this is to say that interactive rituals do not occur online, nor that they do not occur successfully, merely that they are considerably less conspicuous when viewed against the larger canvas of online modern Paganism than their place in the tradition as a whole would seem to warrant. It is one of the tasks of a sociological analysis to discern patterns within the complex matrix of social behavior, but often the significance of such patterns emerges only when held against a sufficiently broad background of activity and observation. This is the case with online ritual. At first blush, it appears to be a much more prominent part of modern Paganism on the World Wide Web than it proves in the end. Furthermore, although there is no reason to suppose that online ritual will not increase in sophistication as Internet access and technology develop, in addition to the digital divide that we have already discussed, I will suggest a number of aspects of the online ritual experience that militate against it challenging in any significant way the pride of place held by its off-line counterpart.

*Conceptualizing Modern Pagan Ritual*

As a way of beginning or as a way of entering their sacred spaces, some basic understanding of how modern Pagans conceptualize ritual is important. Once again, the open source character of these emerging traditions requires that the picture be painted in rather broad strokes. Some modern Pagans see very specific psychological processes at work in ritual; others regard ritual as little more than daily habit and repetition infused with vague notions of magickal intent. Some partition ritual into designated sacred spaces such as circles and groves; others consider the act of living itself a ritual, and press items ranging from teacups to computer mice into service as ritual implements. Some challenge the modern Pagan foundation of personal gnosticism and require that ritual implements and furniture be used in very particular ways ("the altar MUST face east"), whereas others suggest that the most efficacious ritual arrangement is the one that is most significant for the participants.

Writing of the psychological function of ritual, and quoting Jungian writer Tom Chetwynd, Janet and Stewart Farrar contend that "'Ritual is the dramatic enactment of myth, designed to make a sufficiently deep impression on the individual to reach his unconscious' . . . an enacted psychic truth" (1984: 149, 150; cf. Hume 1998). Well-known modern Druid Isaac Bonewits concurs, contending that ritual is "any ordered sequence of events, actions and/or directed thoughts, especially one that is repeated in the 'same' manner each time, that is designed to produce a predictable altered state of consciousness within which certain magical or religious (or artistic or scientific?) results may be obtained" (1989: 264–65). For the all but ubiquitous Silver RavenWolf, ritual is "a focused mental/physical ceremony to either honor or thank one's chosen pantheon, or to perform a specific magickal working or act" (1993: 24). "In Wicca," writes Vivienne Crowley, a well-regarded British Wiccan (no relation to Aleister), "we contact the Divine through ritual and through the enactment of ancient myths which express eternal truths about human beings and the universe we inhabit" (1996a: 41). In *When Someone You Love Is Wiccan*, a book designed to explain modern Paganism to nervous friends and family who find themselves confronted with a newly proclaimed or initiated Witch, Carl McColman writes that the "purpose of these rituals is to honor the Goddess and the God, and to generate magical energy, usually for the purpose of healing" (2003: 40). And, finally, "by definition," write Sirona Knight and Patricia Telesco, somewhat less specifically than any of these others, "a ritual is anything we repeat with spiritual overtones" (2002: 24).

Modern Pagan rituals occur in a number of ways, each of which relates to the organizational context in which it takes place. Here, once again, the most basic division is between the solitary ritualist and the modern Pagan working group. Beyond that, like many other religious traditions, some rituals are open to the public, whereas others are restricted to group members; some rituals occur in the context of given cycles, others are designed for specific purposes and to meet specific needs—handfastings, funerals, wiccanings and paganings, coven initiations, as well as a variety of rituals for divination, guidance, and healing (see Clifton 1993; Starhawk, NightMare, and Reclaiming 1997). Cyclically, although Wiccan seasonal rituals (*Sabbats*) are organized around the eight festivals of the modern Pagan liturgical calendar (see especially Farrar and Farrar 1981; Hutton 1996), the 13-month lunar cycle guides the ritual performance of inter-Sabbat magickal workings called *Esbats*. Noncyclical, purposive rituals often take the form of spellworking cast by the participants as ritual.

None of this, however, tells us much about what modern Pagan ritual *is*, what an observer might witness standing on the edge of a working coven, grove, or magickal circle. In terms of broad structure, modern Pagan ritual, whether online or off-line, differs little from ritual performance in other religious traditions, and it is marked by three distinct, yet intimately connected phases or movements—preparation, performance, and postlude. Each of these is meant to invoke particular responses or experiences in the participants, and each contributes to the fundamental goal of modern Pagan ritual, which is the raising, focusing, releasing, and grounding of psychic energy. Preparation for ritual occurs both personally and spatially. Based on the concept of interconnectedness that underpins modern Pagan cosmology, ritual participants are careful to eliminate or mitigate anything that might adversely affect the energetic process of ritual work. Personally, for example, many modern Pagans will bathe or shower in preparation, often with soft music playing and aesthetically pleasing accoutrements such as candles, incense, or flowers placed in and around the tub. If the ritual is to be performed robed, then fresh clothing is laid out; if ritual participants will be sky-clad (naked), then perhaps only a few drops of fragrant oil, and for the High Priestess a ritual necklace of amber and jet (Farrar 1991, Plate 15; for the appropriate accessories of a sky-clad High Priestess according to Gerald Gardner, see Crowther 1998). As a way of slough-ing the distractions of the mundane world, meditation is a common practice before entering the ritual space. And this space is prepared similarly. If the rit-ual is to take place indoors, floors are swept, carpets vacuumed, and the room thoroughly cleaned. Any unnecessary furniture is moved out of the way, and re-placed by the ritual furniture and tools required by the group. The altar is set up, and the cardinal directions marked with candles or other symbolic items. Decorations appropriate to the ritual—the fruits of harvest for Samhain (October 31) or a Maypole for Beltaine (May 1)—are added to the ritual space. Often, more candles, incense, and music greet the participants as they arrive, contributing to the ambiance that will support the performance of the ritual.

*Ritual Performance*

Once again in broad terms, modern Pagan ritual performance proceeds ac-cording to fairly standard protocols. Once the ritual participants are gathered and the initial greetings concluded, the ritual space is established. In Wiccan and non-Wiccan Witchcraft, this is known as "casting the circle," the creation of a boundary between the mundane and the sacred, between time and not-time, between the phenomenal and the noumenal. In this, a number of ritual actions combine. First, the ritual presider (sometimes, though not always, the High Priestess) asks designated participants to "call the quarters," that is, to ac-knowledge and greet the supernatural guardians of the four directions who symbolize the base elements of the natural world and who will watch over the conduct of the ritual. As she does this, she uses her *athame* (ritual knife) to trace the circumference of the ritual circle. Visualizing the effect of the action and encouraging her co-ritualists to do the same, she establishes a psychic boundary within which the ritual will take place. At each cardinal point, she also traces in the air a pentagram, the five-pointed star that is perhaps the most common symbol of Wicca and Witchcraft. As with all meaningful ritual, these are not simply actions performed for theatrical effect or empty ceremony; there are powerful imaginative influences at play that charge the venue, the imple-ments, and the participants with sacredness and ritual legitimacy. "As she speaks," writes Starhawk, "she traces the invoking pentagram in the air with her knife. She sees it, glowing with a pale blue flame, and through it feels a great on-rush of wind, sweeping across a high plain lit by the first rays of dawn. She breathes deeply, drawing in the power, then earths it through her knife, which she points to the ground" (1989: 70). Starhawk considers the casting of a ritual circle "an enacted meditation," and "in Witchcraft, the function of the circle is not so much to keep *out* negative energies as to keep *in* power so that it can rise to a peak" (1989: 72). Stewart Farrar, on the other hand, contends that "the Circle has a double function: concentration and protection" (1991: 45). The power raised within the circle must be both contained until the appropriate moment of release, and protected from external influences that could dissipate, dilute, or otherwise corrupt its energy. However it is understood, once the circle has been cast and the sacred space created, the deities that are considered appropriate and efficacious for that ritual are invoked. Some rituals call simply on the divine complementarity—in Wicca and Witchcraft, the Goddess and the God—while others invoke deities more specific to the ritual purpose, patron pantheon, or modern Pagan tradition. In a three-hour Yule ritual performed in the Pagan Room on Compuserve in 1994, for example, in addition to the Goddess and the God of Winter, participants also invoked Hecate, the Greek goddess of the underworld, conceptualized in this instance as Belfana, the Italian crone goddess (Dixon 1994). Often, with words borrowed from Starhawk's *The Spiral Dance*, ritual invocations end with the declaration of the cast circle, the acknowledgment by all present that the sacred space has been created: "The circle is cast. We are between the worlds, beyond the bounds of time, where night and day, birth and death, joy and sorrow, meet as one" (Dixon 1994; Starhawk 1989: 71).

Once the ritual space has been created, the core of the ritual embodies liturgically the purpose for which the participants have gathered—healing, seasonal celebration, remembrance, thanksgiving. Beltaine, for example, the festival marking the beginning of summer and the growing season, is often celebrated off-line with bonfires, dancing, and ritual actions intended to promote prosperity and fertility. For a 2002 Beltaine ritual performed at the MSN portal of Online Wiccan Rituals the purposive text reads:

> Wulfslaird —TYPE— Let us now use the need-fire to bless and purify sacred things with the smoke of a new fire—to let go things we no longer need in the flames of purification.
>
> ALL: Visualize the lighting of Belfire.
>
> (You may write whatever it is you wish to release, such as negative energy, hard feelings, unhappiness, etc., on a piece of paper, (light it and place into a fire safe container) and send it to ashes, to be reborn into something of need or desire on the flames of the new fire.) RITUAL PAUSE TO ALLOW BURNING (Wulfslaird 2002)

In an off-line Wiccan circle, purposive energy is often raised through chanting and dancing, the participants visualizing both the intent of the ritual and the energy raised as a "cone of power" contained within the circle. At the appropriate moment, the ritual presider releases the energy towards its intended focus, and then ritually grounds the group in preparation for opening the circle and returning to mundane space and time. Starhawk considers this grounding process "one of the basic techniques of magic. Power must be earthed every time it is raised. Otherwise, the force we feel as vitalizing energy degenerates into nervous tension and irritability" (1989: 59). Once surplus energy has been grounded—returned to the earth just like an electrical charge—the Goddess and the God, in whatever aspects they were invoked, are thanked. Thanks are also given to any other spiritual beings or entities who were called upon during the ceremony. The ritual concludes when the circle is opened—not broken—and the participants, in Wicca and non-Wiccan Witchcraft at least, bid each other farewell with the words, "Merry meet, and merry part, and merry meet again." Often, after the circle is opened, food and drink, ritualized in many modern Pagan contexts as "cakes and ale" and understood as a continuation of the grounding process, are shared among the participants.

There are, of course, individual differences between traditions, some minor, some more significant. For example, in some Wiccan covens, if a participant wishes to leave the cast circle before the conclusion of the ceremony, she must ritually cut a portal into the boundary of the sacred space, closing it behind her as she leaves. Like the spiritual version of a biohazard lab, carefully sealing the circle ensures that nothing pollutes or contaminates the liminal space created by consecration. Druids, on the other hand, do not cast a circle at all. Rather, many modern Druid rituals begin with a procession at the end of which a "grove" is declared. Compared to Wiccan circles, ritual boundaries in groups such as the Ar nDraiocht Fein (pronounced *arn ree-ocht fane*), an independent modern Druid tradition founded by Isaac Bonewits, are considerably more permeable; during the ritual, participants are free to leave and reenter the grove as they please. Ritual gatherings in Asatru, modern Norse heathenism, are called *blots* and *sumbel*; in the former, sacrifices of mead, ale, or cider are offered to the gods. The latter, according to the Irminsul Ættir, "is a sort of ritualized toasting. The first of the usual three rounds is to the Gods, starting with Odin, who won the mead of poetry from the Giant Suttung ... The second round is to ancestors and other honorable dead. The third round is open" (Buck n.d.; Kaplan 1996).

Modern pagan ritual functions on a number of levels, many of which can occur within the context of a single ceremony or gathering. For some, the ritual focus is directed outward, the energy released on behalf of concerns external to the ritual practitioners (see, for example, Starhawk 1988). Others are oriented inward, and focus on issues of spiritual development, self-realization, or personal healing within the group. Some are theologically relational, in that their primary function is worship of the goddesses and gods invoked for the ritual. Others are theologically instrumental, in that the deities are invoked for the services they can offer or the guidance they can provide. All rituals, how-ever, function along two principal axes: a vertical connection with the Divine (however that is understood in the particular ritual context) and a horizontal axis, which connects the participants with others around the world and through time who have performed (or are believed to have performed) similar rituals and invoked similar deities.

### The Reality of Online Ritual: The Coven at Work on the Web

Searching for examples of online modern Pagan ritual yields three interrelated sets of data, which are, in descending order of magnitude: texts of off-line rit-uals that have been uploaded for online reference (i.e., as part of an Internet Book of Shadows), texts of proposed online rituals (that may or may not ever have been performed), and, most important for this discussion, the chat logs (transcripts) of online rituals that have taken place and have been uploaded for archival or illustrative purposes. One transcript, appropriately entitled "A Simple Ritual," has been floating around the Internet for many years. Its author, "Soror N," claims to have adapted the ritual for solitary use after taking part in it online in September 1986. Another text commonly encountered on the Web is the ritual log from the 3-hour Yule celebration that took place in the Pagan Room of CompuServe's New Age Forum in December 1994.

In terms of their content, though, online rituals differ very little from their off-line counterparts; in fact, many ritualists explicitly reference the off-line works that inspired (or have been used in) their online efforts. Ritual prepara-tion and structure are the same; the deities and elementals invoked or invited into the online ritual space are no different from those that populate off-line rituals. In fact, of the more than two dozen online rituals I examined closely, but for the differences in performance that will be discussed below, nothing in the theological substance of the ritual texts revealed that they were designed for use in an online environment at all. That is, to this point, the open source in-vention and wholesale invocation of all manner of "cyber-deities" advocated by modern Pagan authors such as Sirona Knight and Patricia Telesco (2001, 2002) appear not to have influenced the performance of online ritual in the slightest. Indeed, in online Wiccan and eclectic modern Pagan contexts, the circle is cast, the quarters called, and the deities invoked just as they are off-line. Some ritu-als contain interactive components to which participants are encouraged to contribute freely; others take the form of online guided meditations, with little keyboard interaction from the rest of the group; still others are largely an-tiphonal, the presider typing in a line of ritual text, which is then simply re-peated online by each participant. Keyboarding aside, however, none of these general modes of ritual conduct is unique or even particular to online en-vironments. With the exception of problems related specifically to Internet technology—from frozen servers, to unexpected "fatal errors" in one's operating system, to cats who jump on the keyboard and drop the user unceremoniously from the chat room—even the pre- and post-ritual chatter is indistinguishable from that which occurs off-line. That is, there is nothing inherently special about online ritual, other than, as I have said, it gathers together those who might not otherwise meet.

Are there, then, *any* differences that make it worthwhile exploring at all? Is there anything to be learned from such a small portion of the modern Pagan Internet? There is, but in the end I think it is more usefully understood *not* as the performance of modern Pagan ritual, but in more traditional sociological terms as the maintenance of modern Pagan identity and the reinforcement of modern Pagan community. Although this is a topic I will take up in more detail in the following chapter, here I would like to consider more closely three online rituals—two celebrating Ostara, the third Beltaine.

*The Cauldron: Ostara 1997*

Online since December 1997, The Cauldron (www.ecauldron.com) is a modern Pagan Internet portal that hosts a number of discussion forums, chat sessions, an online newsletter, book reviews, a wide variety of information pages, and eCauldron electronic mail. In many respects, it resembles The Witches' Voice (www.witchvox.com), though on a considerably smaller scale. Unlike The Witches' Voice, however, since its inception The Cauldron has sponsored online, interactive, seasonal rituals and has published the chat logs of several of these on its Web site.

In the liturgical calendar shared by a number of modern Paganisms, Ostara is the celebration of the vernal equinox and is held on (or close to) March 21. Named for the Saxon goddess Eostre, many modern Pagans hold that the fertility symbols culturally associated with Easter—bunnies and eggs—actually predate Christianity and are more correctly connected to Pagan celebrations from which it is believed Ostara derived. With two modern Pagans named Elspeth and Ghost serving as co-presiders, nine people participated in The Cauldron's 1997 Ostara ritual, which took place on the site's previous incarnation as The Grove. Organizationally, although Elspeth does make reference to "the Priestess corp" in a different ritual (Cauldron 1998d), in all of The Cauldron rituals for which logs are available, participants go either by their first or their Craft names; there is no online designation of high priest or priestess, and the ritual interchanges are simple and informal. As well, for the 1997 Ostara ritual, participants required only a few implements. "You all have your egg, candle and marker? Or a vision of them?" asked Ghost (Cauldron 1997), to which the others answered, simply, "Yes." To begin, Ghost led the group in a short guided meditation to help the participants visualize the ritual space and its milieu.

.Ghost> Now is the time . . . Journey with me, if you would, to a sheltered glade deep in the Grove . . . shrouded now in night's dark cloak.

.Ghost> Stars burn bright and steady overhead . . . piercing pinpricks of light in the fabric of the night sky.

.Ghost> The pre-dawn air is cool against your skin . . . carrying the wild scent of trees and other growing things that lean close to watch and listen and guard our gathering.

.Ghost> Feel the power rising through the soles of your feet as you take your place in the circle, bringing with it the calming strength and power of the Earth Mother. (Cauldron 1997)

The meditation continued, and Ghost instructed the participants to "type <> when ready to continue our journey" (Cauldron 1997). Whenever participants were required either to visualize a particular aspect of the ritual or to perform some action with an off-line ritual implement, "<>" was the signal that they had finished and were ready to proceed. Once the circle had been cast and the patron deities of the participants invoked, Ghost led another guided meditation, this one involving the egg, the marker, and the candle. Participants were instructed to visualize some aspect of themselves or their lives that they believed needed changing, and then to mark the egg shell with a symbol representing that thing. "The symbol need only have meaning within yourself," wrote Ghost. "Type <> when ready to go on" (Cauldron 1997). The energy imparted to each egg—whether real or imaginative—was released when participants cracked the shell at the point of the ritual mark, and either ate or buried the egg. The deities were thanked, the circle opened, and The Grove's 1997 online Ostara ritual drew to a close.

Unfortunately, the archived versions of all Cauldron rituals have "been edited to remove extraneous comments" (Cauldron 1997), which is problematic because these comments often tell us much more about the process and conduct of online ritual than the liturgical texts themselves. Fortunately, this ritual still contains some of the interaction that occurred immediately following the opening of the circle, and this is important for the sense of participant engagement it reveals. The ritual itself was not long. Though not time-coded, I suspect it took no more than 20 minutes, and the vast majority of the ritual text was typed or pasted in by Ghost. With the exception of Elspeth, whose task it was to call the quarters, and the brief invocation of individual patron deities by some of the other participants, the rest of the group's online responses were limited to "Yes" and "<>." That is to say, following the instructions scrolling up their monitor screens, they participated in the ritual imaginatively. Led by Ghost's poetic meditation, the "sheltered glade" existed nowhere but in their joined imaginations. They had no part in the decision that this would be the image of the ritual space nor the manner in which it was presented to them. Did they feel excluded from the ritual because of this? Left out? Apparently not.

.Ghost> Merry meet, merry part . . . and merry meet again.

.terri> it was BEAUTIFUL Ghost..thank you so much for sharing it with us.

.Elspeth> Merry Meet, Merry Part, and Merry Meet Again!

.roo> {{{hugs ghost}}} that was wonderful!

.Kris> Please forgive my interuption in the middle of everything. :)

.TL> It was wonderful, Ghost!

.Ann> It was marvelous, Ghost! . . .

.Ghost> No prob, Kris . . . sorry you got dumped.

.GF> Merry Meet, Merry Part, and Merry Meet Again! (Cauldron 1997)

There is nothing in the text of the ritual or the comments that follow to indicate that participants were being disingenuous in their praise for Ghost's leadership or the genuineness of their experience. Influenced by a highly idealized mythistory of modern Pagan origins, the ritual scene was consistent with the shared conceptions of many Witches, Wiccans, and Druids. Well-known off-line referents—the "sheltered glade," stars in the night sky, trees—guided the performance of and their participation in the online ritual. The stage, as it were, was familiar and allowed them to play the roles assigned to them by the ritual leader with little or no conceptual dissonance.

Spontaneous co-construction of imaginative ritual space is also possible, though it also tends toward established off-line conventions. Although there was no designated imaginative space for a 2002 "Purification/Protection Ritual" performed by members of the Online Wiccan Rituals group (http://go.to/OnlineWiccanRituals), the rather specific contours of a ritual setting did emerge in post-ritual chatter and was not dissimilar to the scene set in The Cauldron's 1997 Ostara ritual.

"I have an odd question," wrote Willow~Song, a 26-year-old woman from Indiana who was one of the co-presiders, "but when you guys were imagining us in a circle did anyone see stones around them?" "YES!!!!!!!!" replied Sinovess exuberantly, adding as two others agreed with Willow~Song's suggestion, "STONES!!!!!! Like Stonehenge!" Gradually, other participants strengthened this emerging vision, adding trees, a "great big giant moon," and warmer temperatures. It should be noted that the ritual took place in mid-January and the moon was a waxing crescent sliver on that particular night. In this case, though, the ability of participants to co-create a shared imaginative space that resonated with what I would suggest are tacitly authorized visions of modern Pagan ritual settings—Stonehenge rather than St. Peter's Square, and circled in a forest glade rather than floating through the dust clouds of the Horsehead Nebula—is regarded by those participants as evidence of the ritual's success. Elsewhere in the post-ritual conversation, while other members seemed content merely to chat about the event, Willow~Song also invoked other aspects of modern Pagan belief, details that further served to ground and support this particular vision of a ritual environment. "I could feel the energy as well," she wrote, referring explicitly to modern Pagan belief in reincarnation, "and got the distinct feeling I've been in circle with some of you before . . . long ago" (cf. Cowan and Hadden 2004b).

Both of these examples demonstrate that although facilitated by computer technology and taking place through shared visualization, they occurred within conceptual boundaries that explicitly reinforced particular visions of the modern Pagan experience and identity off-line. Even those participants whose online profiles indicate an affinity for Greek or Egyptian pantheons, for example, did not include in (or attempt shifting) the imaginative focus to suggest either the Doric columns of the Parthenon or the great pyramid complex at Giza. Whether they had those visions in mind or not, we do not know; as the shared imaginative space emerged, however, it assumed the very particular contours authorized by the more "vocal" members of the group.

In terms of computer facilitation, Kris's experience in the Ostara 1997 ritual also nicely demonstrates one of the more mundane problems inherent in an online ceremony. For whatever reason, some technical problem obviously dropped her from the chat room for a period of time and she had to be readmitted—an interruption to her ritual consciousness at the very least. To reiterate, however, there is also nothing in the chat log to indicate that the computer, the Internet, or the World Wide Web served as anything other than the basic means of communication for the ritual. It could as easily—and perhaps even more meaningfully—been performed over nine speakerphones set on conference call. That is, the claims of cyber-Pagan entrepreneurs like Knight and Telesco notwithstanding, although computer technology facilitated the ritual, it was not part of it in any significant way.

*The Cauldron 1998: Ostara Evolved*

A year later, the Ostara ritual had developed, matured slightly; the leaders recognized that there might be participants who were unaccustomed to online ritual and included specific instructions to guide them in the process. This year the ritual was led by Elspeth, Ghost's co-presider from the year before. After initial introductions, she called the group together: "Type <> when you are grounded and centered and ready to go" (Cauldron 1998c). Then, with more explicit reference to the computer as a touchstone of community, she began to cast the circle.

.Elspeth> I draw this circle to contain and protect our working. From Keyboard to Keyboard, I connect us. We come in friendship and desire to reach beyond ourselves. By our will let the circle be cast!

.Elspeth>

.Elspeth> Randall?

.Randall> ::draws invoking pentagram of air:: (Cauldron 1998c)

Though the computer never became more than the means of communication for any of the rituals, "From Keyboard to Keyboard" did become a common invocatory refrain in other Cauldron ritual texts. The 1998 Ostara ritual was also more inclusive. Rather than call each of the quarters herself, as she had done the year before, this year Elspeth involved more group members in the performance of the ritual itself. Four others took turns invoking the presence and protection of the cardinal directions. In this, they moved from being marginally involved members of an online audience for whom the ritual was being performed to antiphonal participants in the performance of the ritual itself. And, as I will discuss in more detail below, a number of participants also signaled off-line action meant to influence or contribute to the online ritual. Further on in the ritual, Elspeth continued, "Join with me as we call upon the returning tide of light, life, and growth. Just type the words as I do . . . " (Cauldron 1998c). And as she typed each short line of the ritual text, the other eight participants followed suit. She also included online "chanting" in the ritual as part of the raising and releasing of power.

.Elspeth> While I am 'transforming' I want each of you to stir the liquid [part of this Ostara ritual] and 'chant' by typing . . .

.Elspeth> I desire change . . .

.Elspeth> A Change for me

.Elspeth> As I do will

HALLIEJEAN> I desire change

.Elspeth> So mote it be . . . (Cauldron 1998c)

Though the "chanting" went on for nearly a page of single-spaced text, HALLIEJEAN's initial, preemptive start indicates another problem with asynchronous communication in the online world. As numerous other researchers have pointed out from the beginning of sociological and ethnographic study of computer-mediated communication (cf. Danet, Ruedenberg-Wright, and Rosenbaum-Tamari 1997; Donath, Karahalios, and Viégas 1999; Herring 1999; Liu 1999; Marvin 1996; Rafaeli and Sudweeks 1997; Smith, McLaughlin, and Osborne 1997; Turoff et al. 1999), the cues that regulate turn taking in off-line social interaction—pauses in speech, changes in the speaker's tone or inflection, a glance toward the person whose turn is next—are not present online. Based on the "prime directive" of Internet communication—that information must flow—the fluid architecture of online communication may have meant that, in this case, Elspeth's first three lines of text were routed to their recipients along one path, while the fourth was forced to follow another, slightly longer path. What might have appeared to participants, then, as a communicative pause, which perhaps precipitated HALLIEJEAN's interruption, was in reality a lag in communication caused by the architecture of the technology. This kind of limitation in computer-mediated communication becomes more pronounced in more extended interactions, when participants are required to track several conversation threads, many of which are only quasi-synchronous in terms of communicative turn-taking. For inexperienced Internet users, this can be both awkward and frustrating. Near the end of the ritual, for example, before the circle was opened, the following extended interchange took place. I quote it at some length for the number of issues it raises about the successful performance of ritual online.

> .Elspeth> Did anyone bring food they want blessed? :)
>
> .Terri> no..but I brought a doll.
>
> .Elspeth> ::watching ghost play with fire::
>
> .Elspeth> Want a blessing, Terri?
>
> .Phyllis> me too!
>
> .Terri> please, Elspeth.
>
> .Terri> ::holds up the doll::
>
> .Randall> ::Watches Elspeth watching Ghost::
>
> .Elspeth>
>
> .Dianne> brought my self
>
> .Elspeth>
>
> .Jill> I have some new crystals =)
>
> .Tina> ::holds up Mama doll::
>
> .Elspeth> ::focusing::
>
> .Elspeth>
>
> HALLIEJEAN> I'll observe candle

.Phyllis> ::holds up Mama doll::

.Jill> can I hold up the crystals?

.Elspeth> Sure. :)

.Elspeth>

.Jill> ::thanks::

.Elspeth> By those who watch . . . those who guide . . . those who guard

.Tina> ::and my crystals::

.Elspeth> By all the deity known and unknown . . .

.Elspeth> Send your blessings to these items

.Elspeth> Make them tools of wisdom for us

.Elspeth> That they may aid us on the Path You have sent us on

.Elspeth> ::sketching a symbol of blessing and sending forth::

.Terri> ::smiles::

.Elspeth> :)

.Terri> I felt that. :)

.Tina> :)

.Elspeth> You should have . . . Ghost was helping :) . . .

.Ann> It hit . . . felt it in the back of my skull. Thank you. :) . . .

.Tina> I felt a warmth in my arms (Cauldron 1998c)

Unlike the 1997 ritual, in addition to textualized conversation the 1998 example includes several attempts to indicate participants' off-line activity; for example, Phyllis "::holds up Mama doll::" and Elspeth signals that she is "::watching ghost play with fire::," where double-colons indicate the action performed. One participant, Randall, even uses this device to suggest that he is no longer at his own terminal, wherever it is located physically, but is now "::[watching] Elspeth watching Ghost::." The imaginative sense of the ritual has clearly moved beyond the simple keyboard-and-follow mode of the year before. Unfortunately, whether this shift occurred because the participants knew each other off-line, or had simply become more comfortable with textualized interaction online, is impossible to discern from what remains of the ritual text. Similarly, though, rather than localizing the central rite at each participant's computer, Elspeth invites them into a more interactive ritual space yet by offering to bless various items—food, a doll, a new set of crystals—while they are online together. It is important to point out that she is not blessing these things *over the Internet*; their computers remain the technology of communication and nothing more. It is the psychic and imaginative connection established by their shared ritual world that allows for the blessings to occur.

However, she must still indicate to the other participants that something *is* happening and *when* it takes place, that is, when she is ":::focusing:::" and ":::sketching a symbol of blessing and sending forth:::." In order for the other participants to offer appropriate responses to these actions, they must know what is happening and when. Whether there was intervening chatter or other "extraneous" interruptions in the text quoted above before it was edited for publication on the Web site, we do not know. However, rather like questions of religious historicity in other traditions—did Moses really part the Red Sea? did Gautama really live as an ascetic on one grain of rice per day?—what is more important here is that this is the way the ritual has been remembered by and for the community of which it was a part. In terms of the ritual as remembered experience, this is the "authorized version." As soon as the blessing has been sent forth by a ritual action recognized by the participants as efficacious, they are authorized to respond, which reflexively validates Elspeth's authority as one who can offer blessing. As we can see, one smiles, while two others affirm the positive, physical effect of their leader's action. For all of them, the ritual has been successful; it has confirmed the reality of their belief in the imaginative conduct of modern Pagan ritual and affirmed their place as participants in that belief.

*Beltaine at Online Wiccan Rituals*

The third example is not a ritual log but the text of a Beltaine ritual that was performed in the chat room of Online Wiccan Rituals on April 30, 2002. Celebrating the beginning of summer in the modern Pagan liturgical calendar, the ritual was written and led by a group member named Wulfslaird (2002), and incorporated aspects of his particular modern Pagan paths: Wicca and Native American spirituality. What distinguishes this example from those performed on The Cauldron is that Wulfslaird scripted the ritual, then assigned individual parts based on the number of members who signed up to participate. Rather than remaining in the audience, more cast members were invited to occupy the ritual stage. Thus, initial organization for the ritual and encouragement for new members to participate in it became more important. Onica, for example, wrote that "this will be my first ritual ever and am very excited about it. I've been hesitant to preform one yet being new and not really knowing what I'm doing." Wulfslaird responded that he had been very nervous his first time as well, but that it was relatively easy despite some technical problems. "All I had to do was type my part over the screen at the appropriate time. Well guess what! Everything went well until I got to the End of my part. MY computer failed to print the last two lines and I didn't realize it until it was too late. [High Priestess] Sinovess, being the lady that she is took it in stride and typed it in for me." Encouraged by this, Onica agreed to take an active part in the ritual and Wulfslaird assigned her the "Cakes and Ale" component, a small text recognizing the bounty of the Earth.

The ritual itself incorporated a number of online and off-line elements, some of which the participants performed for themselves, others they were meant to visualize based on the cues provided by Wulfslaird's text, still others they were to recite aloud but not type. As the circle was cast, participants were instructed to light candles and incense around their computers. The quarters were called and the divine complementarity invoked by typing the ritual text—with which all had been provided ahead of time—onto the chat screen. For the "Symbolic Lighting of the Belfire," participants were instructed to "visualize your self flowing back to a life long ago . . ." (Wulfslaird 2002), and then to read a portion of the ritual text aloud, but not to type it. As noted above, the ritual called for group members to burn to ashes a representation of things they wished to release in their lives and for this Wulfslaird incorporated a "Ritual Pause to Allow Burning." This was followed by an aspect of Wiccan and non-Wiccan Witchcraft ritual that is rarely seen online. "Wulfslaird —TYPE— Following the olde ways the Great Rite take place at this time, following is a description of the Rite. (narrates a description of the Great Rite)" (Wulfslaird 2002). The extant text does not indicate whether Wulfslaird meant by this that he recounted the Great Rite aloud or keyboarded a portion of ritual text onto the chat screen. Because the performance of the Great Rite cuts to the heart of the paradox presented by online modern Pagan ritual—an intensely imaginative experience that is meant to be grounded in ritual intercourse, whether actual or symbolic—I will discuss it in greater detail below.

Whatever other value the ritual may have had, it provided an important community reinforcement of Wulfslaird's modern Pagan identity, as well as those of other participants. Prior to the ritual performance, for example, many members commented on how beautiful they thought it was—significant approbation for Wulfslaird since this was his first attempt at writing a ritual. Sinovess, the founder of Online Wiccan Rituals, whose messages convey an unmistakable sense of emotion (see Cowan and Hadden 2004b: 129–30) and whose support as High Priestess is particularly important to the other members, wrote: "Wulf, It's . . . beautiful! Just BEAUTIFUL! I feel very good vibes from it!=) . . . THANK YOU!!!!" (2002). Other members expressed similar sentiments, though some in the context of their disappointment at not being able to take part. After the ritual, which appears to have involved nearly a dozen participants, a brief round of "thank you's" ensued, all of which commented on its beauty and the honor people felt in being asked to participate. Onica, who was uncertain of her ability to participate at all, wrote: "I'll never be able to tell you how much it meant to me."

Whether it takes place online or off-line, whether it is performed by a modern Pagan solitary or a working group, ritual both presupposes and reinforces a *communitas* (in Victor Turner's sense of a "modality of social relationship" [1969: 96]) against the backdrop of which the ritual is performed, and a *veritas* (a belief in "the actual state or nature of things" [Simpson 1968: 636]) in the context of which ritual purpose, performance, and efficacy is conceptualized. For the forerunners of anthropological, historical, and sociological theories of ritual, ritual served some specific function in the context of the social fabric. Whether it increased social density (Emile Durkheim), established the boundaries of social acceptance and marginalization (Mircea Eliade; Mary Douglas), or as "consecrated behavior" (Geertz 1973: 112) served to replicate "the world of the gods that is at the same time a template for the world of men" (Geertz 1983: 29–30), there was a social purpose toward which ritual was directed. In addition to these, in the open source, personally gnostic appropriationism of modern Paganism, ritual instantiates and reinforces modern Pagan identity for those who participate. Writing and directing the Beltaine ritual solidified, as it were, Wulfslaird's identity as a modern Pagan; no longer content simply to participate, he is beginning to assume a leadership role within the Online Wiccan Rituals community. On the other hand, it is hardly inconceivable that the online Beltaine performance presented Onica with her only chance to participate in a modern Pagan ritual at all. In this sense, she is trying out the identity of a modern Pagan, and the willingness of the OWR community—particularly Wulfslaird—to support her in this reinforced her emerging identity. This is a topic to which we will return in depth in the next chapter.

## Performance and Paradox: Parsing the Online Ritual

Although there are obviously a number of analytic directions one could take here, I would like to focus on three that I regard as particularly salient for understanding online ritual in the modern Pagan context: *where* it occurs, the problems inherent in where it occurs as a possible explanation for *why* it doesn't occur more often, and, in the light of Onica's final comment above, what we might call its *deep function* when it does occur.

### Turning a Chat Room into a Temple

"Ritual," writes Jonathan Z. Smith (1987: 103), "is, first and foremost, a mode of paying attention. It is a process for marking interest." That is, there is a particular psychic intentionality about ritual performance that sets it apart from other activities. Reading one's sacred scriptures in bed may be a nightly habit for many people, but reading them aloud in the context of religious worship is an entirely different "mode of paying attention" both to their meaning and to their ontology. Likewise, most people follow some pattern of daily ablution— say, washing one's hands—but when the same act is performed before entering a religious space, whether temple, mosque, or Wiccan circle, it takes on a different character of intentionality. Washing one's hands before a meal is a habit born of concern for cleanliness as a function of physical health; the same act prior to a religious activity is often invested with a much more complex understanding about the relationship between the human and the divine, the manner in which that relationship is negotiated, and the observances that are meant to ensure that the relationship is maintained in proper balance. In this way, continues Smith, as "a fundamental component of ritual: place directs action" (1987: 104). Reading scripture becomes ritually significant because it is read in a church or a mosque; washing one's hands or feet becomes a ritual act because it is linked to entry into or the performance of action within a sacred space. So, to speak with Smith in this context, one of the questions about online modern Pagan ritual is: Where, precisely, does it take place? Where is the attention of participants directed? By now, it seems inadequate to respond simply, "Well, it takes place online"—because "online" is not a place, per se, it is mode of communication.

Though it is based on the conceptualization of clearly established off-line referents, online modern Pagan ritual is, by and large, a theater of the mind. It "takes place" in the imaginations of the participants, though, following Smith, it ought not be considered less real, less efficacious, or less significant for its participants because of this than those rituals that take place in more traditional venues. As we discussed in Chapter 2 with regard to the sacred as a product of social agreement, Smith writes that "there is nothing inherently sacred or profane. These are not substantive categories, but rather situational ones. Sacrality is, above all, a category of emplacement," continuing that "when one enters a temple, one enters marked-off space" (1987: 104; cf. Smith 1982: 54–56). How, then, is this imaginatively constructed sacred space "marked off" online? How is place determined? At this point in its technological development, three principal mechanisms are used to sacralize the space in which modern Pagan ritual occurs online, to separate it from that larger online "space" in which it is embedded. In Smith's terms, three principal "modes of paying attention" turn a chat room into a temple.

First, as we have already encountered, there is the co-constructed visualization, whether it is part of a prepared ritual script or the spontaneous online product of a tacitly authorized off-line ritual venue. Of the nine Cauldron rituals for which logs are available online, more than half were led by a modern Pagan named Randall, who told participants that the different rituals were "not particularly Wiccan" but were drawn, rather, from something he calls his "'Eclectic Druid' ritual" (Cauldron 1998a). In fact, but for very slight changes in wording to accommodate the differences in liturgical season, the sacralizing aspects of the ritual texts are practically identical; the same basic ritual is used season after season. In his 1998 Lughnasadh ritual, for example, an early harvest festival traditionally celebrated on August 1, Randall guided the participants into their sacred space through brief instructions on relaxation and visualization.

.Randall> I want all of you to relax . . . leaving your fingers lightly

.Randall> on the keyboard.

.Randall> Take a deep breath . . . Hold it . . . Let it out slowly . . .

.Randall> Do it again, taking in a calm, peaceful feeling . . . letting

.Randall> out the cares and distractions of everyday life.

.Randall>

.Randall> Another breath and you feel the mundane world drawing

.Randall> away . . .

.Randall>

.Randall> Another breath and you smell the warm bounty of the ripened

.Randall> fields on the winds . . .

.Randall> Continue to breathe and relax . . . until you feel yourself

.Randall> enter that place that exists between the worlds, not in this

.Randall> world and not in the next.

.Randall>

.Randall> This is the Place between the Worlds . . . (Cauldron 1998a)

As I noted above, "between the worlds" is a phrase commonly used by modern Pagans to signal that the sacred space—whether a circle, a grove, or some other form of ritual working group—has been successfully partitioned from the mundane world. With the exception of the seasonal identifier, every ritual Randall led began with this invocation of a sacred place. For Midsummer, "the warm bounty of the ripened fields" was simply replaced by "the warmth and glow of the summer sun" (Cauldron 1998b), for Ostara, by "the first breath of spring bourne on the wings of the March winds" (Cauldron 1999b), and for Beltaine, by "the new growth bursting through the fertile soil of fields" (Cauldron 1999a).

Rituals performed in The Ritual Room, on the other hand (http://thedance .com/rituals), and for which a number of logs are available upon request from the site administrator, use much more elaborate descriptions to create the sacred space. At the beginning of one 1999 ritual, for example, participants entering the chat room for a more traditional Wiccan ritual were greeted by the following introductory text.

The ritual room is a simple space tonight, dark but for candles in sconces on the wall. There are windchimes tinkling faintly in the distance, but you could not find the source of their sound if you tried. In the middle of the room is a circle of floor pillows, soft, plush, and richly colored. Within the circle in a large cauldron. It is surrounded by small pots of lavender and rosemary. Near the cauldron is a small simple altar. On it rests a candle each for the Goddess and God. In the east, there is a collection of feathers. In the southern corner of the altar is a small pot of incense burning. A bottle of waters of the world rests in the west. In the north is a small clay pot of earth. Find a seat and get comfortable . . . perhaps begin to ground and center yourself . . . and we'll begin soon. (Ritual Room 1999).

This example leads to the second mechanism by which ritual place and presence is established: participants locate themselves within the ritual space both textually and imaginatively. The following fictionalized example has been compiled from a number of the chat logs available from The Ritual Room. I have chosen to present it in this format to respect the privacy of the individuals involved. Indeed, this is the only information that I had to obtain through personal contact with a site administrator, and in that it departs a little from the public face of online modern Paganism with which I have been more concerned to this point. Thus, at the request of the administrator of this site, who very kindly provided me with the ritual logs, I am describing these aspects of ritual in more general terms. As each participant enters the room, an initial text similar to the example directly above sets the ritual scene; participants are told how the room is decorated, what ritual furniture and accoutrements are in place, whether music is playing, and how the seating for the ritual is arranged. Occasionally, a host greets them as they enter, and the members use this as a way to emplace themselves both textually and imaginatively.

<Athena> ::Athena is sitting on a brocade pillow near the doorway, softly playing her *shakuhachi* flute as the members gather::

<Jadetiger> ::enters quietly, nodding to Athena as she passes. She chooses a dark green pillow to the north of the altar and begins to center::

<Willow~wisp> ::kisses Athena gently on the cheek and {{{Jadetiger}}}::

<Willow~wisp> Merry meet, JT . . . Athena. ::sits down near the south candle::

<Jadetiger> {{{W~W}}}

<Athena> ::Nods at W~W, but continues playing::

<Raven> Good evening, everyone, and merry meet.

<Raven> ::takes a small sprig of rosemary and settles onto a big purple pillow beside JT::

<Runecaster> Merry meet, my family!! ::looks around the room::

<Jadetiger> ::pats the pillow on the other side from Raven::

<Jadetiger> Come sit here, Runie, it's been too long . . .

<Runecaster> JT!!! ::sits on the pillow beside JT and Raven:: {{{all around}}}

<Angelfish> Merry meet, gentles, have we started yet?

<Angelfish> ::hurries to a pillow beside W~W::

<Raven> Nope . . . we're still gathering

<Jadetiger> No, there's lots of time . . .

<Runecaster> Nah! ::) C'mon in!

)O(

::Athena walks to the altar and lays her *shakuhachi* between the two candles of the Goddess and the God. She picks up her athame and motions everyone to rise::

<Athena> We create this place between the worlds . . .

)O(

<ALL> SO MOTE IT BE

Though this is a manufactured example, it is true to the sense of many Ritual Room logs and represents a significant departure from The Cauldron rituals. Not only is it more interactive, but the participants take much greater responsibility for their own co-constructed emplacement within the visualized ritual space. Familiar off-line social interaction—initial greetings, hugs ({{ . . . }}) and kisses, preferred seating—is textually reproduced in the online environment. And, as often happens at many off-line religious services and ceremonies, some members choose to interact prior to the ritual (Raven, Jadetiger, and Runecaster), whereas others (Willow~wisp) more intentionally separate themselves as a way of preparing for the experience to follow. Whether the fictional Athena is actually playing a *shakuhachi* flute off-line is unknown and largely unimportant; in the co-created ritual space, she *is* playing the instrument and the other participants acknowledge and support this statement of action. Once again, though, it is worth pointing out that there is nothing inherently "cyberspatial" about the ritual spaces created in any of these transcripts; they are off-line spaces reproduced online through guided and co-constructed visualization, and sacralized according to the agreement of the participants.

The third mechanism that signals the invocation of or invitation to create the online ritual space involves an intentional shift in participant identity. Though Lisa McSherry's claim that the cybercoven is "the next step in pagan evolution" (2002: 4) may be overstated, she includes at the beginning of *The Virtual Pagan* a chat log excerpt that illustrates very nicely the importance attached both to identity and to shifts in identity in online modern Pagan interaction. For our purposes here, the significant lines are:

*Imago>* Hey Ma'at!

*Brightayes>* Hugs Ma'at. Good to see you.

*Maat>* Looks like we're all here—shall we begin?

Maat changes her nickname to Lady_Maat.

Lady_Ma'at walks to the East and raises her athame high.

*Lady_Maat>* Mighty Mother! Strike this blade with light

*Lady_Maat>* that I may cast the sacred circle between the worlds.

(McSherry 2002: 3–4)

After a round of greetings as different participants joined the chat room designated for the ritual, Maat's online persona changed in an important way. Her inconsistent spelling notwithstanding, the shift from "Maat" to "Lady_Maat" signaled the establishment of the ritual space; with the transformation of one participant into the High Priestess, the chat room was being changed into a temple. Prior to this shift, McSherry goes by her Craft name, Maat, an Egyptian mother goddess. As High Priestess, however, it is Lady_Maat's responsibility to ensure that the ritual space is established correctly. In direct contrast to The Cauldron's 1997 Ostara ritual discussed above, in this shift of online identities, it is as though she left the group and then reentered in ritual regalia. And, in Lady_Maat's case, it both establishes the ritual space and reinforces McSherry's authority as one who can provide "a thorough education in almost every aspect of being a Witch" (McSherry n.d. [a]). As I will argue more fully below, online ritual is most importantly a function of "paying attention" to one's identity as a modern Pagan. In this case, to creatively misread Jonathan Z. Smith, identity directs action.

## Why Chat Rooms Remain Chat Rooms

Obviously, not all of these mechanisms are present in each ritual, and the total number of ritual logs available for close scrutiny makes any generalization tentative at best. However, given the importance of the imaginative component in modern Pagan ritual, the creative visualizations that lie at the heart of magickal working, the World Wide Web should be an ideal venue for this kind of activity. Why, then, relatively speaking, are online rituals so rare? Describing itself as "an open online Coven," for example, organized originally around the performance of modern Pagan ritual on the Internet, Online Wiccan Rituals operates as both a dedicated Web site (http://go.to/OnlineWiccanRituals) and two Yahoo! discussion groups (groups.yahoo.com/group/OnlineWiccan Rituals[2]). Online since October 2001, the first Yahoo! group has posted more than 50,000 messages, averaging nearly 1,900 messages per month. In fact, the message volume got to be so heavy and the membership so large that, in July 2002, Online Wiccan Rituals 2 was created for the express purpose of "performing and discussing online rituals/celebrations/spells." Though the first group is a very active discussion list, which some members clearly regard as an important part of their social support network as modern Pagans, online rituals are extremely rare; chat logs exist for only two. In the day-to-day operation of the group, much more space is dedicated to the exchange of mundane greetings, information, and modern Pagan chatter. At Online Wiccan Rituals 2, there is no indication that any online ritual has taken place at all, and little of the discussion that does occur concerns the construction or performance of ritual in any way. Indeed, to this point, most of the posts are from one member who cuts-pastes-and-reloads snippets of modern Pagan information gleaned from books she is reading or Web sites she is visiting at the time. Ritual, however, is virtually absent, and I would like to suggest three principal reasons for this: technology, psychology, and physicality.

Technologically, as I have mentioned before, there is the inherent fragility of online interaction in terms of Internet connection, software compatibility and stability, server support, and venue access. Although a thunderstorm or power outage may give off-line Pagans pause about *where* to conduct their rituals, neither will necessarily impact *whether* those rituals take place. A particularly recalcitrant operating system is little more than a nuisance for an off-line Wiccan checking her e-mail before leaving for a Sabbat or Esbat ritual, but it means nothing in terms of the ritual itself. Any of these, on the other hand, can bring online ritual to a crashing halt before it has even begun. "I looked forward to sharing this ritual with you all," wrote Phoenix Thorn, referring to Wulfslaird's Beltaine ritual. "Unfortunately, my computer has other ideas. I can no longer use my mouse which makes navigating extremely difficult and all the windows are shown largely in pitch black, which makes seeing difficult." Phoenix Thorn added that she had spoken with another group member earlier in the day and that because of software issues this member would not be present at the ritual either. Even when a ritual does occur, individual computer technology will continue to bound and limit the manner of participation. Like telegraph operators, meaningful communication will take place only at the speed of the slowest participant. It matters little if three members of a ritual group are on high speed networks if others, especially ritual presiders, are using dial-up connections and older, slower modems. As we have seen, this difference can inhibit the natural flow of turn taking in social interaction and confuse the flow of ritual discourse. Although the greater availability of broadband connections such as DSL, cable modems, or T-1 lines will mitigate the problem to some degree, it is unreasonable to suppose that the technological disparity between users will be eliminated entirely. There is also the issue of people being dropped from chat rooms unexpectedly and having to either log back in themselves or ask to be readmitted by someone charged with gatekeeping the ritual space. Conversely, uninvited visitors pop in and out of ritual chat rooms without warning (Cauldron 1998b, 1998d, 2003). More often than not, when they recognize that the room is not for an open chat these unexpected guests exit quickly. Other times, though, as in The Cauldron's 2003 Beltaine ritual, they try to participate, but have little idea what to do or why, and leave after a few unsuccessful attempts to interact. All of this extraneous activity is distracting, and draws the participants' attention away from the ritual itself.

Psychologically, in addition to the specifically bounded environments within which they occur (that is, the "sacred space"), religious rituals frequently involve complex interactions between sacred texts (used both as mythical substrate and for antiphonal invocation or evocation), magickal implements (both as ritual subject and ritual object), and the physical manipulation of one's body (as well as those of other participants). Online, as O'Leary points out, most of these components are created textually, and interaction is managed in the ritualist's imagination. A scene is described in the text of the ritual—a forest clearing under a full moon, a shadowy cavern lit by torches and candles, a megalithic circle in the dead of winter—but the experience of that scene is imagined, visualized by each participant. Some online rituals call for participants to have certain supplies such as candles and incense on hand; others rely entirely on the power of imaginative focus to set the stage for the ritual performance. Indeed, few modern Pagan primers on ritual and magick do not stress the need for—and the difficulty of—psychological, emotional, and imaginative focus as key components in successful working practice. But in off-line situations, little or no psychological energy is required to visualize the very setting of the ritual itself. Off-line, the candles are in place at the quarter points and the altar faces east regardless of what else transpires in the sacred space; ritual implements such athame, pentacle, and cauldron (in Wiccan contexts) need not be imagined because they exist in time and space; if outdoors, the wind will remind participants of its power quite apart from their ability to imagine it. Online, these different ritual components often have no existence apart from the ability of participants to imagine them. Off-line, the ritual setting is the background against which the ritual is performed, the foundation on which the magickal energy is raised, focused, and released. Online, each of these elements must be manifest imaginatively, drawing psychological energy away from the performative purpose of the ritual itself. Speaking dramaturgically, off-line participants can focus on the performance of the play; online, in addition to the play, they must also hold in their minds the appearance of the stage, the set, and the various props. The ability to maintain these complex visualizations is a highly developed skill, the result of diligent practice, and hardly the province of "cut-n-paste" Internet Pagans.

One fairly basic example of this is the difference between *speaking* (even reading) one's part of a ritual text and *typing* that same part in an online ritual. Few people are as proficient at keyboarding as they are at either speaking or reading aloud; yet many online ritual texts contain long blocks of material that are meant to be typed by participants during the course of the ritual. If a participant is concentrating on typing his or her part accurately—and quickly enough not to bog down the proceedings unduly—that is psychological energy unavailable for focusing on the purpose of the ritual. For other participants, waiting for text to upload, especially if one is uncertain whether one's Internet connection remains intact, could easily draw focus away as well, provoking the online ritual version of the discussion group message: Is anyone still out there? Are we still on?

A few examples of online ritual preserve not only the structure and liturgical substance of the ritual itself, but more important, the interactions between participants before, during, and after the ritual itself. Comparing the prepared texts of proposed rituals with the examples of actual ritual participation reveals one stark and significant difference: interactions are drastically shorter in the logs of rituals performed than they are in proposed ritual texts. Even off-line, those who have some skill in ritual preparation realize the need to keep antiphonal aspects of the performance short. That is, as difficult as it is for ritual presiders to read long portions of text aloud, it is even more difficult for ritual participants or audiences to remain focused during those readings—a problem that is only compounded by computer-mediated communication. Add to this the vast and unavoidable differences in speed and fluency between speaking and typing—reading aloud in off-line ritual and keyboarding text during online ritual—and reasons for the relative rarity of online ritual begin to become clearer. It is simply not as satisfying as ritual conducted in "the real world." Consider as more mundane examples of this the acronymic shortcuts that have become a standard component of online communications. "Talk to you later" has become TTYL; "Laughing out loud," LOL; and "Be right back," BRB. Why do these occur so frequently? Because the phrases they represent simply take too long to type accurately and fluidly, and, in the ritual context, this time lag can easily distract participants from their liturgical focus. As anyone who spends much time in chat rooms can attest, most messages are short combinations of sentence fragments, acronyms, and emoticons. Few exceed three or four lines of text. With occasional exceptions, the longest texts in The Ritual Room transcripts are those that participants read to establish the setting as they enter the ritual space. Quarter calls and ritual invocations are shorter, and interactions between participants during the ritual themselves are shorter yet, often reduced to the fragmentary and the semiotic.

### Drawing Down the Electronic Moon: Translating the Body Online and the Problem of Interphysicality

Physically, the problem presented by the performance of modern Pagan ritual online is twofold. First is the basic tension noted by critics such as Ian Lurking Bear (1994) and Clifford Stoll (1995, 1999) between, as Shawn Arthur puts it, "Technophilia and Nature Religion" (2002), the difference between experience and imagination. Second is the centrality of the body in modern Pagan ritual, most specifically in practices such as Drawing Down the Moon and the Great Rite, and the not-insignificant reality that, Internet hyperbole notwithstanding, we cannot completely escape our bodies, however much we may want to or believe that we can. As modern Pagan elder Macha NightMare notes, "from my limited experience with online ritual, I can say that so far I haven't experienced shivers up my spine the way I often do in terraspace rituals" (2001: 211).

First, as powerful as the imagination is, visualization is still not sensation; seeing the Mona Lisa in one's mind's eye, or even in a photograph, is not the same as experiencing it in the Louvre. For one thing, it is much smaller in real life than one might imagine! Conversely, no matter how detailed the .jpeg file or how sophisticated the computer monitor, no mere image can match the towering grandeur of the giant evergreens in Vancouver Island's Cathedral Grove (rumored to have been the alternative location for the "Forest Moon of Endor" sequences in George Lucas' *Return of the Jedi*). Similarly, in the modern Pagan ritual context, imagining the flickering light of beeswax candles and the sweet smell of incense is not the same as trying to read a sacred text by the unsteady glow of real candles or wash the real smell of jasmine and sandalwood from one's clothes at the end of the ceremony. Visualizing snow piled in drifts among the dolmens may cause online participants to shiver in their workstation chairs, but the experience is hardly the same as trying to keep warm while celebrating the winter solstice knee-deep in that same snow. Images, whether real or imagined, are not the phenomenon, or, as Jonathan Z. Smith would say, "the map is not the territory" (1993; cf. NightMare 2001: 211–12).

Similarly, there is a significant difference between reading a written text and hearing the spoken word. Online textual communication can be layered with a number of different social interaction cues—"smiley-faces" and other emoticons, acronyms to signal nonverbal components of conversation such as laughter, and the use of "{{{}}}" to indicate when one participant is hugging another

—but the text itself remains two-dimensional; it has no quality of sound. Few ritual presiders would contest the power of the human voice and of human presence to convey considerably more substance than simply the written word that is read silently to oneself. If this were not so, arguably we should be as satisfied with reading *Henry V* as we are hearing and seeing it performed by Laurence Olivier (1944) or Kenneth Branagh (1989). If this were not so, a Puccini libretto would mean as much to opera lovers as Renata Tebaldi's 1961 performance of *Tosca*. The plain fact of the matter, though, is that they do not.

Ian Lurking Bear adds an ethical component to this particular problem, contending that "it is too easy to create an experience of beautiful scenery, peace, and harmony while ignoring environmental destruction outside, and forgetting about the legions of underpaid third worlders that make the infrastructure on which virtual reality depends possible" (1994; cf. Arthur 2002). In his view, technology such as the Internet and the World Wide Web is not facilitating the relationship between modern Pagans and the most basic ground of their belief system—the natural world—it is actually separating them more completely from it. Extending Lurking Bear's concern, though the Internet is only one source of information on which modern Pagans draw, and some research indicates it is hardly the most significant (Berger and Ezzy 2004), can those modern Pagans who *have* learned about their faith either exclusively or predominantly through online interaction ever appreciate the profoundly embodied character of modern Pagan ritual and practice? Although few modern Paganisms combine all of these elements, dancing and feasting, ritual nudity (which sometimes includes elaborate costuming), sexual activity either actual or symbolic, and ritually mandated physical interactions during particular ceremonies, all speak to modern Paganism as an embodied spirituality (see Pike 2001 for some excellent examples of this). Which brings us to the issue of what I am calling "interphysicality," ritually oriented physical interaction between participants. These interphysical actions can range from a brief "kiss of peace" in the Christian tradition to fully realized *yab-yum*, the physically embodied union of masculine and feminine principles, in Vajrayana Buddhism.

*Translating the Body Online*

Within the Wiccan and non-Wiccan Witchcraft traditions, two specific rituals demonstrate this interphysical embodiment more clearly than any other: the rite of Drawing Down the Moon and the Great Rite, both of which find their modern roots in Gardnerian Wicca (Farrar 1991; Farrar and Farrar 1981, 1984; though see Hutton 1999: 245 for a discussion of Gardner's source for, and creative misuse of, the former). In the rite of Drawing Down the Moon, the spiritual energy of the Goddess is physically embodied in the High Priestess of the coven, either through her own action or, in more traditional settings, in concert with the actions of the High Priest and other members of the working group. According to the Farrars, though always bearing in mind the open source, personally gnostic character of modern Paganism as a whole and the manner in which this rite has been either modified or eliminated by other traditions, Drawing Down the Moon remains a critical component of modern British Wiccan ritual and illustrates, at least, the embodied nature of that ritual. "After the Circle has been cast," wrote Stewart Farrar (1991: 57), "every meeting starts with Drawing Down the Moon. In fact the whole of the Circle casting ritual enters into this, but the heart of it is the calling of the Goddess to descend into the body of the High Priestess, who then continues to personify the Goddess until the Circle is finally banished." Once this has been performed, the High Priestess delivers the Charge of the Goddess, a ritual invocation that constitutes part of the ceremonial work of the Wiccan coven. Elsewhere, the Farrars write that, although the High Priestess' embodiment of the Goddess ought not be confused with possession, but is more akin to conscious channeling, they also note that the outcome of the rite is often unexpected. "The Goddess *does* come through, in the tone and emphasis of the delivery of the Charge—often to the surprise of the priestess delivering it. Janet [Farrar] admits frankly that she 'never knows how it will come out'" (Farrar and Farrar 1984: 68; cf. Harvey 1997: 39–40). To get a sense of the interphysicality of the rite, its dependence on the physical relationship between the ritual participants, I quote part of the rite at length from one of the Farrars' accounts (1981: 40–41; cf. Greenwood 2000: 99).

> The High Priest now proceeds to 'draw down the Moon' on the High Priestess. She stands with her back to the altar, with the wand in her right hand and the scourge in her left, held against her breasts in the 'Osiris position'—the two shafts grasped in her clenched fists, her wrists crossed, and the shafts crossed again above them . . . He kneels before her. The High Priest give the High Priestess the Fivefold Kiss, kissing her on the right foot, left foot, right knee, left knee, womb, right breast, left breast and lips. (When he reaches the womb, she opens her arms to the 'blessing position.') As he does so, he says:
>
> 'Blessed be thy feet, that have brought thee in these ways.
>
> Blessed be thy knees, that shall kneel at the sacred altar.
>
> Blessed be thy womb, without which we would not be.
>
> Blessed be thy breasts, formed in beauty.
>
> Blessed be thy lips, that shall utter the Sacred Names.'

For the kiss on the lips, they embrace, length-to-length, with their feet touching each other's. The High Priest kneels again before the High

Priestess, who resumes the 'blessing position,' but with her right foot slightly forward. The High Priest invokes: '*I invoke thee and call upon thee, Mighty Mother of us all, bringer of all fruitfulness; by seed and root, by bud and stem, by leaf and flower and fruit, by life and love do I invoke thee to descend upon the body of this thy servant and priestess.*'

Whether they were designed for use online or off-line, many ritual scripts that have been lodged on the Web include either a reference to or a liturgical text for the rite of Drawing Down the Moon. Yet, none of the ritual logs (transcripts) indicates that it has been performed as part of an online ritual, and, indeed, it is difficult to imagine how this might be accomplished. Though McSherry includes a definition of the rite in her glossary (2002: 154), she does not include it in any of her sample online rituals and does not indicate how it might be performed. NightMare, who describes the rite as part of the ritual process of "aspecting" (2001: 82–94 *passim*), discusses it in greater detail, but still does not say how it could be performed effectively online. Though Knight and Telesco mention the importance of full moon ritual in both their books on "cyber-witching," neither includes reference to the explicitly interphysical rite of Drawing Down the Moon. Although there is the distinct possibility that the rite has been deemphasized by the very few groups that perform rituals online, that its interphysicality would be difficult to replicate in a chat room environment should not go unnoticed. Though she is not addressing the issue of online ritual specifically, Silver RavenWolf points out the inherent difficulty of maintaining focus during the rite. In her brief discussion of Drawing Down the Moon, she notes that "this is usually a silent, physical action. I say silent because it is difficult to concentrate on mentally and emotionally accepting the energies of the moon into oneself while speaking aloud" (1998: 73). One can only imagine how much more difficult this would be when one is required either to type or to follow a computer-mediated liturgical text during this period of intense focus and concentration.

This problem is even more pronounced in the Great Rite, the modern Pagan version of the *hieros gamos* (sacred marriage) and one of the central liturgical acts in traditional British Wicca. As I mentioned above, midway through the Beltaine/Self Healing Ritual celebrated at Online Wiccan Rituals, Wulfslaird (2002) was required to type: "Following the olde ways the Great Rite take place at this time, following is a description of the Rite (narrates a description of the Great Rite)" Unfortunately, nothing in the ritual transcript reveals how he accomplished this, and there is no indication how the body was translated online during the ceremony. Though a number of modern Pagan traditions, particularly in North America and particularly those influenced by feminist epistemologies, have deemphasized or eliminated the Great Rite from their ritual praxis (see Salomonsen 2002: 180–81), that it shows up in Wulfslaird's liturgical text indicates that it has not disappeared entirely.

Like many of the ritual motifs that appear in modern Paganism, the Great Rite finds its Wiccan origins in the works of Gerald Gardner, specifically the initiation of a covener into the third degree of the Craft, but also at the conclusion of certain Sabbat observances. In terms of British Traditional Wicca, initiation into the third degree means that the candidate is considered fully qualified to found his or her own coven, to initiate coveners and teach them as he or she sees fit, and, in the words of the Farrars, be "fully independent, answerable only to the Gods and his or her own conscience" (1984: 31; cf. Adrienne 1993; Crowley 1996b: 91–92; Farrar 1991: 72–80; Farrar and Farrar 1981: 48–54). The rite itself consists of either actual or symbolic sexual union between two coven members, an act that embodies the union of the God and the Goddess. When it is symbolically performed, which is also known as "in token," the High Priest holds the ritual chalice (which represents the female aspect of the divine complementarity) while the High Priestess inserts into it the athame (the male aspect). When performed actually, which occurs by all accounts far less often than symbolically, the participants in the Great Rite either leave the ritual circle and then return when their intercourse is completed, or are left alone in the ritual circle by the other members of the coven. Either way, the interphysicality of the rite is obvious. Although the performance of the Great Rite "in token" could more easily lend itself to online ritual, its absence in all but one of the two dozen ritual transcripts I looked at closely suggests that this particular problem of translating the body online through computer-mediated text is one that has yet to be solved by modern Pagans.

## Modern Pagan Ritual Online and Off-

All told, there is so little substantive difference between the content of ritual that occurs online and that which takes place off-line that, apart from the fact that participants who might never meet otherwise have the opportunity to interact, there seems no compelling reason to perform rituals online—especially in the face of the other various frustrations inherent in online communication. Put differently, if online ritual offers nothing more to the ritual experience, if it does not enhance it in some way—a claim, by the way, which I saw made nowhere in either discussion groups or ritual chatter, and one which is explicitly challenged by modern Pagans such as Lurking Bear and NightMare—then there seems little benefit to the extra effort required by the online environment. Every ritual that I looked at used off-line referents, both environmental (trees, standing stones, a full moon) and ritual (egg, candle, water, juice). The computer itself contributed no more to the ritual than would a telephone party-line. In fact, because the participants would have been able to hear each other, to distinguish tone and inflection, the party-line would have arguably allowed for even more effective ritual interaction.

In terms of creativity, while many texts for online rituals are posted, few differ in any way from ritual texts found in off-line sources. In some cases, they have simply been copied onto the Web site directly from a book, sometimes with an attribution, often without. Given the rampant online replication of other modern Pagan sources, this should not surprise us. Though the issue of creativity is hardly limited to the online world, I suspect that few who have tried to write original ritual texts, especially on anything close to a regular basis and in the symbolically meaningful style so valued by modern Pagans, will contest the claim that it is not an easy task. During my time in graduate school, for example, my wife managed a large denominational bookstore; among the dozens of clergy who frequented her shop, however, the most popular volumes by far were prepackaged liturgies and sermon collections. Online or off-line, using "canned" rituals written by others is rarely as fulfilling as performing those created by or within the participant group. In the face of all these issues, for all but a very few technopagans, computer-mediated ritual is likely to remain at very best a poor second cousin to real life circles, groves, and kindreds. And if this is so, what then does it do, if it *does* anything at all? This is the point at which we begin the next chapter.

# CHAPTER 6

# Coming Out of the Online Broom Closet
## *Identity and Authority on the World Wide Web*

Just as we are not restricted by our names, we are not bound by our bodies. We can move easily through the entire spectrum of gender and sexual identities when we are online. We can be female, male, androgynous, old, young, slender, round, strong, delicate, fair, ruddy, dark, short, tall. Skin, hair, eye color, and body configuration can all be assumed in an online configuration . . . We may even transcend species, becoming a goat, a butterfly, or a juniper.

Macha NightMare (2001: 91)

### From Dabblers to Demagogues: Identity, Disclosure, and Investment Online and Off-

Few aspects of computer-mediated communication have been noted with more regularity than the issues of identity, anonymity, and the potential for online deception that lodges in the space between them. As observers ranging from Rheingold (1993) and Turkle (1995) to NightMare (2001) and McSherry (2002) have suggested, Internet technology has challenged us to reevaluate what we mean by the very concept of "identity," to reconsider the ways in which identity is being created and recreated electronically, and, in some cases, to rethink the very boundaries of the human "self." This is certainly true in some respects, and predicated on the perception of anonymity afforded by online communication, this allegedly wholesale reinvention of personal identity appears in both dystopian and utopian guises. On the one hand, dystopically, there is the specter of online deception, which ranges from identity theft

153

(Ihejirika 2004; Levin 2003) and cyberstalking (Anderiesz 2004; Harris 2003) to betrayal, rape, and even murder in MUDs, MOOs, MMORPGs, and beyond (Dibbell 1994; Lazlow 2003; Ravetz 1998), and from fraudulent claims to professional credentials (Donath 1999) to the debate over the ethics of disclosure in online research (Cavanaugh 1999; Ess 2002; Sharf 1999). Indeed, as an ethical concern, a technological problem, and a foundation for online deception and self-deception, lack of privacy on the Internet occupies a significant portion of the discussion about the future of electronic communications.

On the utopian hand, because of the perception that anonymity has somehow leveled the communicative playing field, Internet enthusiast logic runs that online access means significantly enhanced personal agency, often well beyond anything that may be accomplished off-line. Internet visitors can disclose or disguise whatever aspects of their identity they choose and therefore assume multiple identities as these are deemed conducive to participation in a variety of electronic forums. Online, we can be who we want to be, free from the constraints of who we are or who we are told to be off-line. In its most hyperbolic form, this claim posits a limitless, decentered "self" that can be endlessly recreated across a wide range of socially constructed identifiers—gender, class, race, religion, physical appearance, cultural outlook, social philosophy, and even species—none of which are regarded as having any ultimate hold on the identity constructed and any of which may be freely exchanged in the construction of a new identity.

As indicated by the epigraph above, this more utopian vision fits well with the modern Pagan concept of identity. Rooted in the recovery of a "true persona," modern Pagan identity is often regarded as the instantiation of a more authentic self, a self that reflects the spiritual path one has chosen to follow and is often reflected in the Pagan name by which one has chosen to be known. Thus, the presider at an online Beltaine ritual is not "Bob Smith," but Wulfslaird, a modern Pagan whose religious beliefs and practice include an affinity for *Canis lupus* and the Native American myths that incorporate them. Lisa McSherry is Lady Ma'at, an indication of her kinship with members of the Egyptian pantheon. And "Barb Jones" is Celtic Star, a modern Pagan astrologer with a spiritual interest in all things Scots, Irish, and Welsh. Although Craft names certainly do function as security measures to protect modern Pagan practitioners from the real world consequences of inadvertent "outing," rather than intentional deception, identity in modern Paganism is an almost ludic process, a playful sloughing of mundane reality in favor of a magickal recognition of those elements by which the modern Pagan self is more authentically characterized. While the Internet may have permitted Wulfslaird, Lady Ma'at, or Celtic Star to present their modern Pagan selves more openly online—indeed, I would suggest that this is one of the Internet's most important contributions to modern Paganism—it is the open source nature of modern

Paganism itself, its flair for the ritually dramatic and the personally charismatic, that allowed for their re-identification in the first place. A very prominent example of this identity play has taken place entirely off-line in the ongoing re-identification of Tim Zell (b. 1942), the founder of the Church of All Worlds. Since the beginning of the CAW in the mid-1960s, Zell has gone through a variety of modern Pagan incarnations: Otter G'Zell, Otter Zell, Oberon Zell, and, at the time of this writing, Oberon Zell-Ravenheart (Guiley 1999: 387–90; Hopman and Bond 1996: 217–25; Vale and Sulak 2001: 130–53). Each name marks a transition in his modern Pagan journey, and, consequently, an evolution in his modern Pagan identity.

## The Continuum of Identity

As it does in many other social and cultural arenas, identity making in modern Paganism occurs along a continuum bounded by interested nonidentification at one end and complete, public identification at the other. Those who browse modern Pagan titles at a local bookstore, for example, but who would never identify themselves as Wiccans, Witches, or Druids, populate one end of the spectrum, whereas those such as Starhawk, Isaac Bonewits, Oberon Zell-Ravenheart, and Laurie Cabot, whose entire identity is concerned with being a publicly acknowledged modern Pagan, populate the other. Along the path from interested observer to dedicated participant, however, lie several major stages of identity formation, crisis periods through which prospective converts pass, between which they often vacillate, and in the midst of which they not infrequently stall. The most significant of these is between internal identity formation and external identity presentation—telling myself I am a modern Pagan in the privacy of my own thoughts versus demonstrating that identity to others in the rough-and-tumble of the real world. Put this way, there seems a rather obvious correlation between identity, disclosure, and investment.

Internally, identity making often begins as casual interest, as an unspoken seekership. For whatever reason, a person is drawn to some particular path within modern Paganism (or Buddhism, or Christianity, or Judaism) and begins a process of exploration on the basis of that sense of internal resonance. Though the initial boundaries of this religious territory may be drawn by cultural convention or social pressure—Merton's "anticipatory socialization" (1968), for example, or Bourdieu's "games of culture" (1984a, 1993)—what ultimately resonates with one individual and not another remains something of a mystery, just one of the many challenges faced by the academic observer. As a function of cultural production, for example, the haunting beauty of Loreena McKennitt's music or the lyric romanticism of Marion Zimmer Bradley's *The Mists of Avalon* (1982) may encourage some inquirers to explore the Celtic revival that both underpins and depends upon works of art such as these. For others, the mere prospect of bagpipes at a modern Pagan moot (gathering) is enough to put them on an entirely different path. For some, the elaborate rituals of Gardnerian Wicca fulfil a yearning for the theatrical; for others, the simpler one's religious practice the better.

Externally, however, as an initial foray into the real world of modern Paganism, perhaps the inquirer attends a large public ritual or a gathering such as Pagan Pride Day. At the beginning of this exploratory process, she may not consider herself a modern Pagan; that is, despite some initial internal resonance, she may not have identified herself even internally as a Wiccan or a Witch, and simple participation as an audience member in public rituals, meetings, or other events does not necessarily change that. Indeed, no matter how heartily one participates, simply going to a modern Pagan ritual—whether public or private—does not make one a modern Pagan if one does not identify as such internally. This might seem a rather obvious point, but given the reliance of at least some modern Pagans on putative data such as the "readership of relevant materials" as indicators of modern Pagan growth (see Chapters 4 and 7), its importance cannot be overstated. If the "readership of relevant materials" were extended to include "visiting relevant Web sites," then who knows how many millions of modern Pagans there are? Of course, "reading relevant materials," "visiting relevant Web sites," attending a public ritual, even leaping the Beltaine fires does not, *necessarily*, make one a modern Pagan. In the emerging lore of new religious movements scholarship, for example, there is the well-known story about a small group of millennialists that had been infiltrated by so many scholars that the observers all but outnumbered the actual participants (see Festinger, Riecken, and Schachter 1956). Put differently, simply going to a Mormon church service in coat-and-tie would no more make me a Latter-day Saint than bowing before a roadside shrine in Tokyo—both of which I have done—would make me a follower of Shinto. External participation does not necessarily indicate internal identification. In terms of identity and investment, there is an important difference between personal participation in external behavior and the external presentation of a self-identified persona.

In the trajectory of identity, disclosure, and investment, internal identification precedes external presentation. That is, prior to any outward display of belief or behavior that is meant to instantiate identity, based on internal resonance and unspoken seekership cognitive decisions are made about the time and manner in which one publicly reveals aspects of one's emerging internal identification. This is the personal and social process of conversion, of gradually escalating levels of identification and commitment.

In a social context that supports the values of religious freedom and religious pluralism, and in which conversion is not necessarily a singular event, internal identity formation in the process of conversion is often marked by an evolving conformation of worldview. Here, I am not referring to one's comprehension of theological minutiae or exposure to ritual esoterica, but to a broader sweep of identification that is governed by less precise processes of resonance and affinity. We see something and we want it for ourselves; we encounter someone and we want to be like them, to have what they have; we think something is fashionable and believe we will be fashionable if it becomes part of our identity; we realize at some point that the explanations and answers offered by a particular worldview resonate with our own experiences and questions. A very common sentiment on Yahoo! and MSN discussion groups, for example, especially those that encourage the participation of modern Pagan "newbies," is an expression of familiarity, even déjà vu, about the beliefs and practices these "newbies" are exploring. In the personally gnostic world of modern Paganism, this subjective resonance is often regarded as objective validation for the path one has chosen. Through this evolving conformation of worldview, we begin to see the world through the lens of our new path. Gradually, as the conversion process continues, the way in which one conceptualizes and responds to the world begins to reflect and be governed by the beliefs and ethics—if not necessarily the behaviors—of the worldview under exploration. Those who are in the process of converting to the Church of Jesus Christ of Latter-day Saints, for example, may come to see the value of the well-known Mormon "Word of Wisdom," which prohibits such things as tobacco, coffee and tea, and alcohol. Those who are exploring a nature religion such as Wicca may begin to pay more attention to the seasons, to the phases of the moon, or even to their own physical bodies.

Numerous scholars have suggested that conversion to religious movements, new or established, has an important relational component (see, for example, Bainbridge 1978; Barker 1984; Rochford 1985; Stark and Bainbridge 1985). As our relational ties to group members become stronger than ties to nonmembers we begin to identify more closely with the group. Although this social support is certainly part of the conversion process to modern Paganism, especially as converts move into an intentional working group such as a coven (see, for example, Berger 1999; Curott 1998), gradual self-identification as a modern Pagan has important literary and cultural components that were not part of at least some of the groups on which this earlier research was based. That is, the shelves of local bookstores were not well-stocked with Hare Krishna texts, and television series and movies did not popularize being a member of the Unification Church. Instead, over the past few decades, when they have been noticed at all, the majority of new religious movements have been unfairly demonized in the popular and religious media (cf. Cowan and Hadden 2004a; Dart 1997; Palmer 1999; Richardson 1995; Richardson and van Driel 1997; Wright 1997). Identifying oneself as a modern Pagan, on the other hand, whether Wiccan, Witch, or whatever, has become increasingly fashionable in the light of such media fare as *Charmed*, *Sabrina the Teenage Witch*, and *Practical Magic*, and whole sections in bookstores both large and small are now devoted to various aspects of modern Paganism. And, of more immediate concern to our discussion, at the time of earlier research into the dynamics of conversion to high commitment movements such as ISKON (Rochford 1985) or the Unification Church (Barker 1984), the Internet did not exist as an intermediate venue to "try on" one's identity as a Hare Krishna or a Moonie, but it does so for those who are experimenting with modern Paganism.

Over time, as the conversion process continues, this internal conformation of worldview begins to affect external behavior, often prior to overt external identification. Potential Mormons stop drinking coffee, stop buying beer or wine, and at least attempt to quit smoking. In the Mormon context, complete external identification comes with a prospective member's ritual presentation to and acceptance into the LDS community. Similar processes can be detailed in the conversion to many different religions. In the process of successful conversion, inquiry (which, in terms of modern Paganism, is marked for many by "Wicca 101" classes, such as the one I took at our local communiversity) leads to a conformation (or confirmation) of worldview, which is positively reinforced either by personal experience, social acculturation, or both. This leads to an internal identification as an adherent and an evolving conformation of external behavior. Conformation of external behavior leads to external identification as an adherent, which may occur with or without relinquishing religious positions formerly held. External conformation of behavior—whether that manifests itself in ritual activity, manner of dress, or lifestyle—follows the internal conformation of worldview. In modern Pagan terms, this includes such important mechanisms of identity making as taking on a Craft or magickal name, dedicating oneself to a patron god/dess or pantheon, and choosing to follow a designated modern Pagan path. And, in terms of the process of conversion leading to complete, overt identification as a modern Pagan—"coming out of the broom closet"—the venue in which one chooses one's Craft name can serve as an indicator of identity disclosure along the internal-external continuum.

In their typology of audience cults, client cults, and cult movements, Rodney Stark and William Sims Bainbridge (1985) provide a very helpful heuristic based on increasing levels of organization and member dedication. Audience cult "membership remains at most a consumer activity," they suggest, whereas the client cult "resembles the relationship between therapist and patient or between consultant and client" (Stark and Bainbridge 1985: 26). Cult movements, on the other hand, the most complex level of organization in the typology, "are full-fledged religious organizations that attempt to satisfy all the religious needs of converts" (Stark and Bainbridge 1985: 29). Although this category was developed more than a decade before the popular advent of the Internet, we can still readily recognize the consumerist aspect of the audience cult in the way the World Wide Web provides a venue for the relatively risk-free exploration of one's internal spiritual resonances.

Building on the basic concepts of the Stark and Bainbridge typology—participation and commitment—I would like to suggest that the World Wide Web presents a number of intermediate stages of modern Pagan identification and investment that precede, and in some cases, preclude, the off-line presentation of oneself as a modern Pagan (see Figure 6.1). However, similar to the essential difference between internal identity formation and external identity presentation noted above, a further distinction now needs to be made between self-identification as a modern Pagan that takes place entirely online and self-presentation that either moves or occurs off-line. As numerous observers have noted, the initial anonymity of the Internet means that participation on-line entails significantly less risk than that which takes place off-line. Thus,

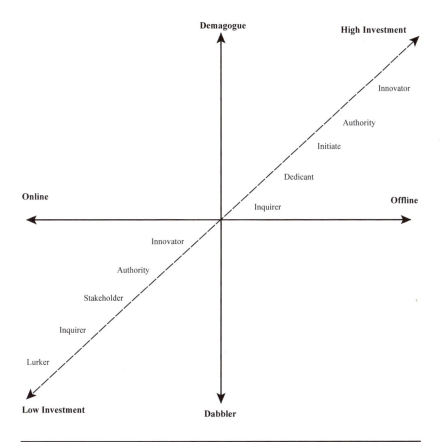

**Figure 6.1** Trajectory of identification online and off-

there is a salient difference between presenting oneself as a modern Pagan named Celtic Star in an otherwise anonymous chat room, and even walking into a modern Pagan moot at a local coffee shop or bookstore. In the trajectory of identity and investment outlined below, even someone who operates as an Internet demagogue, pronouncing and pontificating on any and all manner of modern Pagan topics, but who remains hidden behind a Craft name online and solidly in the broom closet off-line, is less invested than a curious neophyte who, through participation in rituals, engagement with the larger modern Pagan community, and external performance of modern Pagan belief and practice, is willing to instantiate her modern Pagan identity in the real world.

Here, the question could be raised whether exclusively online modern Pagans are less invested or merely differently invested than those who disclose their identities off-line. I would like to suggest that both are the case. Because there is so much less risk attached to the performance of a modern Pagan identity on the Internet, those who do so exclusively are both less and differently invested in what we might call the emerging modern Pagan project. They are less invested, because no matter how many hours they spend in a MUD, MOO, or chat room they cannot live their entire lives online. They are differently invested because their participation is restricted to the norms, conventions, and limitations of the online world, not the larger, more complete modern Pagan experiences that take place in the real world. Online, the trajectory of identification and investment is marked by five stages or levels of interaction: lurker, inquirer, stakeholder, authority, and innovator. As always, though, these stages need to be regarded as fluid rather than static, and heuristic rather than categorical. As well, as I did in previous chapters, I will discuss the instantiation of modern Pagan identity as it appears in discussion groups, then proceed to a consideration of Web sites and homepages.

*Lurkers*

In online discussion forums, *lurkers* are the least involved and least invested constituents, online voyeurs whose commitment to the interactional process is limited to having joined the group. As I pointed out in Chapter 4, 60 percent of the Yahoo! discussion groups surveyed posted less than one message per month per member and thus are populated largely by lurkers. Between September and December 2003, for example, the Bella Luna Cyber Coven posted just over 250 messages. Of these, though, nearly 80 percent were from either the moderator or the co-moderator of the group; 20 of the other 95 members accounted for the remainder, with most posting only one or two messages each. Despite the claims of its moderators to a "family feeling" on the Bella Luna discussion group, nearly three-quarters of the membership simply lurked during this period of time. Similarly, with over 500 members, the Yahoo! group _Wicca posted roughly the same number of messages in one month. Although considerably more members took part in the various discussion threads, the number of different participants was still less than 10 percent of the total membership; for that month, just like the Bella Luna Cyber Coven, if members logged into the _Wicca group at all, over 90 percent chose to lurk, to remain entirely uninvested in the discussions. Lurking as a social phenomenon is not unique to the Internet, but it is considerably more prominent in online discussion groups for a number of reasons. For some, the ease of enrolment in electronic discussion groups may lead them to join far more groups than they can possibly participate in. For others, the novelty of online communication quickly wears thin, and problems with hardware, software, and Internet access discourage more frequent participation. Also, though precise data on this would be very difficult to generate, it is clear that some lurkers are pursuing their modern Pagan interests in clandestine fashion, and logging on to discussion forums or chat rooms has to take place when parents, children, or significant others are out of the house. Occasionally on discussion forums, for example, a member will reappear after an extended absence and explain, "My dad caught me on the Wicca Web and took my computer away; I haven't been able to get online for a month!!!" All of this is matched by the comparative ease of nonparticipation and the lack of accountability in the online environment. Because there is no way to determine if a group member is online, there is no way for a lurker to be explicitly invited into a discussion or called to account for nonparticipation. Lurkers themselves must make the initial contact, and they must maintain proactive contact if they want to participate.

Off-line, on the other hand, if a newcomer appears at a coffee shop for a modern Pagan moot, she will be noticed whether she says anything or not. In the real world, active participation in a discussion is not a necessary index of physical presence at a gathering. Online, however, the only indicator of presence is participation (Cowan 2000; Donath, Karahalios, and Viégas 1999). If you don't post, no one knows you're there. Even in a chat environment, though a particular user may have logged in to the chat room, unless he continually contributes to the conversation, the other participants have no way of knowing if he is still sitting in front of his computer, is away getting a drink and a snack, or has left for the evening but forgotten to log off. Finally, because they disclose nothing, it is impossible to know what lurkers on modern Pagan discussion groups believe; if it exists at all, their identity as modern Pagans remains completely hidden.

*Inquirers*

In terms of investment and identity, those I am calling *inquirers* use the Internet as a way to explore their initial interests in modern Paganism. Off-line, some have already begun to identify themselves as modern Pagans, either internally or externally; others have not. Often referred to as "newbies" online, these group members introduce themselves, ask questions, and seek resources, but do not always engage the answers beyond a simple courtesy response. That is, they do not make the transition from online inquirer to stakeholder, a point to which we will return. Online since 1999, for example, the Yahoo! group Wiccans of Kansas City MO Area subtitles itself "A place for Wiccan networking." With 80 members currently subscribed, however, it is a very quiet group, posting just over 400 messages in 5 years. "I've been an 'official' Pagan for a few weeks," wrote Shieldwolf in his first post to the group, "but I think I've been or felt the call since before the sixth grade . . . Feel free to contact me. My Pagan name is Shieldwolf, and I've been told I'm a good listener. I'd love to make some friends in the Pagan community." His post generated only one response: "This is a rather quiet list, but if you ask questions . . . you generally get answers" (Morgaine). Two days later, Shieldwolf did post a question, a request for information that went ignored by the other members entirely. He did not contribute again and is no longer a member of the group. Despite his initial enthusiasm, there was little encouragement for him to remain or to transition from inquirer to stakeholder.

Granted, Wiccans of Kansas City MO Area is a relatively small group with a light volume of posts. Inquirer interactions, however, do not appear to be significantly different on many groups with larger memberships and more substantial message traffic. On Solitary Druid Spiritual, which has more than 150 members and nearly 4,500 total posts, Druidprincess2 wrote, "I'm a newbie looking for like minded peeps, I have a lot of questions." Though she revealed nothing of herself beyond being a "newbie," and though one of the list moderators and two other members welcomed her to the list, she did not post again. Similarly, Niamh Celtic Mist, a 39-year-old newcomer to the Yahoo! group The Witches Cottage (nearly 400 members and over 4,300 total posts), wrote: "I have just started this path. I am leaning towards the Celtic Tradition. I am hoping to be an active member but, at the moment I have more questions than actual knowledge." Only one member of the group, RavenHarte, responded, assuring her that "the people here are warm, friendly, and knowledgeable, and most willing to share information." No one else acknowledged Niamh's presence in the group and, though she is still listed as a member, she has not posted since her introductory message.

Unlike both of these examples, some inquirers already have some off-line sense of themselves as modern Pagans when they come to a particular discussion group. They are new to the group, but not to modern Paganism itself. Often disclosing significant amounts of information in their initial posts, they use the Internet to explore at least the possibility of online and off-line relationships with "like minded peeps." On the Yahoo! group Christian Wicca, for example, which has posted more than 20,000 messages since 1999, one inquirer disclosed her religious orientation (a mixture of "Shamanistic Native

American," Roman Catholic, and Wiccan), her sexual orientation, and the difficulties she encounters in her hometown because of both; further, she wondered whether anyone on the list lived close enough to her for some kind of online/off-line fellowship. Though there are nearly 450 members in the group, only one member answered her introductory post, with a very general comment about the openness of the Unitarian Universalist church to gay men and lesbians. The inquirer posted once more, then disappeared from the list. Despite at least some sense of identity as a modern Pagan, in terms of online investment she too remained an inquirer and did not transition to a group stakeholder.

*Stakeholders*

In this particular model of identity and investment in modern Pagan discussion groups, *stakeholders* are those who generate the bulk of list traffic—asking questions, engaging the answers, perpetuating discussion, and providing resources, advice, or personal information. They are the participant core upon which the life of the group depends, and often include modern Pagans who have been practicing their Craft for many years both online and off-. However, since many self-identified "newbies" who post introductory messages never return to the lists beyond their first tentative questions or courtesy responses, the shift from inquirer to stakeholder appears significant in terms of online investment and identity. The salient question here, of course, is: What encourages or facilitates that transition from inquirer to stakeholder in these discussion forums? What inhibits the transition? Though this is obviously open to further research, three interrelated factors suggest themselves initially: (1) proactive invitation to further participation by current stakeholders; (2) responsive formation of significant online relationships between inquirers and stakeholders; and (3) performative use of the Internet by inquirers for a successful instantiation of modern Pagan identity.

First, because I would argue that, in many respects, the dynamics of entry into new social spaces are not radically different online than off-line, inquirers who are proactively invited to contribute to ongoing discussions will be more likely to make the transition to stakeholders than those who are simply greeted or ignored. Just as it is in the off-line world, if inquirers are not made to feel welcome or valued by current stakeholders—especially those with acknowledged authority, such as list owners and moderators—there is less motivation for the inquirers to remain and participate. None of the inquirers discussed above received this kind of proactive invitation; instead, although the responses to their introductory posts certainly did not *dis*courage participation, they were sufficiently nonspecific that they did little to encourage further contributions. Vague, generalized responses such as "we're all learning here, so jump right in, and ask some questions" or "tell us more about yourself" are not conducive to further participation, especially for those who are so new to modern Paganism that they are not sure what questions to ask and do not want to embarrass themselves by asking the "wrong" questions. As well, if inquirers are participating on the list clandestinely—that is, they fear negative consequences if their involvement is discovered by significant others off-line—admittedly innocent requests to disclose personal information could easily be construed as barriers to further interaction. It is not the case that their participation is discouraged; rather, in an attempt to encourage involvement, stakeholder respondents are, in fact, asking the wrong questions. Finally, some responses do simply discourage participation. Consider, for example, this open message directed to inquirers on the Yahoo! group Moonwitch. "I am starting to get tired of 'young ones' e-mailing me for spells and such," writes Lady Pagan, who then posted the following general notice to inquirers. "Merry meet all the young, newbies and beginners: Please go to the following link and read this essay . . . 'The Little Witch' . . . it is worth your time!" Whether it is worth their time or not, sending potential stakeholders to another Web site, instead of engaging them personally and inviting them to participate, offers no incentive for inquirers to pursue any further involvement in the group. Instead, I would suggest that it is a disincentive. Off-line, it would be the equivalent of sending a newcomer to a monthly Pagan coffee shop moot away to a local bookstore before interacting with them any further.

Second, relationally, if no one on a particular list responds to an inquirer's post, or there is no indication from those initial responses that any significant relationships will form quickly, or, as in the case above, inquirers are deterred from participation by current stakeholders, it is hardly surprising that they stop posting and either move on to another group or remain as uninvested lurkers. In this, the formation of online relationships as a function of increased investment appears little different from the influence of affinitive ties on group participation off-line. That is, if online relationships between group members and newcomers are established quickly and more deeply than a simple exchange of introductions, there is a greater likelihood that inquirers will make the transition to stakeholders. If the relationships formed on discussion group "X" are more fulfilling than on groups "Y" and "Z," then inquirers are likely to become more invested in "X." Continuing this line of argument, not unlike the dynamics of conversion, participation, and religious growth off-line, it becomes the responsibility of stakeholders to encourage the formation of online relationships with inquirers—if they want those inquirers to remain. Finally, if inquirers to group "X" are met there by stakeholders they either know off-line or know from other online venues, there is a greater potential for a transition from "newbie" to active stakeholder because of the implicit accountability structured into these preexisting relationships.

Third, performatively, for those who are new to modern Paganism it is the very discussions in which inquirers become involved that continue to instantiate their online identities as modern Pagans. The more these discussions positively reinforce emerging modern Pagan identity, the more likely inquirers will continue in a group and transition to stakeholders.

Despite the fact that a significant number of the messages on the Bella Luna Cyber Coven are posted by the two moderators, this Yahoo! group also provides a good example of an inquirer making a successful transition to stakeholder. In late 2003, a teen named JDMerlin77 joined the group and expressed an interest in witchcraft. "I'm not really a witch," he wrote, "or whatever it is y'all call guy witches." At this point, his modern Pagan identity is tentative at best, his inquiry at the level of interest rather than experiment. He concluded his introductory message: "Now i've heard that these internet covens don't like amatures bugging them like this, and i'm sorry. I'm sure that y'all have important people with real problems that y'all prefer to deal with. But if you're interested in helping someone new out, then I'm all ears. So please help me y'all. anything you think someone just starting out sould know, I'd love to hear. so please write back." Since that initial post, he has become a regular participant in group discussions, taken responsibility for greeting other newcomers, and raised new questions for discussion. He has transitioned from inquirer to stakeholder.

Based on the factors affecting this transition, a number of aspects are worth noting. His introductory message indicates that, while he wanted a response from someone, he was not at all sure that he would receive one. Certain that group members have more important things to do than correspond with interested "newbies," he did not ask specific questions, but simply wanted someone to "write back." Thus, for him, a simple response from group members constituted his threshold of acknowledgment. Within one day he had begun conversations with another newcomer to the list and the list owner, Bella Luna, and within a week with the other moderator, WulfWuman. As these conversations progressed, his relationship with the group moderators developed. At one point, he raised a question about Christianity, specifically his interpretation of a similarity between the Trinity and triple aspect of the Goddess as Maiden, Mother, and Crone. He prefaced his question, however: "Now before everyone starts scolding me for daring to post something with 'that word' [i.e., Christianity] in the subject . . . " Consciously or unconsciously, JDMerlin77 was testing the boundaries of acceptable participation in the Bella Luna group. Would his questions bound him out or would he find continuing acceptance from other stakeholders and group authorities? Given the antipathy of many modern Pagans toward Christianity (recall the discussion of this in Chapter 2), his concern was not unreasonable. "Hi JD," replied the list owner, Bella Luna. "No one here should 'scold' you for your post, so don't worry about that. Frankly, that's one of my personal pet-peavs: Christian-bashing Pagans." In this simple response, Bella Luna did three important things. By affirming that JDMerlin77 was well within the boundaries of acceptable participation, she confirmed his importance as a member of the group. By confirming this importance, she encouraged his continued involvement in group discussions. And, by identifying personally with his question, she reinforced the relationship that they were in the process of developing. All of these contribute to his transition from inquirer to stakeholder. While other messages posted by JDMerlin77 continued to request validation of his participation in the group, they also evidenced an emerging instantiation of modern Pagan identity. "I've been at Wicca for a little while now," he wrote a few months later. "I've learned a lot, but now I'm in a pickle." Having defined his modern Pagan path more precisely than in his introductory post, he wanted information on a personal relationship with Deity that was not necessarily limited to ritual performance. "I hope this doesn't sound too corny," he concluded. "Dearest JDMerlin77," replied Amberwhisp, another newcomer to the group, though one who knows Bella Luna off-line as well, "First of all there is no such thing as a corny question." Bella Luna concurred, once again offering to take a personal interest in his spiritual development and his acceptance of himself as a modern Pagan. Since then, he has emerged as a regular participant and stakeholder in the group.

## Authorities

Asserting one's identity as a modern Pagan *authority* occurs in a number of ways in online discussion groups, both positive and negative, and marks the next stage or transition in this model. Most obviously, there is the acknowledged authority of group owners and moderators, illustrated by Bella Luna's interactions with JDMerlin77, and, on Online Wiccan Rituals, Wulfslaird's acknowledgment of Sinovess as high priestess during preparations for his Beltaine ritual (see Chapter 5). Similar to the development of off-line relationships, this is an achieved authority, established as a result of interaction, trust, and the recognition of expertise and experience. Authority is also instantiated online in less obvious ways: some establish their authority as a source of modern Pagan knowledge through volume posting and reposting of information from books and Web sites; others skip the stakeholder phase and, by contesting the nature or content of group discussions, seek to demonstrate their identity as modern Pagan authorities on the basis of superior knowledge or greater experience; and still others seek to instantiate their identity as "legitimate" modern Pagans in the midst of online argument and insult, which can be interpreted as struggles for authority. Finally, some offer to use online discussion groups as venues for teaching various classes in modern Paganism, instantiating their identity and authority through pedagogy.

Known affectionately to the group as "Wulfie," we met WulfWuman first in Chapter 2 in her guise as Crzy Wulf and her dedication to the Egyptian goddess Sekhmet. She is also one of the moderators of the Bella Luna Cyber Coven and posts significantly more messages than any other single member—arguably more than all other members combined. Indeed, of the more than 250 messages posted between September and December 2003, 54 percent were from her. Of these, though, more than three-quarters were spells, chants, deity information, and tidbits of modern Pagan wisdom she gleaned from such sources as Llewellyn's *Witches' Spell-a-Day Almanac*, various online discussion groups, and other Web sites, then reposted to the Bella Luna list. Though she occasionally engages in ongoing discussions, it is clear that WulfWuman regards these volume posts as her contribution to the group, both as a stakeholder and as a modern Pagan authority. And it is equally clear that other members support her in this role. At least one, though, did not. Penny joined the group in late 2003, though it was 3 months before her only post—a direct challenge to the volume of messages from WulfWuman. With neither preamble nor salutation, Penny responded to one of JDMerlin77's notes of thanks to WulfWuman for her guidance with two lines: "must U post SO much SO many times? do you have a life?" Though clearly hurt by the comment, WulfWuman responded by suggesting that Penny change her group settings so that she did not receive individual e-mails and offered to help her with this. Bella Luna, on the other hand, responded more sternly. "WulfWuman is my co-moderator," she wrote, "& helps make this list an information-filled cyber coven for all involved . . . I highly suggest you post a sincere apology to Wulfie, if not, then please leave. The choice is yours" A number of other members, including JDMerlin77 and Amberwhisp, were quick to jump in and defend their beloved "Wulfie." Indeed, this was one of the longest discussion threads of the previous 6 months, and all the respondents praised WulfWuman for her contribution to the list. Her role as a respected resource for the group instantiates her identity as a modern Pagan authority.

Not infrequently, however, online authority is asserted in less positive ways, ways that demonstrate the fluid nature of the various stages in this model. For example, instead of seeking information, inquiries and introductions can mask instantiations of identity and dominance. One such episode occurred over a 2-day period on Druid_Celtic-Sidhe, the Yahoo! "home of men and women of Celtic/Druid Spirituality." In her introductory post, Patience wrote that "I may only lurk for a while but I am here." At this point, she revealed very little about herself and nothing about whether she was a practicing Pagan, although she did end her message with the common closing, "merry meet and merry part and merry meet again." Several members welcomed her to the group. A few days later, she answered another member's question about the popular television medium, John Edwards, and it seemed as though she might transition from inquirer to stakeholder. Two weeks after her initial post, however, she identified herself more clearly as an authority. Responding to another member's request for information on off-line Druid teachers, Patience wrote: "I have been lurking for a while now and I haven't heard or seen too much that I find useful from this site. I live with a Grandfather Druid and I seem to know more than this group can share. I don't see the benefit of argueing the 'benefits' of a commercial trisscale. My Grandfather Druid practices in the Old Ways and I only hope that you all are practicing in the Druid way. He has been practicing for over 25 years and learned from his Ancestors by word of mouth in Ireland." She signed this note, "Patience (Lost)."

Although a number of members responded—some graciously, others less so—all acknowledged in one way or another that Patience may have something positive to offer the group instead of simply criticizing it. Though some objected to the tone of her post, no one even intimated that her claims to a lineal transmission of Druid teachings were not completely legitimate—her appalling misspelling of *triskele* notwithstanding. The harshest criticism came from Tara, the list moderator, who reacted not unreasonably to the insulting tone of her post. Surprisingly, though, other list members rose to defend Patience, who responded that she "didn't write to insult anyone, just to make them think. As to asking questions, it seems that I got some of the answers I was looking for. I wondered if anyone practiced what they preached . . . I am going to unsubscribe to this group so that anyone who has found insult with my writings won't be insulted further." At this, Tara relented, apologizing to her profusely and asking "Dearest Patience" to remain. "I beg you to please stay and be my friend," he wrote, "please teach me and hopefully I can teach you something as well . . . you have nothing to feel bad about, I think other group members stood firmly beside you and what you were trying to say . . . It was I that misunderstood your purpous." It is, of course, entirely possible that Tara's final reply was meant sarcastically, though, read in the context of the entire exchange, there is no indication that this is the case. Patience never posted again; in her instantiation of modern Pagan authority, there was no need. Playing nothing more than her (unsubstantiated) claims to lineal teachings and her dissatisfaction with the list on the basis of those, she had successfully trumped Tara's authority as moderator and other group members had supported her in this. Tara yielded the hand to her and Patience retired from the list, her authority both intact and reinforced, before being asked to play again and demonstrate that she actually knew what she was talking about.

In other cases, just as they do in off-line interaction, struggles for authority in online discussion groups often seek to instantiate the legitimacy of one's own modern Pagan identity at the expense of another's. When this occurs in the course of a simple exchange of insults, the results are less clear-cut. The MSN group Wiccan Gauntlet describes itself as "a wiccan online coven for the solitary and coven practicing WICCAN(s)," in which anyone may participate without the permission of the moderator. Though it has been online since July 2001 and counts more than 90 members, it has seen very light message traffic. In mid-2003, however, Juggalettewitch, a young Pagan who also goes by the online name Evilprincess, wrote: "hello I have been a witch for the past 10 years iam looking for others in the chicago area to have a wiccan seminar so we are notice cause we are noot at all we are basically fairytale in peop;es eyes so please let me know thankyou." For some reason, Wen_Nefer, a Wiccan in her fifties who claimed to have been practicing "for a very long time," took exception to the post. "Young lady," she replied, "Please try getting a life before attending to true paths. I might be qualified as an old fart but I believe I speak for all of us that don't watch bewitched or charmed. We *are* out there and when you grow up . . . we still will be. Yours in Magick and truth and light, Wen_Nefer." In this belittling response, Wen_Nefer chose to instantiate her authority in three ways: a claim to the experience of age, a claim to speak for the entire group, and an explicit denigration of Juggalettewitch's claims to her own tenure as a modern Pagan. Basically, "you go play with your official *Charmed* spell book, dearie, and leave real Witchcraft to real Witches." Although none of Wen_Nefer's claims is self-evidently authoritative, Juggalettewitch (responding in her persona as Evilprincess), fired back: "ok dear why don't you try getting a real name cause yours is from a movie so don't try telling me some thing ok." Wen_Nefer chose not to respond. Unlike the contest between Patience and Tara, in which a hierarchy of acknowledged authority was rather clearly established, we might call this brief exchange of insults a draw—at the time of this writing, neither had posted to the discussion group again.

Finally, by offering classes ranging from "Wicca 101" to "Advanced High Magick," there are those who seek to instantiate their online identities as modern Pagan authorities pedagogically. This is the moment that I would suggest presents the most risk in terms of one's emerging authority—not necessarily because of the nature of the instruction provided, but whether the proffered instruction is actually provided. Despite occasional claims to esoteric teachings only available to serious initiates—a particular instantiation of authority that will be discussed further below—most introductory information available on the Web is either drawn from or based on standard modern Pagan sources. Thus, in this case, it is not the quality of the teaching that is at stake. Rather, a product has been offered for consumption by Internet participants, and if that product is not provided the authority of the one who made the offer could be seriously compromised. Recall the experience of the MSN group Calendula's Garden Coven discussed in Chapter 4.

However, some modern Pagans do seek to instantiate their authority through claims to both pedagogy and esoterica. The MSN group Holy Dragon Fire, for example, describes itself as dedicated to "the High Magick aspect to Wicca. High Magick is more powerful than Witchcraft. In this community we will help you learn about high magick, and spellcasting." Shortly after the group went online in mid-2002, the manager, who goes by the name Lady Pyralis (and the MSN e-mail name Deathz Mistress), wrote that "the first lesson will be held tomorrow . . . It will be held in the chat room in this community. Be there." Although it is unclear whether anyone actually showed up to chat that night—and the lack of gushing list chatter about the success of the event implies, at least, that the lesson did not go as planned—two days later Lady Pyralis posted that "there are new lessons, check the lessons page." The next day, she asked, "No one gonna sign up for lessons?" Identifying herself in another message as "Lady Pyralis, 15, and I practice High Magick," she also operates a Web site called "Dragon's Blood" (www.angelfire.com/darkside/wiccanmagick/Homepage.html). On the MSN discussion group, she describes the site as "about Wicca in general. Very good for beginners, and also for intermediate and advanced witches/warlocks." The fact that "warlock" is regarded as a very derogatory term among modern Pagans notwithstanding, there is the rather obvious question of what qualifies a 15-year-old girl who runs an MSN discussion site that is open to anyone as a teacher of High Magick. Despite this, Wraith wrote: "guys I was reading the lessons page, and seeing that the lessson discriptions weren't links does that mean you need to ask for lessons?" To which Lady Pyralis responded: "no, it just means i've been kinda lazy and not been updating stuff . . . " Three months later, the thread continued. "I am now wondering if any of the lessons will ever be opened," complained Basstrina. "Could somebody please let us know one way or the other." To which Lady Pyralis, who boasted that "High Magick is a way of life" and that she would be offering "tons of Lessons," responded: "well ya there will be lessons but not now . . . everything is kinda screwed up . . . the people who were supposed to help me don't have computers or are really buzy at the moment . . . and all that . . . what kinda lessons do you wanna take excatly?" Not surprisingly, Basstrina left the group. When Dragonhawk asked, "How about lessons in Draconic tradition?" Lady Pyralis responded with three messages. First, "ya sure why not . . . I wil get everything in order soon," and a day later, "just a heads up people . . . this is Lady_Pyralis . . . I just changed my name to Deathz Mistress." And, finally, six weeks later, "imgiving lessons on draconic magick . . . lets say . . . Saturday. What time will be good for y'all? and for the people who cant make it I will post the lesson up . . . no worries :)."

The "lessons" that Lady Pyralis/Deathz Mistress eventually posted are cut-pasted-and-reloaded from another Web site, the "On-line Ritual Book of the Clan of the Dragon" (www.geocities.com/jkarrah), a site that has been formatted to prevent—as much as possible—the unauthorized use of the material. The site's author, and head of the Clan of the Dragon, J'Karrah Ebon Dragon, has a note on the page that anyone who wants to use the material should contact him (her?) for permission. There is no indication that Lady Pyralis/Deathz

Mistress did anything but simply take the material and upload it to her MSN site. The layout, graphics, and text are all but identical. She simply removes any reference to J'Karrah, and presents the lessons as her own teachings.

Although it is tempting to dismiss discussion groups and Web sites like these as the misguided exuberance of adolescence, this extended example points to a number of important factors in the discussion of modern Pagan authority and identity, both online and off-. Even though she is simply taking material from other Web sites, reposting them on MSN as though they were her own, and then "teaching" them to list members as though she is something significantly more than an adolescent dilettante (cf. Berger and Ezzy 2004 on how serious teen Witches appeared to them), Lady Pyralis/Deathz Mistress is, nonetheless, asserting her identity as a modern Pagan authority within the context of the small community she has gathered around her. All those who uploaded personal profiles to the Holy Dragon Fire group—including those who requested lesson information and remained on the list—are around her age. Thus, though few others in the broader Pagan community may give credence to her authority, her list peers, at least, acknowledge her ability to teach. As I have pointed out throughout this book, the open source nature of modern Paganism, and the personally gnostic way in which it is authorized, enables if not encourages this form of spiritual and material plagiarism. And, though none of her material can be regarded as even remotely original, Lady Pyralis/Deathz Mistress does point toward the most invested stage of this model, the online *innovator* of modern Pagan identity.

*Innovators*

*Innovators* not only function as online authorities but also seek to create new resources which may then be appropriated and extended by the open source culture of modern Paganism. When Jeffrey Hadden and I first wrote about modern Paganism online, for example, we pointed out how two modern Pagans from Virginia were creating their own tradition as "The Temple of Duality," a "cyber version of what we would like to build, an interfaith church of Nature Spirituality" (Cowan and Hadden 2004b: 127). Other modern Pagans have similar online ambitions. The introductory notation for the MSN group Light of the Goddess, for example, reads: "This tradition was started on October 31, 1999 by Lady Jessica Lujan. This branch of witchcraft recognizes and honors both goddess and god. We have no set limit on the size of the coven. we welcome anyone to join." Though as an MSN discussion list, Light of the Goddess is no longer operational, Lujan does operate a Web site for her emerging tradition which will be considered in more detail below.

"My name is Raven Firewolf," writes the list owner of the active MSN group The Order of the Luminous Path. "As a 3rd degree High Priest I grew tired of my friends creating covens as though they were clubs, abandoning them if they were bored or if nothing 'cool' happened. I then decided to create a coven based on the ideals that I was taught by the High Priest I learned under. Along with my second-degree High Priestess, Lady Avalon, We hope to create an atmosphere of brother(and sister)hood." Indeed, his plan is ambitious, to say the least, and includes a ten-degree "ranking system" ranging from apprentice to elder, the latter available only after a person has been a coven member for 15 years. At the time of writing, however, nearly a year after the group was formed, Raven Firewolf remains the sole member of the online group.

As the participant data from both Yahoo! and MSN discussion groups indicate, few of these innovations will bear significant online fruit and fewer still will make the all-important transition from online discussion group to off-line working group that remains essential for long-term durability. More, however, make the shift from discussion group to site-based instantiations of modern Pagan identity. In this particularly, the Internet and the World Wide Web provide an important intermediate venue for the process of identity making. It is *intermediate* because, in terms of identity, the process of conversion often remains hidden in the online world. Coming out of the off-line broom closet as a fully identified modern Pagan is clearly something many online Pagans are not willing to do. In the chat rooms and discussion groups, an online Wiccan named Paganwolf *is* Paganwolf. Once he has logged out, however, and shut his computer down for the night, his identity as Paganwolf diminishes; in the family context, he returns to being Jeremy, or Bob, or Charlie. If the utopian rhetoric about the value of the Internet is all but entirely hyperbolic, as I believe it is, and a survey of what is actually woven out there on the Web proves to be considerably less original and considerably more replicative than one might initially suppose, then I think that the Internet's position in terms of an intermediate venue for identity making, testing, and validating is one of the most important contributions that it provides modern Paganism.

*Trying on the Craft: Identity in Conversation*

Through interaction in discussion groups, alt.-lists, and chat rooms, identity testing and the reinforcement of modern Pagan authority occurs in a readily identifiable discursive loop. Participants test their modern Pagan identities online as a function of moving from internal resonance to external performance and conformation; other participants reinforce their identity as modern Pagan authorities by answering questions, providing resources, and weighing in on any topic available. To creatively misread Sherry Turkle as a way of understanding the effects of the Internet on modern Pagan personae, I would like to suggest that although identity construction, maintenance, and reinforcement can, indeed, "only be understood as part of a larger cultural context" (1995: 10), that cultural context is not the consistent reinvention of the online self that Turkle suggests. Instead, it is the precisely bounded conceptualization of what it means to be a modern Pagan in the off-line world that control identification and performance online. Just as we have seen online modern Pagan literature replicate off-line resources and online ritual reproduce off-line liturgical texts and environmental referents, online identity is configured according to implicit and explicit cultural codes that differentiate modern Pagans from other religious adherents and allow modern Pagans to recognize that difference. Just as modern Pagan conversation would be less than successful in a chat room located at www.Come-to-Jesus.com (recall Chapter 3), so, too, someone who entered a modern Pagan chat room with the screen name "Elijah the Prophet" (who slew the 400 pagan priests of Baal in 1 Kings 18: 17–40) might find himself duly excluded from the discussion. The point is that the contextualizing boundaries of modern Pagan identity have very little to do with the Internet, and although they may seem infinitely elastic to the casual observer, they have fixed (though often tacit) limits. In the ongoing definition, presentation, and performance of the modern Pagan self, both online and off-line, the salient factors are *negotiation* and *co-construction*.

Modern Pagan belief in the malleability of online identity occasionally rivals postmodern hyperbole, and, for all its sincerity, presents no fewer problems. Returning to the epigraph that began this chapter, for example, in a passage worth quoting at length for the clarity with which it illustrates some of these problems, Wiccan elder Macha NightMare writes (2001: 91):

> Another way that sacred techniques intersect with computer culture is through our bodies. Just as we are not restricted by our names, we are not bound by our bodies. We can move easily through the entire spectrum of gender and sexual identities when we are online. We can be female, male, androgynous, old, young, slender, round, strong, delicate, fair, ruddy, dark, short, tall. Skin, hair, eye color, and body configuration can all be assumed in an online configuration. Through the Net, we are free to switch our gender or race and to make other 'body changes' of the sort that can be done in terraspace rituals. In doing so, we have much to learn from the 'edgewalkers' among us—those who are gay, bi, or transgendered, priest/esses in particular. We may even transcend species, becoming a goat, a butterfly, or a juniper.

Unfortunately, in NightMare's almost Castanedan musing, she does not disclose precisely how someone of our species might come to understand what it means to be any of these others, quite apart from our inimitable penchant for anthropomorphizing almost any social, cultural, or physical phenomenon. Nor does she consider the practical, ethical, or moral implications of her claims.

How does one assume an identity online with which he or she has no experience and no affinity off-line? I could try to assume the identity of an African-American Wiccan priestess who in mundane life works for the telephone company, but the reality remains that I am a middle-aged, male academic of Scots-Irish descent and no particular religious affiliation. And when does that assumption cross the line from identity play to deception and fraud? Whether we are willing to admit it or not, we are, in fact, bound by our bodies, or at least limited in the identities these bodies will allow us to assume. As Wynn and Katz (1997) point out so trenchantly, academic authors such as Turkle (and, arguably, Brasher), who depend on postmodernism to carry the analytic day, operate so far outside the framework of social interaction theory—and the inevitable impact of social interaction on the construction, presentation, reflexive modification, and re-presentation of the "self"—that their observations bear little resemblance to life either online or off-line. Identity is not the sole property of the individual actor. It is not infinitely mutable, endlessly malleable, or always under our control. Any belief that it is is part of the Western social fiction of boundless potential left to us by parents, teachers, and a horde of well-meaning others, the lie that says "we can be anything we want to be." In point of fact, we can't, and let me give you a couple of examples why not. At 5'7" and 200 pounds, I'm a classic mesomorph. That is, no matter how much I may want to, the entirely understandable bias of the NBA toward the tall and the ectomorphic means that I will never be a starting center for any of their teams. Put even more frankly, as a biological male with a Y-chromosome in each of my diploid cells, I will never be a biological female.

Although I realize how quickly and easily I can be taken to task—and quite rightly so—for stating the matter this bluntly and simplistically, I do so to point out the inevitable framework of restriction and proscription within which the elements of identity construction that do exhibit some flexibility are negotiated. I want to highlight that not every element of identity is negotiable, as some of the more hyperbolic interpretations of online interaction suggest. Identity is not limitless, no matter how many personae one pursues online. Instead, following the work of theorists ranging from Simmel (1950) to Mead (1962), from Berger and Luckmann (1966) to Blumer (1969) and Goffmann (1959, 1967, 1971), and as others have pointed out with particular respect to the process of its presentation on the Internet (Miller 1995; Miller and Mather 1998; Sannicolas 1997; Wynn and Katz 1997), identity is a negotiated, co-constructed product that exists within fixed and definable limits. Although the range of culturally acceptable identifiers may be much more narrowly proscribed within a Hare Krishna community than within modern Paganism, the reality of greater performative breadth in the latter does not alter the fact that boundaries of acceptability exist just as they do in the former. Rather, the negotiation and coconstruction of identity reflect both a framework and a process of *potential, choice, reflexivity,* and *modification,* an interpenetrating and mutually reinforcing array of influences that emerge within and as a result of social action and interaction. Instead of the open-ended, online shapeshifting suggested by Internet enthusiasts, and even in a culture as playfully fluid as modern Paganism, as Wynn and Katz point out, participants "are engaged in a constant effort to structure experience together and to establish order in conventions of discourse so that shared meanings are possible" (1997: 302).

As it relates to the negotiation and co-construction of identity, of "self" in a social situation bounded by shared meanings and conventions of discourse, *potential* is nothing more than the range of choices available to an actor at a specific time and in a certain setting. It is axiomatic here that not all choices are available to all actors at all times. Such choices as are available, however, are determined largely but not entirely by the type of situation in which the actor is operating, the social and cultural constraints imposed by the situation, the manner and focus of interactions he or she has with other actors in the same situation, and the effects he or she seeks to create by virtue of his or her social interaction. Among the important things we learn as we create or modify our identities are the contextually specific boundaries of acceptability for those identities. As we saw in Chapter 4, for example, identifying oneself as a covener on the Yahoo! group Solitary Witches 13 transgresses the group's boundaries of acceptability. Though Hemptress, the list owner, would not deny other modern Pagans their open source right to gather in covens, circles, and groves, in the particular situation of that discussion group the acceptable potential is more limited.

*Choice* is the ongoing selection each of us makes based on internal resonance, desired effect, observation of the range of available and appropriate options, and imitation of certain components drawn from that range of possibilities. Two key concepts from social learning theory are important in terms of the choices we make: observation and imitation (Bandura 1977, 1997). We observe in order to learn the modes and norms of behavior in different situations; we imitate certain of those behaviors in order to participate meaningfully in those situations. We do not, however, imitate everything we see nor do we replicate it in precisely the same way. However closely our behavior may conform to situational norms, we are not slaves to imitation. We choose, consciously or not, which behaviors we will imitate and which we will not. We observe extensively; we imitate selectively. *Reflexivity* assesses the effects of our selections, evaluates them in the context of those expected outcomes and situational norms, and suggests new choices in the ongoing process of identity construction and re-presentation. And, finally, *modification* recognizes that the range of choices available, the criteria for selection and performance, and the manner of evaluation occur within confines prescribed by those particular social domains and situations, and may require adjustment in the way one re-presents one's identity if one wants to maintain meaningful interaction.

### Peeking Out of the Broom Closet: Disclosing Modern
### Pagan Identity Online

In terms of the trajectory of modern pagan identity and investment, discussion groups, alt.-lists, and chat rooms can be conceptualized as "entry level" venues of disclosure, as identity made visible in conversation. Though they are important venues for inquirers to experiment with their modern Pagan identity, for stakeholders to gather around them a modern Pagan community they may lack off-line, and for would-be demagogues to attempt imposing their particular modern Pagan vision on the rest of the online community, they disclose identity very differently than Web sites. If these discussion groups, alt.-lists, and chat rooms are venues for interactive, *conversational* identity, Web sites provide online stages for a unidirectional, *performative* identity. I say "unidirectional" because, as Wynn and Katz also point out, "the home page seems to bend over backward to pretend to be interactive by being preemptively disclosive about the self . . . Who-I-am tends to be expressed in a photograph, a list of interests that are active by being clickable, and a list of friends that is also active" (1997: 320).

In the context of the framework of negotiation and co-construction discussed above, and to speak with Wynn and Katz further, what is of interest in terms of these particular modern Pagan "preemptive disclosures of the self" are the "conventions of discourse" according to which Pagans perform identity online. Among other things, these conventions include personal Books of Shadows, photographs, journals, poetry, and artwork, as well as a goodly amount of replicated modern Pagan shovelware—all of which are performed within the context of boundaries established by a tension between the identity norms of modern Paganism and the degree to which one's modern Pagan identity requires the Internet for its performance. That is, if one is not out of the broom closet off-line, not only does the online performance of modern Pagan identity become, possibly, the only outlet for that identity, but the manner of performance is often different from one for whom the Internet is simply another venue of disclosure. In the latter case, not surprisingly, more personal information is available for disclosure; in some instances of the former, Web sites are remarkable for their lack of personal disclosure. In both cases, however, disclosure is preemptive because we rarely learn anything substantial about the individuals behind the identities performed. What we see on the Web are the players, robed and masked for their online performance as Wiccans, Witches, or Druids; we rarely see the actors in their dressing room, preparing their masks, rehearsing their lines, deciding which part in the modern Pagan play they will perform. We see the choices they make from the potential by which they are surrounded, but only occasionally gain insight into the breadth of potential they felt was available to them and the decision-making processes that led to their particular choices. In other instances, however, from the various masks, props, and soliloquies by which the modern Pagan stage is populated online, it is possible to piece together substantial mosaics of the people behind the parts.

*Performing Identity: The Online Masks of Modern Paganism*

As examples of this variety of online performance of identity, consider these three personal Web sites: Endless Forest (http://endlessforest.freespace.com), The Realm of the Shadow Witch (www.shadow-witch.com), and Word from the Bird, the personal Web site of a modern Pagan named Raven Spirit (www.wordfromthebird.com). Each illustrates in a different way how levels of modern Pagan disclosure are instantiated online, and that the level of disclosure is linked not only to the manner in which the owner's identity is performed, but also the relationship between what we might call the online and off-line broom closets. For those whose modern Pagan identity is solidly hidden (or at least inhibited) off-line, the Internet provides an opportunity for expression that might not otherwise be available outside the few friends who share a similar secret. For others, the online expression of one's modern Paganism is simply one more aspect of identity that is shared with those who visit the owner's personal Web site. For those who live as public Pagans both online and off-line, some Web sites are not meant to disclose identity explicitly but do so in the choice of material and the manner in which it is presented; others provide the stage on which the owner's modern Pagan identity continues to be performed definitively.

According to the typology developed in Chapter 4, Endless Forest is an information site that calls itself a coven online. First uploaded in February 2001, it was originally the project of two adolescent Pagans, Nightingale and Willow (who now goes by the name Justice or Lady Justice). And although at first blush the site appears to contain little more than modern Pagan shovelware, much of the material related to faeries and gnomes—the magickal creatures of choice for the ownersappears original to the site and is extremely creative. Nightingale, however, the author of much of this original material, is no longer with the "coven," and we can infer from some of Justice's comments that the two had some sort of dispute. "This is a so far nonpracticing coven," she writes (Justice n.d. [a]), "because there is only one of the founding members left, and that is me Justice. I've recently discovered that many people don't have the dedication or don't connect with the religion enough to stay with it. Oh well I suppose. We are a more internet coven to help connect people on the web with similar beliefs." While it remains unclear just how Endless Forest would do this —there is no interactivity beyond a few standard hyperlinks—Justice's own online profile reveals a more important purpose behind the site: the ludic performance of a modern Pagan identity online that is subdued and suppressed off-line.

"My magick name was Willow," she writes, taking this perhaps from the very popular character on the television program, *Buffy the Vampire Slayer*, "and was recently changed to Justice [no reason given]. I have been a practicing witch for four years now. I recently also decided on a tradition to follow, and that's Celtic Paganism. My patron Goddess is Morgan Lefay. She is the goddess of the sea, general magick, the Isle of Avalon, Faeries, and many other things . . . I'll be 18 on Thanksgiving . . . My favorite book is The Mists of Avalon" (Justice n.d. [a]). This is the extent of personal information revealed on the site. Unlike many other modern Pagans' personal sites, with one exception that will be discussed below, there are no pictures, no personal disclosure beyond her age, and no reference to off-line activities beyond turning 18 at Thanksgiving and her love for Marion Zimmer Bradley's justly celebrated *The Mists of Avalon* (1982). Endless Forest is focused on her modern Pagan identity as Justice.

Like Oberon Zell-Ravenheart and the Church of All Worlds, whose philosophy and polytheology are quite self-consciously drawn from works of speculative fiction such as Heinlein's *Stranger in a Strange Land* (1961) and Zell-Ravenheart's own visionary experiences (G'Zell 1971), part of the identity Justice performs online is fantasy-oriented modern Paganism (see Chapter 2), informed by works of fiction such as *The Mists of Avalon*, which she appears to regard as an authentic depiction of "Celtic Paganism," and her love for fay creatures like faeries and gnomes. An enormously popular book among modern Pagans, *The Mists of Avalon* raises another open source question for the emerging tradition: which came first, the literary chicken or the performative egg? Margot Adler holds up *Mists* as "the most extraordinary example of a book that became a best-seller even though it had thoroughly Wiccan themes and was written by a Wiccan priestess" (1986: 418; Vale and Sulak 2001: 22–26). Despite some question as to Bradley's religious pedigree (Rabinovitch and Lewis, for example, claim she was an Episcopalian [2002: 28–29]), does *The Mists of Avalon* read for modern Pagans like Justice as though it is "thoroughly Wiccan" because it is, or because many modern Pagans, influenced by the beauty of its narrative, imagery, and mythology, have so incorporated these into their beliefs and practices that it now appears as though the novel actually reflects belief and practice rather than grounds it? One might be tempted to say that at this stage in Justice's life, her performance of a modern Pagan identity is informed more by fantasy than practice, more by the romantic sweep of adolescent imagination than the rather harsher realities of off-line life, but such an evaluation would be premature at best.

Setting aside the modern Pagan respect for the power of the imagination, there is indication that her religious experimentation with modern Paganism —and specifically its off-line consequences—is one of the reasons Justice has uploaded the information. "My main goal on this page was to eventually trans-fer my entire Book of Shadows on the this site. It was my most treasured poss-esion. It was about 700 pages long and had been my project for three years, almost four. Well it was found be parents that didn't want it in their house. It was thrown away . . . I'm trying to rebuild a new one" (Justice n.d. [b]). That is, through her online Web project, she is seeking to reinstantiate part of a mod-ern Pagan identity to which she had devoted significant amounts of time, and that she feels was unjustly taken away from her by her parents. Though, with only one member, the Endless Forest is not a coven; it is the online perform-ance of a modern Pagan identity, the very props for which must apparently re-main hidden in the off-line world.

"Welcome!" writes Inanna Lightbringer, owner of The Realm of the Shadow Witch and an early-30s woman who claims in her online journal to be a "Witch by birth, magickal practitioner for 23+ years, general Pagan for 5ish years," but definitely "*not* Wiccan." "Overall," she continues, "I have to say that this site is more for my own gain, to get the stuff out of my head and onto a tangible medium, than for actual education of the masses—but if someone finds what I put here helpful, then that's certainly okay too" (Lightbringer n.d.). And in many ways, what she has put up is the quintessential personal Web site. Bringing together a number of aspects of her off-line life—her family, her pets, her likes and dislikes, photos of her wedding and her tattoos, artwork that she considers representative of her personality, and a mass of modern Pagan shov-elware, some of which is original to her site, some of which is simply reloaded from other online and off-line sources—she discloses her modern Pagan iden-tity as part of a much larger whole. Unlike Justice, however, whose modern Pagan identity at this point in her life depends on the Internet for significant instantiation, for Inanna Lightbringer the Web is simply one more performa-tive venue in which to present her life, and modern Paganism simply one more aspect of the characters in that presentation. Whereas Justice revealed very lit-tle of her off-line self, Inanna Lightbringer—whose online journal lists her as "Lucifera Shadow," an obvious pun—discloses a considerable amount of information, only part of which is concerned with her life as a Witch. Indeed, while her modern Pagan identity is a motif that appears in a number of ways, her Web site presents a more complex picture of the woman behind the per-formance. She is a proud mother and devoted wife, a fan of horror films such as *Hellraiser* and *The Evil Dead*, a fire-eater who was married in a very tradi-tional white gown, and a modern Pagan whose patience with the populariza-tion of "the Craft" appears to have just about run out.

Both in her online Book of Shadows and other sections of the Web site, the most substantial portions are dedicated to things that irritate or annoy her, and to people she considers less intelligent than she—which appears to be just about everyone. Indeed, reading through Inanna Lightbringer's numerous rants (www.shadow-witch.com/rants.html), during which she rails at the stupidity of everyone from "The Bitch at Target" and "Morons at Radio Shack" to "Fluffbunny Know-It-Alls" and "Dysfunctional Pagans," and in which she displays little more than vulgar intolerance and self-indulgence, one could easily be forgiven for wondering why anyone should care what she thinks at all. One answer, of course, is that no one should care. If we are to take her at her word, The Realm of the Shadow Witch is for her enjoyment alone; according to the front page disclaimer, "I don't do this for you, I do it for me, because I enjoy it . . . Deal with it or piss off." On the other hand, all performance is meant for an audience, and performance on the Internet is meant for an audience potentially far larger than any she might encounter at Radio Shack, the Target parking lot, or a modern Pagan moot in Wilmington, North Carolina. As opposed to identity constructed in conversation, the performative aspect of identity on a Web site such as this avoids the more obvious components of negotiation and co-construction that inform interactive communication. Though visitors are invited to correspond with her through e-mail, instant messaging, or an online guest book, she can easily choose to ignore their input and continue to present herself as she sees fit. Though she locates herself as an authority within modern Pagan conventions of discourse, few of the consequences that structure more interactive communication—whether positive or negative—obtain in the unidirectional communication of the personal homepage.

Finally, Word from the Bird is the Web presence of a modern Pagan named Raven Spirit, and "is dedicated to those who seek the grail of wisdom and immortality that comes from finding the connection to Spirit within yourself." Like Inanna Lightbringer, he does not hide his modern Pagan identity; unlike her site, however, Word from the Bird (which is also called Raven's Realm) does not present his modern Paganism as simply one thread woven among many. Like Justice's, his Web site is entirely devoted to his identity as a modern Pagan; unlike Justice, Raven Spirit is a visible part of the modern Pagan community in a major Midwestern city—out of the broom closet both online and off-line. He is a third-degree Wiccan high priest of Mystic Moon Coven (see Chapter 4), as well as a board member and local organizer for Pagan Pride Day activities.

Whatever form they take, though, and there are considerable variations on each of the three types discussed in this section, online representations of identity are still precisely that: representations. They "exist as artifacts of that being that types them in" (Wynn and Katz 1997: 305), artifacts carefully chosen and arranged to produce a desired effect. They remain performances.

### The Modern Pagan Entrepreneur: Hieratic Authority and Spells for Sale

Among the most concrete instantiations of religious identity and authority, either online or off-, are those that occur when one begins to offer oneself as a teacher, when one purports not only to be a modern Pagan but to mold the identity of those who would be as well. This last category of identity perform-ance, which I have called "the modern Pagan entrepreneur," appears in two major forms online: claims to hieratic authority lodged in the possession of es-oteric knowledge or modern Pagan innovation, and claims to pedagogical au-thority manifest in offers to teach modern Paganism, often for a price. Once again, although neither of these is unique to the Internet, expanding access to the World Wide Web gives many modern Pagans the opportunity to claim identities online that might never be supported off-line.

*HPs.com: Hieratic Authority and the Forbidden Power of the Esoteric*

Hieratic authority often lodges in claims to superior or advanced knowledge. In traditional Wiccan covens, for example, leadership is usually vested in the High Priestess and, often, the High Priest. Although they may delegate certain duties at certain times, they are ultimately responsible for the day-to-day administration of the coven, the initiation and proper training of coven mem-bers, and, depending on the tradition, ensuring adherence to the established precepts of ritual, magick, and spellworking. As we have seen, though, claims to an authoritative identity online can occur when someone simply calls her-self the High Priestess of an online coven that is nothing more than a Yahoo! discussion group. In some cases this claim is warranted by off-line training and experience and is affirmed by other members of the online group; in other cases, there is no group to acknowledge these rather plaintive attempts to assert authority and identity. Though nuanced in different ways, in the performance of identity that takes place on personal Web pages this assertion of a hieratic authority takes two major forms: claims to superior or advanced knowledge that are couched in admonitory terms, or claims to the authority of modern Pagan innovation.

Recall Justice, whom we discussed above. According to her online perform-ance of identity, she has been a modern Pagan since she was 14, had collected a substantial off-line Book of Shadows, and, influenced by *The Mists of Avalon*, had chosen "Celtic Paganism" as her religious path. In her introduction to Endless Forest's online Book of Shadows, however, Justice instantiates her identity as a hieratic authority by posting a warning about some of the content on her site, knowledge that she believes is too powerful for the uninitiated or the uneducated to control. "**Welcome to our online Book of Shadows,**" she writes (Justice n.d. [b]), the boldface letting readers know just how serious she is. "**If you don't know what that is then please don't use any of these spells, rituals, and the like at home. We aren't here to give out these things to novice witches who don't know how to use them. To the rest of you out there come in and look around.**" Elsewhere, a similar warning: "Like stated on the other page please do not use this information if you don't know what you are doing" (Justice n.d. [c]). The rather obvious epistemological problems with these warnings notwithstanding, in the *dramatic personae* of modern Paganism Justice has scripted herself as an authority, as keeper of the Endless Forest esoterica— one who not only knows what she is doing, but who has arrogated to herself the responsibility to save the uninitiated and uneducated from themselves.

Or consider Deathz Mistress, whom we also met earlier in this chapter. Under the "Book of Shadows" link on her MSN site, Holy Dragon Fire, she writes: "This is where our coven spells are going to be. We are gonna have a lot of different spells here. It's always better if you make your own spells, but if you aren't really much of a poet or are a beginner its best to get some spells outa here. I also have Black Magick spells, DO THEM AT YOUR OWN RISK!!! I don't know how many times I need to stress that, but they are dangerous and shouldn't be attempted by anyone but those advanced." The issue of her own verbatim use of spells, rituals, and magickal explanations written by others aside, like Justice she implies that she has the magickal knowledge to upload "Black Magick spells" and is sufficiently advanced in the Craft to make use of them. Now, is plagiarism and open source appropriation unique to a 15-year-old girl who styles herself a High Magick adept on a public MSN Web site and discussion forum? Of course not. But it illustrates a number of problems with which modern Paganism will continue to contend, both online and off-line.

Whereas Justice simply warns her visitors that inexperienced Witches or Wiccans should use caution, and Deathz Mistress alludes to "Black Magick spells" for which she assumes no responsibility, the elders of Coven of the Silver Light (members.lycos.co.uk/covensilverlight) warn potential users that "This page contains spells that are only to be used if all mundane methods fail, and these spells should therefore only be used as a last resort when this happens." Further, according to elders Cirrus and Snakewolf, both of whom appear to be in their early '20s, "the coven of the silver light take no responsibility for the consequences of the information concealed on the following page has on those casting any of the hexes or curses or the intended person they are aimed to-ward." These rather banal and grammatically atrocious disclaimers precede a section in their online "Spellbook" entitled "Hexes & Curses." "Lucifer's Touch," for example, is "A Hex for putting on an enemy . . . [which] should be performed at midnight," and requires that "you should be worked up into a frenzy of anger and thinking of the darkness about to descend upon your enemy." The "Spell for Hexing Enemies" requires, among other things, some personal item belonging to the intended victim, chimney soot, and the "urine of a black cat"—although no instructions are given on how to obtain this last ingredient. And, during the "3 Nights of Hell" curse the practitioner is required to "visualize the wax burning sore into the body of thine enemy," a condition that will last, apparently "for a period of 3 strange days."

As I have noted earlier, a number of modern Pagan Web sites and discussion groups either do not include negative magickal practices such as hexes, curses, and the like, or insist that no "real" modern Pagan would indulge in such workings. On the one hand, it is hardly inconceivable that many modern Pagans would look at sites like these and shake their heads sadly, marveling that the religious tradition they are working so hard to see culturally legitimated is being overrun by poseurs and dilettantes; on the other hand, given the open source nature of modern Paganism, especially as it exists online, Justice, Deathz Mistress, Cirrus, and Snakewolf do form part of the modern Pagan community whether modern Pagans like it or not, and there are those who will find their "curses and hexes" and take them seriously. Indeed, in the context of modern Pagan epistemology—especially as it conceptualizes the fundamentally interconnected and energetic nature of reality, as well as the ability of the modern Pagan to affect that reality through intentional focus—there is every reason to take them seriously. Though it seems that the subtitle for this section could easily have been, "Seen *The Craft* one too many times, have we?," instantiations of hieratic authority such as these are examples of "what passes for knowledge" in at least some of the modern Pagan community.

Finally, there is modern Pagan innovation that bridges the instantiation of hieratic authority through admonition and its pedagogical instantiation through commerce and commodification. "In 1999," writes one Web site operator, "Jessica Lujan created a new tradition. I dreamed of a coven, which was a blend of the Celtic pantheon and the Egyptian pantheon to bring together those people who were torn between the two pagan paths" (Lujan n.d. [b]). To this end, Lujan has created two Web sites for what she now calls the "AnkhaCross Tradition": Light of the Goddess (www.geocities.com/lightofthe-goddess), which purports to offer a fairly standard three-degree training program, and Witches Brew (http://clik.to/mythic), an assortment of modern Pagan shovelware, with a couple of interactive options. Beyond a claim that it exists, though, there is very little information about the AnkhaCross Tradition on the first site, and with no index or internal hyperlinks visitors must click through the site one page at a time—a feature that does little to encourage those visitors to stay. At the end, however, Lujan, who also goes by the name Lady Moonstone, writes, "I will be adding more in time to come I am working on things for my off-line coven now so if you would like to join the off line coven click the botton that says click. Then you will be taken to the membersShip form print it out fill it out and send it to me" (Lujan n.d. [a]). The membership form has a variety of payment options: $35 annually for a "Basic Active Membership," $50 for a Basic Active Family Membership, $30 for a Full Time Student/Financial Hardship Membership—though it's not entirely clear how saving that $5 is going to alleviate anyone's financial hardship. All active members receive a copy of the member newsletter; those who do not want to join the coven but still want the newsletter pay "only" $18. Twenty dollars gets one something called the "Light of the Goddess Journal of AnkhCross Witches," which is apparently not a journal at all, since the sizes range from x-small to x-lg. Lujan is also willing to accept donations ranging from $25 to $200. The only information she requires of potential coven members is name, address, and telephone number. None of the other standard information—age, length of time in the Craft, reasons for wanting to join this particular coven— are present. Though it is by no means an infallible indicator, a Google search for "AnkhaCross" returned only one of Lujan's pages and an entry in The Witches' Voice coven listings for Ohio. Finally, at the bottom of the membership application page, there is a link to a Yahoo discussion group (groups.yahoo.com/group/lightofthegoddess), which is also nonexistent.

Lujan's second site, Witches Brew (http://clik.to/mythic), is much more elaborate, though like the Yahoo! group, many of the links (e.g., Flaming Pentagram Press, Online Classes) are inoperative. Under "Ask a Witch," she offers "more than 2000 spells" that are available by calling or e-mailing her "anytime." Like Justice and the others considered in this section, she asserts identity as a modern Pagan authority through reference to the "dangers" of Witchcraft. "Before proforming any rituals or invokations," she writes on a page entitled "Making Invocations," " it is a good thing to do a lot of reading so you know what you are doing. Trying to do these without the experiance you need is *very dangerous*."

Much of this site, though, contains other examples of modern Pagan plagiarism masquerading as the assertion of hieratic and pedagogical authority. In the introductory paragraph to a section entitled "Warnings & Cautions for the New Wiccan or Witch," she writes, "I have been asked to discuss the not-so-nice things that can happen [in Witchcraft]. I'm not trying to scare anyone off, just give you enough information so you can make an informed decision" (http://clik.to/mythic). This disclaimer is followed by several paragraphs on shadows, vampires, the unpredictability of magick, and the "dark side" of magickal power—all of which, including the background, have been taken verbatim from another site, The Celtic Connection (www.wicca.com/celtic/wicca/cautions.html). On that site, the document is "signed" and copyrighted by "Erik, Herne and The Celtic Connection." Those clicking in to Lujan's site, however, could very easily be persuaded that she wrote the "Cautions" page in response to questions posed to her either online or off-line; that is the plain sense of the text. Nowhere does she suggest that the page has its source elsewhere, nowhere does she cite an author. Of course, she is not the only person who has used this page without attribution on a Web site; in addition to at least three other sites that use the same document, it has appeared as a cut-and-paste message on numerous Yahoo! discussion forums. The striking difference here is the commercial aspect of the site, the fact that online and off-line she is charging not insignificant fees for material that she has apparently plagiarized.

The question becomes, at this point, is this a religious scam? Or something more? Does Lujan expect to be taken seriously, or is this simply a ploy to benefit from the current popularity of all things Pagan? Trying to give the benefit of the doubt to a 20-something woman from a small town in Ohio who claims to have been a witch since she was 10, I suggest that it remains an issue of identity; like Justice, Deathz Mistress, and the rest, it is the open source character and the personally gnostic authorization of modern Paganism that allows her to perform online and off-line as a modern Pagan innovator, authority, and pedagogue.

### Spells for Sale: Pedagogical Authority and the Online Marketing of Modern Paganism

Perhaps, to this point, readers will be disappointed that I have not discussed in more detail other usages of the Internet by modern Pagans: online shopping (www.magickware.com), occasionally massive information sites (www.witchvox.com), institutional Web sites (www.cog.org), and modern Pagan search engines (www.avatarsearch.com). It is not that these are unimportant, obviously, but because the World Wide Web is really not so much an information superhighway as it is an information supermall, their presence is like saying there are stores and kiosks in a shopping center. Accurate, but ultimately rather obvious.

In this last section, I would like to discuss some of the ways in which modern Pagans are using the Internet to instantiate their identities entrepreneurially. At Pagan Adventures (www.paganadventures.com), for example, "High Priestess Willow Brooke" presents herself as an all-around New Age modern Pagan, "a Teacher of the Pagan Path with 19 years experience in esoteric and religious studies," whose "heritage is Irish, Scottish, Apache Nation, and Mexican. Her Irish family is one of the original clans of Ireland. She is a High Priestess, Minister, Quantum Holistic Healer, Reiki Master, Herb Specialist, Tarot Master, Rune Master, Crystal Seer, Astrologer, Psychic, and Witch." Though Pagan Adventures does offer an "Online Free Spellcasting Request," Willow Brooke also markets "spell kits" for $40 each. For a $20 enrolment fee and $15 a month, the College of The Sacred Mists ("An Online Wiccan College"; www.workingwitches.com) assures potential students that they will receive information and training unavailable anywhere else, online or off-. Similarly, at the School of Magick (www.schoolofmagick.com) "a team of highly experienced Witches" offer courses in everything from general magick to Reiki, and from aromatherapy to shamanism—all for a $9 monthly membership fee. Like the Universal Life Church, the Esoteric Theological Seminary (www.northernway.org), which claims to be "the educational institution of the Metaphysical Interfaith Church" and which also goes by the name "University of Esoterica," will ordain anyone who applies; unlike the ULC, however, ordination costs $150. With credit for life experience, a "2000 word thesis on any topic of a spiritual nature that appeals to you," and a $600 fee, applicants can receive either a Doctor of Divinity or Doctor of Theology degree.

Traditionally, no money changed hands for coven training; it was considered knowledge freely received that was to be as freely shared. With the growing popularity of modern Paganism, however, and the willingness of eager inquirers to purchase books, tapes, CDs, DVDs, and now monthly subscriptions to Web sites, the Internet provides a venue for the commodification of religion unparalleled in history. Contrary to Starhawk's wishes, modern Paganism has become a mass market religion, and the World Wide Web has contributed to that. Consider just two examples: "Lady Raya's Cottage," and the rather elaborately named "Cougar Silvermoons School of Celtic Shamanism, Witchcraft & Magick."

For the most part, Lady Raya's Cottage (www.ladyraya.org), which is subtitled "your source for all things Wiccan," is a multipage advertisement for the Wiccan writings of its namesake, most notably her book, *13 Lessons for Pleasing the Divine: A Witch's Primer* (Lady Raya 2001). According to the introductory page, "Lady Raya is a family trad witch of Black Forest heritage. She is one of eight elders of the tradition of Elijan Wicca, and the only elder who is public about her religion. In practice, she is High Priestess of White Wolf Temple of the Olde Religion" (Lady Raya n.d. [c]). According to her online resume, she also has a Harvard MBA and a bachelor's degree in electrical engineering. Reading like the pitch of a modern Pagan motivational speaker, the advertisement for *13 Lessons* proclaims: "Learn wizardry and witchcraft as the masters practice it! Lady Raya's simple and easy to follow, step by step instructions take you to the height of your abilities! Learn the self empowerment practiced by the highest achievers in human history! . . . PLUS, this book includes private access to Internet covens where witches meet AND a music CD of chants and drums which reveal the hidden ways! You've always wanted to know. Now, the door is being opened. Don't miss this once in a lifetime opportunity" (Raya n.d. [a]). The site also contains links for a variety of discussion lists, including a password-protected group devoted to *13 Lessons*, and an online seminary and Wiccan training program, the texts for which are, not surprisingly, Lady Raya's books. Though the various discussion lists have nearly 300 members, message traffic patterns reflect those found on Yahoo! and MSN: few members reveal any personal information, less than 10 percent post to the various discussions, and the vast majority of posts are from Lady Raya herself. Elsewhere, under "Lady Raya's Spells of Self Empowerment," she writes: "Yes, it's true that you can't use a spell out of a book. Every spell is unique, and has to be designed for your situation, to speak uniquely to your dreaming brain" (Lady Raya n.d. [b]). Apparently, whereas one "can't use a spell out of a book," using one of the more than 20 spells supplied on Lady Raya's Web site is acceptable, and to make it that much easier visitors are encouraged to purchase kits containing all the requisite ingredients for the spells. Unfortunately, at the bottom of each advertisement is the banner: "Buy the materials for this spell—SOLD OUT!!—Back order"—which is an e-mail link to Lady Raya.

Finally, building on the claim to hieratic authority lodged in forbidden or esoteric knowledge, recall the Trad of the Sacred Cauldron and the exaggerated air of mystery it invoked on its Web site (see Chapter 4). The coven's "council elder" is the Rev. Cougar Silvermoon, who claims to be a University of California BA, MA, and *juris* Ph.D., and who offers a variety of modern Pagan courses for sale over the Internet at Cougar Silvermoons School of Celtic Shamanism, Witchcraft & Magick (http://celticshaman.cjb.net). In a passage worth quoting at length for the different aspects of identity instantiation it illustrates, Silvermoon reinforces her own claims to an esoteric authority by denigrating other "teachers of shamanism."

> Let's get something straight right from the begining. Shamanism is NOT safe! It is a very dangerous practice if you do not have a personal teacher to guide you!!! You can't learn Shamanism from a book or a website!! [Though, apparently, you can . . . from her books and her correspondence courses.] Anyone who tells you it's safe or that you can learn how to be a Shamanic Practitioner through any other means than a personal teacher does not know what they are talking about, is a fake and is a liar. So does this mean that DJ Conway, Amber Wolfe, and John Matthews lied in their books when they told you it was safe to learn from books they have written? Is the Pope Catholic? Of course they lied!!! . . . Authors who write these books are just raking in the money while they cry all the way to the bank and their private Lear jet about how they swindled you out of your hard earned cash! . . . Mental hospitals, hospices, emergency rooms and nursing homes are filled with people who attempted to practice Shamanism and many forms of Ceremonial Magick without a teacher. Does that mean that you or your family can sue these authors? No, the books have all sorts of legal disclaimers in them . . . Even I have disclimers on my pages and my course materials to protect myself from someone who lies about their medical condition, state of mind, addictions or age. (Silvermoon 1996a)

In "What Shamanism Can Do For You," however, the introduction to her own 3-year course of study that leads to becoming a "Certified Celtic Shamanic Practitioner," Silvermoon (1996b) assures potential students that, "if you spend your time working on the exercises I give you, your life in this realm will get better. You will have increased prosperity in all areas of your life. You will be able to improve your finances, health, relationships with others, your communications skills, increased physical energy, you will be able to help and heal others, and more" (Silvermoon 1996b)—all of which will be news to traditional shamanic practitioners (see, for example, Eliade 1964; Maskarinec 1995). Her own courses are available by correspondence (postal or electronic) and online apprenticeship, which offers little more than the option to modify lessons and schedule chat sessions with Cougar Silvermoon. Courses range from $175 for 12 "beginner" lessons ($250 for online apprenticeship) to $400 for 12 "advanced" lessons. According to her credentials page, in addition to her ordination in the Universal Life Church, the Rev. Cougar Silvermoon has "been a practicing shaman for over 30 years. I was taught the ways of the Shaman by my Grandfather. I was raised in a 'traditional' pagan family, and at the age of 12, I began practicing Ceremonial Magick (Qaballah & Babylonian systems) with my mentor who was a trained elder. I have also extensively studied Miyamoto Musashi's system of Zen (do not confuse with Buddhism). I have been teaching Shamanism for 15 years" (Silvermoon 1996c).

In terms of the online performance of modern Pagan identity, one very important question is begged by a number of these examples. As the house lights come up, as the masks are set aside and the players gather at the edge of the stage, who *are* these people? How much more do site visitors, inquirers, or potential students know about Willow Brooke, Lady Raya, or Cougar Silvermoon? In reality, of course, very little. For a few dollars a month anyone with Internet access can register a domain name—www.Doug's-Religion.com—and even a few hours spent with software like Frontpage or Dreamweaver can produce a very attractive Web site on which to publish any type of content one desires. In point of fact, visitors to many of the sites we have considered throughout this book have no way of knowing anything about site creators beyond the often very limited amount of information those creators present. As Wynn and Katz point out (1997: 320), though these sites "bend over backward to pretend to be interactive by being preemptively disclosive," they are eminently performative. Even such interactive options as there are often do little more than reinforce a particular performance of identity. Though site visitors are encouraged to e-mail Lady Raya, for example, she writes that there is "no guarantee your e-mail will be answered by her directly. However, I have been assured you will at least receive an answer from the Faerie Domain. If you don't hear from The Lady [Raya], watch for the signs of Mother's Hand in coincidence and circumstance" (Lady Raya n.d. [d]). That is, for those who are predisposed to see the interconnectedness of energy and events, the interpretation of happenstance following an e-mail to Lady Raya becomes a confirmation of her identity as a modern Pagan authority. Though Cougar Silvermoon (2002) assures potential students that she will answer paid-up members of her various classes within 2 days, she bluntly tells others who ask for advice or information to "meditate twice daily for several years, then contact me. I just do not have the time."

In many cultural domains, performances of identity and putative authority such as these would be regarded as little more than spiritual cozenage, transparent scams meant to bilk credulous and unsuspecting consumers. Comparatively speaking, however, and recognizing that in the cultures of modern Paganism identity and authority are measured differently than elsewhere, participation in religious ventures the uninitiated might consider questionable is hardly unique. As Lorne Dawson and I point out elsewhere (2004: 3–4; Srinivasan 2002), the Internet serves a number of not dissimilar religious needs in a number of different religious traditions. On the one hand, for example, rather than travel several hundred miles from her home near Mumbai to placate a Hindu god an astrologer has told her she has angered, Anasuya Dhanrajgir went online and was able to make the appropriate *puja* "with the click of a mouse and a credit card charge." On the other hand, for decades Christians around the world have been encouraged via radio, television, direct mail, and now the Internet to contribute "love gifts" to a growing assortment of televangelists in return for a variety of prayers, promises, and preferential treatment. It is not the case that one situation is inherently less credible than another, but that what "passes for knowledge" in each of these contexts is simply different from what passes for knowledge in others. So it is among modern Pagans.

Within modern Paganism, online at least, credentials are as much about claims to authority as they are about the empirical demonstration of either knowledge or experience. Recall Patience on the Druid-Celtic Sidhe list. Despite the ungracious tone in her post challenging the commitment of list members to the Druid path, no one—not even the list owner—challenged her about the veracity of her own claims. In this instance, and in others throughout this chapter, as instantiations of authority online, three performative dynamics emerge as some modern Pagans (1) present the appearance of knowledge, (2) employ culturally accepted symbols of pedagogy, and (3) attempt to differentiate one's own religious product through presentation, not revelation.

First, as a cultural product, *knowledge* is that which addresses or purports to address the concerns and questions extant within particular cultures. Thus, not surprisingly, what explicitly "passes for knowledge" in one culture will be just as explicitly rejected by another; evangelical Christians would no more go online to make an Internet *puja* to an outraged Hindu god than a devout Hindu would mouse-click hard-earned rupees to a religiously xenophobic televangelist. Many of the Web sites considered in this chapter make explicit claims to re-solve the concerns and questions they regard as extant among their modern Pagan constituents. One interactive pretension that has been a standard feature on Web sites since the popular advent of the Internet a decade ago is the hum-ble FAQ, the "Frequently Asked Questions" page. In terms of the instantiation of modern Pagan identity, however, whether the "frequently asked questions" have actually been raised by site visitors or not matters little. The FAQ is sim-ply another mechanism, another prop by which the appearance of knowledge is presented. "Asked," for example, to resolve the problem of how the White Wolf Temple of the Olde Religion could be a Wiccan church with "all this Jesus and Mary stuff on your website," Lady Raya (n.d. [d]) "responds" in true open source fashion:

> We began as a wiccan coven, in the traditional manner of wicca. We chose Zeus and Aphrodite as our Deity Names. We invoked Zeus. He showed up. He told us how it was going to be. Mother said, 'Do whatever He tells you.' We apologize sincerely to our wiccan brothers and sisters, but we're sure you are aware of how it is when Zeus decides something . . . Zeus is God. If He wants to be Jesus, He can be Jesus. And if there ever was a real Jesus, then he assuredly was Zeus. This must be true, because there is only one God . . . So Zeus, ever the Morality Enforcer, and the Sum of All Gods Cahuna, decided to take it on Himself to become Jesus and get this Show on the Road. This, of course, make Jehovah the mani-festation of Chronos, which is fairly self-evident anyway . . . It really ties up quite neatly. (Ellipses added)

Again, whether any of this is self-evident or not, or whether it is tied up neatly or left as a rat's-nest of conjecture, conflation, and concatenation, mat-ters little in terms of modern Pagan knowledge as a cultural product. Lady Raya performs her online identity as a modern Pagan authority through her claims to be a *savant*, not necessarily her demonstration of those claims.

Second, whether lodged in an *ad hoc* chat room or offered as part of a larger institution, modern Pagan entrepreneurs, both online and off-line, employ culturally accepted symbols of pedagogy—the school, the seminary, the col-lege, the university—as a way of performing their identities as religious au-thorities. Like the symbols of power and prestige discussed in Chapter 4, these institutions are recognized in our culture as venues in which learning takes place, in which those who know teach those who would know. It is significant that for all the open source appropriation in modern Paganism, its fascination with exotic deities, sacred locales, and mystic practices, the performance of pedagogical authority online resorts to very traditional off-line models. Online educational venues are not called *gurukalas* or *ashramas*, for example, they are the "University of Esoterica" (www.northernway.org), the "Blue Moonlight Coven Seminary of Living Earth Religions" (www.bluemoonlightcovensemi-nary.com), and "The College of Sacred Mists" (www.workingwitches.com). Moreover, though initiation and degree training in many modern Paganisms has traditionally been provided without charge—not least to avoid precisely the kind of religious entrepreneurship we see here—some modern Pagans have adverted to the larger cultural fiction that payment for something guarantees (or at least implies) a higher-quality product.

Finally, in the rapidly expanding modern Pagan marketplace, there is a growing need for entrepreneurs to differentiate themselves in order to attract potential consumers to their product over someone else's. After all, why study shamanism online with Cougar Silvermoon when you can study with any number of other modern Pagan or New Age practitioners who claim to offer similar services? In the almost inevitable competition for students, what sets her apart as a teacher? Whether they occur online or off-, attempts to instanti-ate authority always take place in the context of a struggle with others who seek to instantiate a similar authority. As we have seen, some of these struggles de-volve into simple insults, others play out in more complex fashion. In addition to disparaging other popular teachers of modern Pagan shamanism, though, Cougar Silvermoon also instantiates her identity by alluding to her putative monopoly on authoritative information. In a FAQ devoted specifically to her training program in Celtic Shamanism, for example, she was "asked" whether she required "outside reading materials" for her courses. "No," she responded, "in fact I discourage outside sources as they will interfere with my teachings." In the online world, with its rampant replication of resources, monopolizing authoritative teachings becomes a function of representation, rather than rev-elation. That is, potential entrepreneurs must *represent* that they are in control of authoritative resources, but not *reveal* the content of those resources lest on-line replication rob them of the monopoly on which their very claims to au-thority rest. In this instance, the open source character of modern Paganism is not well served by the World Wide Web, but instead is in tension with the need to differentiate one's own modern Pagan product from that of entrepreneurial competitors. Cougar Silvermoon's shamanic secrets, passed down to her by dint of lineage and training, will remain solidly in her grasp until the money order or certified check arrives. Those who would challenge either Cougar Silvermoon's authority as a teacher or her choice to charge for her services are told in no uncertain terms: "You need to understand that the Internet was NOT invented to exploit knowledgeable people" (2002). One of the problems with the Web, however, which is only exacerbated by the current popularity of Wicca, Witchcraft, and other aspects of modern Paganism, is that it does seem to be open season on the uninformed, the unintelligent, and the unsuspecting.

# CHAPTER 7

# (In) Conclusion
## *A Web of Dangers, Benefits, and Research Directions*

I watched charmed two weeks ago and they had to go to an island called valhalla where the women collected the spirits of men who were warriors when they were alive and they were training them for the big fight between good and evil, I never realised that valhalla was actually connected to wicca, I just thought they made it up.

Nikki, e-mail to Bella Luna Cyber Coven

### Growth and the Illusion of Growth: A Cautionary Tale for Scholars and Pagans Alike

Once upon a time, it was common knowledge among social scientists that people in North America were becoming less religious, less inclined toward their various gods, rituals, and religious institutions. They were secularizing, choosing the rational explanations and dubious comforts of modernity over the traditional consolations offered by religious belief and practice. As worship attendance became less of a priority for many of their parishioners, Christian churches that once boasted thousands of active members were suddenly struggling to meet their annual budgets. Rather than successful venues for religious socialization, Sunday schools seemed to turn into brightly decorated storerooms designed to keep children out of the sanctuary so their parents could worship in peace. And as those children grew up, many of them opted out of the sanctuary for good. Toward the end of the 1960s and into the 1970s, as membership decline in mainline Protestant denominations became more obvious, scholars explained this phenomenon as a "secularization" of society, a gradual drift away from the need for religion as a social force, a cultural resource, and a personal wellspring of strength and inspiration.

As we know now, though, the problem with this explanation is that it wasn't true. Not all churches were losing members. Some were gaining. Indeed, many denominations with a more conservative theology or churches that demanded higher levels of commitment as part of the cost of membership were growing by leaps and bounds. Not to mention the fact that, as Jeffrey Hadden pointed out in retrospect some years later (1989: 13), the so-called theory of secularization did nothing to explain the "effervescence of new religious movements in the very locations where secularization appears to cut deeply into established institutional religion." People were not, in fact, becoming less religious during those decades, but they were becoming very differently religious. As Hadden concluded, however, secularization as an explanation had come to wield the force of an entrenched ideology as opposed to a theory that remained open to challenge and empirical investigation. I offer this well-known episode in the sociology of religion as a cautionary tale both for scholars of modern Paganism and for modern Pagans themselves.

*The Undeniable Growth of Modern Paganism*

Recall the claims of modern Pagans discussed in Chapter 4 that their religious traditions, especially Wicca, are among the fastest growing in North America, Australia, and parts of western Europe. Returning from a modern Pagan festival, for example, Windwalker reports to the nearly 200 members of the Yahoo! group Solitary Witches 13 that one lively topic of conversation among festivalgoers was the phenomenal growth rate of modern Paganism—"supposedly doubling in size every (there's debate on this figure) 18 months." While popular modern Pagan authors such as Phyllis Curott and Raymond Buckland may be less willing to suggest such a specific rate of growth, a number of them make similar claims. And there are both popular and demographic indications that modern Paganism is on the rise. Modern Pagan books have swelled the shelves of bookstores; a media-savvy Wiccan is one of the characters on a "reality TV" show called "Mad, Mad House"; and, in some contexts, being a Witch or a Wiccan is culturally fashionable, something membership in any number of other new religious movements could never hope to achieve. According to the 2001 national census—at least as the statistics were reported in the media— modern Paganism is among the fastest growing religions in Australia (Burke 2003; Wallace 2003). And, finally, though there is no explicit mention of modern Paganism in its discussion of findings, data from the 2001 American Religious Identification Survey (ARIS 2001), conducted under the auspices of the Graduate Center of the City University of New York, indicate that the number of self-identified Wiccans in the United States rose from 8,000 in 1990 to

134,000 in 2001. Respectable numbers indeed—depending, of course, on what they mean. If the lesson of secularization has taught us anything, however, it is that we ought to approach any claims like this with a healthy hermeneutic of suspicion. It's not like we haven't been fooled by statistics before.

That modern Paganism *is* growing, both in popularity and in participant numbers, I don't think is in serious dispute. How *fast* it is growing, on the other hand, especially in light of some of the more hyperbolic claims, is a matter for careful investigation rather than premature declaration. Setting aside, for example, the distinct possibility that many survey respondents filled in "Wiccan" or "Pagan" as a culturally fashionable joke—recall that nearly 400,000 Britons responded to their 2001 census as "Jedi Knights" (70,000 did so in Australia)— there are a number of other issues to consider. First, in terms of both the ARIS data and the Australian census, increase in disclosure does not necessarily mean a corresponding increase in population. That is, it is possible that many of those who participated in these surveys are not new Pagans, but for the first time have been given the opportunity to answer questions about their religious affiliation *as* Pagans. For those in this category, then, the apparent growth of modern Paganism is not a function of religious conversion, but of an expanding cultural acceptance of religious choices they have already made. There is also a derivative issue of first-time survey respondents, young adults who chose a modern Pagan path as teens, but who are entering the survey population for the first time. Put differently, though the increase according to the ARIS data is substantial, there is insufficient context and longitudinal information to say precisely what it means. Second, and conversely, there is the inherent problem of surveying the modern Pagan population at all, either online or off-. Off-line, as any number of discussion forum messages make clear, many modern Pagans still experience a significant sense of cultural marginalization, whether real or imagined. Will modern Pagans such as these answer survey questions truthfully under those circumstances? Online, on the other hand, there have been a number of attempts to utilize the Internet to survey various Pagan populations. These suffer from their own set of problems, many of which relate to the digital divide and to the self-selective nature of online survey instruments. At this point in time, for example, no one should be surprised if an online survey of modern Pagans returns results that skew toward white, middle-class and upper-middle-class participants (cf. Hadden and Cowan 2000a; Bainbridge 2000). If, as one correspondent in the *Circle Network News* forum on "Virtual Paganism" wrote, "the Internet is not much more than a global notice board for the privileged" (Sant 1996), then only those so privileged will constitute the survey population. Third, as we have seen, the appearance of online activity does not necessarily mean an active online reality. Thousands of modern Pagan discussion groups on Yahoo! and MSN do not translate into hundreds of thousands of modern Pagans chatting away when less than half of those groups have more than a handful of participants and comparatively few groups post more than one message per month per member. None of these issues is definitive in terms of skewing the rate of modern Pagan growth one way or the other, but together they suggest the value of a more restrained approach to claims about that growth until more usefully contextualized data is available. Given the often hyperbolic claims that migrate over the Web, however, a "restrained approach" is often an alien concept.

### The Internet as a Channel for Problematic Research

Whenever I teach my course on cults, sects, and new religious movements at least one student wants to write a research paper on religion and the Internet. Occasionally, what I receive is an essay in which the student has tracked the number of search engine hits generated by a particular search term and tried to interpret these data in some significant way. Over the course of the semester, for example, what was the weekly rate of change on Google for the word "druid" or "witch" or "wiccan?" I have also encountered this method in the academic peer-review process and in online discussion forums. "Hey, you guys," wrote Deepcstar to the Beginner's Wicca group, "I jus cheked out witch on the Internet and got ove a million sites! WoW! we're really out there!"

Out there, indeed.

Perhaps, though, the problem with this kind of a statistic is not immediately apparent. Because it fundamentally misunderstands the technology of a Google search, this method of tracking Internet activity generates a seriously flawed picture of Web usage. When I first drafted this paragraph one evening, Google returned about 990,000 hits for the search term "wicca." When I revised the paragraph the next morning, the return result was about 991,000. Does that mean that there are nearly a million separate, distinct Web sites about Wicca, which is at least implied by the research method I've just described? Or that more than 1,000 new sites appeared in less than 12 hours? No, in both cases. Google returns the number of hits which fit its search parameters for the total Web sites that are part of its search index. That is, it does not necessarily search the entire Web, nor even the entire Web that is sourced in North America. More important, though, search terms very often return multiple hits for the same Web site, creating a serious misperception about Internet use if one relies on the raw hit total.

The problem only gets worse when researchers try to make definitive statements about Internet growth or decline based only (or principally) on search engine hit returns. Using a search term like "religion," for example, without contextualizing it through a specified limitation of search parameters, renders any statistical result all but meaningless. There is no way to know whether the hit refers to a site that deals with religion negatively or positively, explicitly or tangentially; whether it is a passing mention of religion in a poem, story, or song lyrics posted in a reader's review on Amazon.com; or whether it is one of a number of fan sites dedicated to the grunge band Bad Religion. Now, some could argue that these distinctions really don't matter. I disagree. In terms of a workable research hermeneutic for the Internet, context is everything. Sites that are explicitly critical of Wicca, for example, will be returned in a Google search of "wicca" just as surely as those that are positively disposed, yet could not be used necessarily to argue for the growth of Wicca on the Web or in the world.

As a channel for dubious research methods, this problem is exacerbated on the Internet by debatable authority and suspect data, the replication of unsubstantiated and decontextualized information, and Web visitors who may not know enough about the topic at hand to know that they really don't know anything at all. First, when scholars such as Loretta Orion and modern Pagans such as Windwalker base statistical claims for modern Pagan populations on variables as problematic as the "readership of books published on related subjects" (Orion 1995: 279 n.2), they bring two particular types of authoritative pressure to bear, the weight of cultural expectation and the weight of subcultural disposition. That is, because Orion is an academic there is a cultural expectation that she will be careful in her research, rigorous in her analysis, and judicious in her evaluation. Anyone who works in academia knows that this is rarely a complete reality in any research project, but these ideals remain in force as larger cultural expectations. We expect academics to speak with authority in their areas of expertise based on the soundness of their research. In the context of modern Paganism as a religious subculture, there is also the authoritative weight of disposition. That is, because many modern Pagans want to claim extraordinary growth rates as evidence of cultural authority and religious legitimacy, they are willing to give credence to suspect data simply because it supports desired results. To be sure, this phenomenon is hardly limited to modern Pagans. In fact, manipulating information to appeal to the extant preferences and prejudices of particular target audiences is the most basic definition of propaganda, whether religious, political, or commercial (Cowan 2003a, 2004). As I noted in Chapter 4, arguments from growth are more compelling for those who are already disposed to believe them, or who have a vested interest in believing them, than for those who are not so disposed. And because the Internet provides an increasingly intuitive menu designed to suit participants' tastes based on the search choices they have made, it results in a self-limiting construction of reality grounded in those extant preferences and prejudices.

Second, there is the putative authority of replication, a topic we have considered in detail throughout the book. Perhaps the most basic mechanism of successful propaganda, repetition relies for its persuasive force on the ease with which people forget that which they have been told or shown (see Berger 1967).

In many cases, unrestrained Internet replication establishes a deceptive data-base, which to the unwary or the unconcerned gives the appearance that there is considerably more information available about a particular topic than there is in reality. In the flow of an online discussion thread, for example, "census" becomes "survey," which changes at some point to "surveys," and a single source like ARIS or the 2001 Australian census loses its provenance through unre-strained replication. Rather than one indication that modern Paganism is on the rise, suddenly all indicators point to its phenomenal growth. Or enthusias-tic modern Pagans quote an online source such as the Ontario Consultants on Religious Tolerance (Robinson 2003; www.religioustolerance.org) and simply repeat the highest figures they find there. Gradually stripped of provenance and context, these too are replicated across the discussion threads of the World Wide Web.

Third, there is the problem of simple ignorance among those who rely on the Internet to "fill the gaps in [their] knowledge with ready-made, instant info bites" (Wright 2000: 51). More specifically, those who use the Internet in this manner may not know enough to know that they don't know anything at all. "I never realised that valhalla was actually connected to wicca," writes a young modern Pagan named Nikki, recalling a recent episode of *Charmed*, "I just thought they made it up." Though her correspondents on the Bella Luna Cyber Coven responded to a number of other issues in her post, it is significant that no one challenged the problems inherent in her basic assumption. That is, *Charmed* is a fictional television program written and produced for a primarily adolescent and young adult market; there is no connection between Wicca and the Norse hall of the slain; and, as such, they *did* make it up. It appears that in many of these online modern Pagan venues what Jeffrey Hadden and I pointed out elsewhere remains firmly the case today: "In e-space, there is no authorita-tive peer-review process, no editorial chain up which a book or article must be sold, no reliable mechanism by which information is vetted. And this is the Net's gift as well as its cost" (2000a: 6).

## Potential and Performance: The Benefits of the World Wide Web

Lest anyone think that the Web is all illusion and hyperbole, however, nothing could be further from the truth. For religious groups of all types, the Internet presents a number of possibilities and potential benefits. Though significant amounts of misinformation flow along a multitude of Internet pathways, in some cases benefitting most those who employ the Web for just this purpose (Cowan 2004), religious groups and movements such as modern Paganism also have the opportunity to present themselves in a positive light. A very common component of Pagan shovelware is an FAQ that addresses the popular confusion between Wicca, for example, and Satanism. Internet visitors who are curious about modern Goddess worship will almost certainly come across dedicated countermovement Web sites like those maintained by some evangelical Christians, but the breadth of the Internet means that they need not rely on these sites for their information. The Covenant of the Goddess (www.cog.org), The Witches' Voice (www.witchvox.com), the Ar nDraiocht Fein (www.adf .org), and a host of others provide admirable emic perspectives. Two other particular benefits that we have discussed in depth throughout the book are the potential for community represented by the Internet and the stage for the experimental performance of identity that it provides.

## The Potential for Community

Social and cultural marginalization often leads, quite understandably, to a concomitant sense of personal isolation and alienation. With no one to talk to about their feelings, thoughts, hopes, and fears, for example, gay men and lesbians who are still in the closet often feel profoundly alone in their experience. Suicide among closeted gay teens is only one tragic result of this sense of isolation. Conversely, a common theme in any number of support group situations is an equally profound sense of relief that one is *not* alone, that there are indeed others who share similar experiences.

Similarly, one very common aspect of discussion threads among modern Pagans online, especially newcomers to the various traditions, is the sense of relief they display when participants find like-minded Wiccans, Witches, Druids, or Asatruar with whom they can exchange information, trade gossip and opinion, or simply share a sense of community. Over the Internet, it is clear that many modern Pagans see these connections as evidence, not only of personal interaction, but of a larger global phenomenon. Recall Elder (1996), who wrote to the *Circle Network News*'s forum on "Virtual Paganism" that "meeting Pagans from around the world online, this new Pagan group will snowball and a new paradigm of Earth-centered spirituality will displace the Earth-raping, Nature-castrating monotheism which seems an unchangeable part of our society today." As I noted at the time, while we might question the plausibility of his prediction, there is no doubt that for modern Pagans with Internet access, the World Wide Web provides a potential for connection, interaction, and community that is unparalleled in history.

At this stage in the evolution of the World Wide Web, both technologically and in terms of social penetration, I suspect that far more attempts to create modern Pagan community online will fail than will succeed. Web sites that have not been updated in months or years, discussion forums that disappear for lack of members and message traffic, chat rooms that devolve into little more than acronymic name-calling—all testify to the fragile and experimental nature of modern Pagan community in this new communication space. This does not mean, however, that attempts to create community will cease, or that there will not be successes registered. Obviously, there are modern Pagan groups that are thriving online, though most of these have significant off-line components woven into the fabric of their relationships. As groups like Lisa McSherry's JaguarMoon Cyber Coven gain experience in what it means to function as a ritual working group that meets among the electronic dolmens of Cyberhenge and not the local wooded grove, they will undoubtedly mature. They will learn what works online, and what must remain in the real world if it is to serve their religious path. Although, in broad terms, I doubt that online religion will ever represent a significant threat to its off-line counterpart—especially in a religious tradition that is so closely tied to the physical world as modern Paganism—the fact that there is another venue for the crucial conversations on which religious faith, belief, and practice are built cannot be ignored.

## The Performance of Identity

In the performance of modern Pagan identity, the potential benefits represented by the Internet are inevitably twined with some of its very real problems. Take, for example, "Celtica," a 50-something modern Pagan from Rhode Island and a member of the Online Wiccan Rituals group. In her online profile, she indicates that from earliest childhood she had been interested in aspects of what she now recognizes as modern Paganism. "All the other kids liked superheroes—I wanted to be Merlin!" Ontologically, of course, no matter how much she may want to be Merlin, she is not. She is not a sixth-century "shaman" from either the Scottish Lowlands (Markale 1995) or the Welsh hills (Matthews 1991); neither is she a "Druidic wizard," "later thinly Christianized as the resident wise-man of King Arthur's court," but who actually "learned all his magic from the Goddess" (Walker 1983: 650). In short, though she might claim some manner of metempsychotic link (and there is no evidence that she does), she is not what any number of historians, novelists, modern Pagans, or New Agers have imagined Merlin to be. She remains a 50-something real estate agent from Rhode Island, and to suggest otherwise would invite psychiatric diagnosis just as it would if one claimed to "be" Jesus, Cleopatra, or Napoleon. Performatively, however, within the context of a supportive community willing to validate her choice of identity, she can conduct herself according to her understanding of what it means to "be" Merlin. On the modern Pagan stage, especially in the electronic theater of the World Wide Web, surrounded by a supporting cast of other modern Pagan players and informed by shared conceptions of role requirements and responsibilities, she can assume the persona of Merlin.

On the other hand, it is important to remember that cyberspatial declarations about the disembodied person free from the prison of flesh are no more realistic than the body/spirit dualism by which a number of religious traditions have been marked and haunted. And what a number of commentators have missed in the hyperbolic rhetoric that surrounds online interaction and its impact on identity is that *saying* we are a particular thing is not the same as *being* it—either online or off-. Ultimately, our bodies are not separate from our experiences and our imagination; instead, they contribute in essential ways to the quality of those experiences and they shape both the contours and the limits of those imaginings. A young modern Pagan who is dangerously obese, for example, might choose the Craft name "Diaphanous Wind" to escape the unpleasant reality of her physical state. However helpful that may be to her psychologically, it does not change the salient physical reality. In fact, arguably, it was her physical reality that shaped her choice of modern Pagan identity. And that is the point that gets lost in so much of the discussion over online identity play. Despite Macha NightMare's contention that in the online world, "we may even transcend species, becoming a goat, a butterfly, or a juniper" (2001: 91), after several hours online, every one of us returns to the reality of the off-line world that is defined at least in part by our bodies. Our human eyes are dry and gritty from staring at the monitor, our lower back and shoulders stiff from keyboarding. These, and the often overwhelming need to go to the bathroom, remind us that we are ineluctably embodied.

### Modern Paganism Online and Off-Line: A Web of Research Possibilities

Just as computer-mediated communication as a widespread social and cultural phenomenon is in its technological and practical infancy, scholarly investigation into this activity has begun to stand up in the crib. More and more, scholars are taking seriously the need to consider an interdisciplinary approach to the problem of religion and the Internet, weaving the history and sociology of human participation in technology together with the substantive topic areas over which they have command. Thus, rather than simply layer commentary about the World Wide Web on top of one's particular research field, scholars are now asking how each domain influences, interacts with, and indeed changes the other (see, for example, Bunt 2000, 2003; Dawson and Cowan 2004a; Hadden and Cowan 2000b; Højsgaard and Warburg forthcoming). In the glossary to *The Virtual Pagan*, Lisa McSherry—Lady Ma'at of the JaguarMoon Cyber Coven—defines "web witching" as the practice of "networking with other magickal people to gather information of mutual interest" (2002: 170). Throughout this book, we have found that it is considerably more than that, and we are beginning to see the contours of the research yet to be conducted.

Most important, how will communities continue to develop in electronic communication spaces? At this point, for example, we lack the longitudinal data to know whether JaguarMoon Cyber Coven will survive as an online ritual working group. Its parent body lasted only a few years, and there is every indication that participation levels were never very high. We do not know what changes will be required in order to ensure—or at least to encourage—the survival of groups like this. Over time, enough online groups may emerge that have maintained sufficient levels of durability to allow for detailed comparative studies. In these cases, a number of important questions obtain. How successfully are new members integrated? What is the ratio between enrolment and attrition? What is the relationship between online and off-line interaction, and has that shifted one way or the other over the course of the group's career? That is, will the performance of modern Pagan identity online allow for more successful performance off-line? À la Telesco and Knight, has the technology of the Internet woven itself into religious ritual and practice as constituents of that practice, or has it remained simply the mechanism by which that practice is facilitated? How is conflict handled online and off-? Will online "witch wars" continue to reflect off-line tensions, or will they assume patterns and characteristics more unique to the electronic environment? Given the open source character and personally gnostic authorization of modern Paganism, how will the Internet change the balance of power within the various traditions? And, finally, as modern Paganism fades from cultural fashion, as it almost inevitably must, how will its electronic reflection change? All of these are questions that await answers.

# Bibliography

N.b. When referencing Web sites, I quote the URL of the site at the time I accessed it during this research and then provide the date that I accessed it. Though I have not referenced individual e-mail posts drawn from discussion lists, I have tried to include enough contextualization within the text for readers to follow up on my treatment should they wish.

1001 Spells. (2002). "Free Tour;" retrieved from www.1001spells.com/tour, September 4, 2003.

Abanes, R. (2001). *Harry Potter and the Bible: The Menace Behind the Magick.* Camp Hill, PA: Horizon Books.

_____. (2002). *Fantasy and Your Family: Exploring* The Lord of the Rings, Harry Potter, *and Modern Magick.* Camp Hill, PA: Christian Publications.

Abbate, J. (1999). *Inventing the Internet.* Cambridge, MA: The MIT Press.

Adler, M. (1986). *Drawing Down the Moon: Witches, Druids, Goddess-Worshippers, and Other Pagans in America Today.* Revised edition. Boston: Beacon Press.

Adrienne. (1993). "Sex, Wicca, and the Great Rite," *The Blade & Chalice* 3; retrieved from www.wildideas.net/temple/library/greatrite.html, January 20, 2004.

Aldred, L. (2000). "Plastic Shamans and Astroturf Sundances: New Age Commercialization of Native American Spirituality." *American Indian Quarterly* 24 (3): 329–52.

Anderiesz, M. (2004). "Of Mice and Men: Women Are Routinely Abused in Internet Chatrooms, yet Receive Scant Protection from the Cyberpolice." *Observer Magazine* (January 18): 56.

Andrews, T. (1993). *Enchantment of the Faerie Realm: Communicate with Nature Spirits and Elementals.* St. Paul, MN: Llewellyn Publications.

Apollolover, H. (2003). "My Path;" retrieved from www.geocities.com/emaho20/mypath.html, November 2, 2003.

Archer. (2003). "The Search for the Perfect Coven." *newWitch: not your mother's broomstick* 5 (October 03–January 04): 56–59.

ARIS. (2001). "American Religious Identification Survey." The Graduate Center, CUNY; retrieved from www.gc.cuny.edu/studies/introduction.htm, November 28, 2003.

Arthur, S. (2002). "Technophilia and Nature Religion: The Growth of a Paradox." *Religion* 32 (4): 305–316.

Ashcroft-Nowicki, D., and Brennan, J. H. (2001). *Magical Use of Thought Forms: A Proven System of Mental & Spiritual Empowerment.* St. Paul, MN: Llewellyn Publications.

Ashmore, L. (1977). *The Modesto Messiah: The Famous Mail-Order Minister.* Bakersfield, CA: Universal Press.

Autumn Storm. (1996). Letter to the Editor. *SageWoman* 36 (Autumn): 85.

Aycock, A. (1996). "'Technologies of the Self': Foucault and Internet Discourse." *Journal of Computer-Mediated Communication* 1 (2); retrieved from www.acsusc.org/jcmc/vol1/issue2/aycock.html, March 12, 2003.

Badham, J. (1983). *Wargames*. Hollywood, CA: MGM Studios.

Bainbridge, W. S. (1978). *Satan's Power: A Deviant Psychotherapy Cult*. Los Angeles and Berkeley: University of California Press.

_____. (2000). "Religious Ethnography on the World Wide Web." In *Religion on the Internet: Research Prospects and Promises*, eds. J. K. Hadden and D. E. Cowan. Amsterdam and London: JAI/Elsevier Science.

Baker, P. (2001). "Moral Panic and Alternative Identity Construction in Usenet." *Journal of Computer-Mediated Communication* 7 (1); retrieved from www.ascusc.org/jcmc/vol7/issue1/Baker.html, July 10, 2003.

Bandura, A. (1977). *Social Learning Theory*. Englewood Cliffs, NJ: Prentice-Hall.

_____. (1997). *Self-Efficacy: The Exercise of Control*. New York: W. H. Freeman.

Barker, E. (1984). *The Making of a Moonie: Choice or Brainwashing?* London: Basic Black.

Battaglia, D. (1995). *Rhetorics of Self-Making*. Berkeley and Los Angeles: University of California Press.

Bauer, W. (1971). *Orthodoxy and Heresy in Earliest Christianity*, 2nd ed., trans. Philadelphia Seminar on Christian Origins, eds. R. A. Kraft and G. Krodel. Mifflintown, PA: Sigler Press.

Bell, D. (2001). *An Introduction to Cyberspace*. London and New York: Routledge.

Bentov, I. (1977). *Stalking the Wild Pendulum: On the Mechanics of Consciousness*. New York: E. P. Dutton.

Berger, H. A. (1999). *A Community of Witches: Contemporary Neo-Paganism and Witchcraft in the United States*. Columbia, S.C.: University of South Carolina Press.

Berger, H. A., Leach, E. A., and Shaffer, L.S. (2003). *Voices from the Pagan Census: A National Survey of Witches and Neo-Pagans in the United States*. Columbia, S.C.: University of South Carolina Press.

Berger, H. A., and Ezzy, D. (2004). "The Internet as Virtual Spiritual Community: Teen Witches in the United States and Australia." In *Religion Online: Finding Faith on the Internet*, eds. L. L. Dawson and D. E. Cowan. New York: Routledge.

Berger, P. L. (1967). *The Sacred Canopy: Elements of a Sociological Theory of Religion*. New York: Anchor Books.

Berger, P., and Luckmann, T. (1966). *The Social Construction of Reality: A Treatise in the Sociology of Knowledge*. London, England: Penguin Books.

Berland, J. (2000). "Cultural Technologies and the 'Evolution' of Technological Cultures." In *The World Wide Web and Contemporary Cultural Theory*, eds. A. Herman and T. Swiss. New York: Routledge.

Berners-Lee, T., with Fischetti, M. (2000). *Weaving the Web: The Original Design and Ultimate Destiny of the World Wide Web*. New York: HarperBusiness.

Bharati, A. (1961). *The Ochre Robe: An Autobiography*. Garden City, NY: Doubleday & Company.

_____. (1976). *The Light at the Center: Context and Pretext of Modern Mysticism*. Santa Barbara, CA: Ross-Erikson.

Birnie, S. A., and Horvath, P. (2002). "Psychological Predictors of Internet Social Communication." *Journal of Computer-Mediated Communication* 7 (4); retrieved from www.ascusc.org/jcmc/vol7/issue4/horvath.html, January 10, 2004.

Blumer, H. (1969). *Symbolic Interactionism: Perspective and Method*. Berkeley and Los Angeles: University of California Press.

Bohm, D. (1980). *Wholeness and the Implicate Order*. London and New York: Routledge.

Bonewits, P. E. I. (1989). *Real Magic: An Introductory Treatise on the Basic Principles of Yellow Light*. Rev. ed. York Beach, ME: Red Wheel/Weiser.

Bourdieu, P. (1977). *Outline of a Theory of Practice*, tr. R. Nice. New York: Cambridge University Press.

_____. (1984a). *Distinction: A Social Critique of the Judgement of Taste*, trans. R. Nice. Cambridge: Harvard University Press.

_____. (1984b). *Homo Academicus*, trans. P. Collier. Stanford, CA: Stanford University Press.

_____. (1993). *The Field of Cultural Production: Essays on Art and Literature*, ed. R. Johnson. New York: Columbia University Press.

_____. (1997). *Pascalian Meditations*, trans. R. Nice. Stanford, CA: Stanford University Press.

_____. (1998). *Practical Reason: On the Theory of Action*. Stanford, CA: Stanford University Press.

Bourdieu, P., and Wacquant, L. J. D. (1992). *An Invitation to Reflexive Sociology*. Chicago: University of Chicago Press.

Bradley, M. Z. (1982). *The Mists of Avalon*. New York: Ballantine Books.

Brasher, B. E. (2001). *Give Me That Online Religion*. San Francisco, CA: Jossey-Bass.

Briggs, J., and Peat, F. D. (1984). *Looking Glass Universe: The Emerging Science of Wholeness*. New York: Cornerstone Library.

Brint, S. (2001). "*Gemeinschaft* Revisited: A Critique and Reconstruction of the Community Concept." *Sociological Theory* 19: 1–23.

Brooke, J. H. (1991). *Science and Religion: Some Historical Perspectives*. Cambridge, MA: Cambridge University Press.

Brooke, T. (1997). "Lost in the Garden of Digital Delights." In *Virtual Gods*, ed. T. Brooke. Eugene, OR: Harvest House.

Bruce, R. (1994). "Treatise on Astral Projection"; retrieved from www.astralpulse.com/guides/oobe/Treatise.pdf, January 3, 2004.

_____. (1999). *Astral Dynamics: A New Approach to Out-of-Body Experiences*. Charlottesville, VA: Hampton Roads Publishing.

_____. (2002). *Practical Psychic Self-Defense: Understanding and Surviving Unseen Influences*. Charlottesville, VA: Hampton Roads Publishing.

Bruteau, B., comp. (1996). *The Other Half of My Soul: Bede Griffiths and the Hindu-Christian Dialogue*. Wheaton, IL: Quest Books.

Buck, P. (n.d.). "Asatru, An Ancient Religion Reborn"; retrieved from www.irminsul.org/arc/016pb.html, January 10, 2004.

Buckland. R. (1974). *The Tree: The Complete Book of Saxon Witchcraft*. York Beach, ME: Samuel Weiser.

_____. (1987). *Buckland's Complete Book of Witchcraft*. St. Paul, MN: Llewellyn Publications.

_____. (1991). *Scottish Witchcraft: The History & Magick of the Picts*. St. Paul, MN: Llewellyn Publications.

_____. (1995). *Witchcraft from the Inside: Origins of the Fastest Growing Religious Movement in America*. Third edition. St. Paul, MN: Llewellyn Publications.

Budapest, Z. (1989). *The Holy Book of Women's Mysteries: Feminist Witchcraft, Goddess Rituals, Spellcasting, and Other Womanly Arts . . .* Oakland, CA: Wingbow Press.

Bunt, G. (2000). *Virtually Islamic: Computer-mediated Communication and Cyber Islamic Environments*. Cardiff, Wales: University of Wales Press.

_____. (2003). *Islam in the Digital Age: E-Jihad, Online Fatwas, and Cyber Islamic Environments*. London, England: Pluto Press.

_____. (2004). "Islamic Expression Online." In *Religion Online: Finding Faith on the Internet*, eds. L. L. Dawson and D. E. Cowan. New York: Routledge.

Burke, K. (2003). "No Rest for the Wicca—Growing Pagan Population Shows its Political Spirit." *Sydney Morning Herald* (June 30): News and Features, 3.

Cabot, L., and Cowan, T. (1989). *Power of the Witch*. New York: Delta.

Capra, F. (1975). *The Tao of Physics: An Exploration of the Parallels Between Modern Physics and Eastern Mysticism*. New York: Random House.

Carr-Gomm, P. (2002). *In the Grove of the Druids: The Druid Teachings of Ross Nichols*. London, England: Watkins Publishing.

Carr-Gomm, P., ed. (1996). *The Druid Renaissance: The Voice of Druidry Today*. London, England: Thorsons.

Castells, M. (2001). *The Internet Galaxy: Reflections on the Internet, Business, and Society*. New York: Oxford University Press.

Cauldron. (1997). "1997 Ostara Ritual Log"; retrieved from www.ecauldron.com/riteostara97.php, January 11, 2004.

_____. (1998a). "1998 Lughnasadh Ritual Log"; retrieved from www.ecauldron.com/ritelammas98.php, January 23, 2004.

_____. (1998b). "1998 Midsummer Ritual Log"; retrieved from www.ecauldron.com/ritemidsum98.php, January 23, 2004.

_____. (1998c). "1998 Ostara Ritual Log"; retrieved from www.ecauldron.com/riteostara98.php, January 11, 2004.

_____. (1998d). "1998 Samhain Ritual Log"; retrieved from www.ecauldron.com/rite-samhain98.php, January 12, 2004.

_____. (1999a). "1999 Beltane Ritual Log"; retrieved from www.ecauldron.com/ritebeltane99.php, January 13, 2004.

_____. (1999b). "1999 Ostara Ritual Log"; retrieved from www.ecauldron.com/riteostara99.php, January 13, 2004.

_____. (2003). "2003 Beltane Ritual Log"; retrieved from www.ecauldron.com/ritebeltane03.php, January 25, 2004.

Cavanaugh, A. (1999). "Behaviour in Public? Ethics in Online Ethnography." *Cybersociology* 6; retrieved from www.cybersociology.com, July 10, 2003.

Cesara, M. (1982). *No Hiding Place: Reflections of a Woman Anthropologist.* London and New York: Academic Press.

Christie. (1997). "Don't 'New Agers' Belong Here Too?" *SageWoman* 39 (Autumn): 89–90.

Church of All Worlds. (2001). "Neo-Paganism and the Church of All Worlds: Some Questions and Answers (Part 1 of 2)"; retrieved from www.caw.org/articles/cawquest.html, September 25, 2003.

Clark, L. S. (2003). *From Angels to Aliens: Teenagers, the Media, and the Supernatural.* Oxford, England: Oxford University Press.

Clarke, A. C. (1977). *Profiles of the Future: An Inquiry into the Limits of the Possible.* New York: Popular Library.

Clifton, C. S., ed. (1993). *Witchcraft Today, Book Two: Modern Rites of Passage.* St. Paul, MN: Llewellyn Publications.

Cobb, J. (1998). *Cybergrace: The Search for God in the Digital World.* New York: Crowne Publishers.

Coleman, J. W. (2001). *The New Buddhism: The Western Transformation of an Ancient Tradition.* Oxford, England: Oxford University Press.

Collins, A. (2002). *Gods of Eden: Egypt's Lost Legacy and the Genesis of Civilization.* Rochester, VT: Inner Traditions.

Conway, D. J. (1990). *Celtic Magic.* St. Paul, MN: Llewellyn Publications.

_____. (1995). *By Oak, Ash, & Thorn: Modern Celtic Shamanism.* St. Paul, MN: Llewellyn Publications.

Coven of the New Moon. n.d. "Wicca Terms"; retrieved from www.geocities.com/Athens/Rhodes/2544/glossary.html, August 31, 2003.

Cowan, D. E. (1998). "Too Narrow and Too Close: Some Problems with Participant Observation in the Study of New Religious Movements." *Method and Theory in the Study of Religion* 4: 391–406.

_____. (2000). "Religion, Rhetoric, and Scholarship: Managing Vested Interest in E-Space." In *Religion on the Internet: Research Prospects and Promises*, eds. J. K. Hadden and D. E. Cowan. Amsterdam and London: JAI/Elsevier Science.

_____. (2003a). *Bearing False Witness? An Introduction to the Christian Countercult.* Westport, CT: Praeger Publishers.

_____. (2003b). *The Remnant Spirit: Conservative Reform in Mainline Protestantism.* Westport, CT: Praeger Publishers.

_____. (2004). "Contested Spaces: Movement, Countermovement, and E-Space Propaganda." In *Religion Online: Finding Faith on the Internet*, eds. L. L. Dawson and D. E. Cowan. New York: Routledge.

Cowan, D. E., and Hadden, J. K. (2004a). "God, Guns, and Grist for the Media's Mill: Constructing the Narratives of New Religious Movements and Violence." *Nova Religio: The Journal of New and Emergent Religions* 8 (2): 64–82.

_____. (2004b). "Virtually Religious: New Religious Movements and the World Wide Web." In *The Oxford Handbook of New Religious Movements*, ed. J. R. Lewis. New York: Oxford University Press.

Crowley, A. ([1938] 1976). *The Book of the Law.* York Beach, ME: Samuel Weiser.

Crowley, V. (1994). *Phoenix from the Flame: Pagan Spirituality in the Western World.* London: Thorsons.

_____. (1996a). *Wicca: The Old Religion in the New Millennium.* London: Thorsons.

_____. (1996b). "Wicca as a Modern-Day Mystery Religion." In *Paganism Today*, eds. G. Harvey and C. Hardman. London: Thorsons.

Crowther, P. (1998). *High Priestess: The Life & Times of Patricia Crowther*. Blaine, WA: Phoenix Publishing.

Cubitt, S. (2000). "Shit Happens: Numerology, Destiny, and Control on the Web." In *The World Wide Web and Contemporary Cultural Theory*, eds. A. Herman and T. Swiss. New York: Routledge.

Cummings, J. N., Butler, B., and Kraut, R. (2002). "The Quality of Online Social Relationships." *Communications of the ACM* 45 (7): 103–108.

Cunningham, S. (1988). *Wicca: A Guide for the Solitary Practitioner*. St. Paul, MN: Llewellyn Publications.

_____. (1993). *Living Wicca: A Further Guide for the Solitary Practitioner*. St. Paul, MN: Llewellyn Publications.

Curott, P. W. (1998). *Book of Shadows: A Modern Woman's Journey into the Wisdom of Witchcraft and the Magic of the Goddess*. New York: Broadway Books.

_____. (2002). *Witch Crafting: A Spiritual Guide to Making Magic*. New York: Broadway Books.

Danet, B., Ruedenberg-Wright, L., and Rosenbaum-Tamari, Y. (1997). "'Hmmm . . . Where's That Smoke Coming From?': Writing, Play and Performance on Internet Relay Chat." *Journal of Computer-Mediated Communication* 2 (4); retrieved from www.ascusc.org/jcmc/vol2/issue4/danet.html, January 10, 2004.

Dart, J. (1997). "Covering Conventional and Unconventional Religion: A Reporter's View." *Review of Religious Research* 39 (2): 144–52.

Davis, E. (1995). "Technopagans: May the Astral Plane Be Reborn in Cyberspace." *Wired* 3.07; retrieved from www.wired.com/wired/archive/3.07/technopagans_pr.html, June 10, 2002.

_____. (1998). *Techgnosis: Myth, Magic, and Mysticism in the Age of Information*. New York: Three Rivers Press.

Davis, P. G. (1998). *Goddess Unmasked: The Rise of Neopagan Feminist Spirituality*. Dallas, TX: Spence Publishing.

Dawson, L. L. (2004). "Religion and the Quest for Virtual Community." In *Religion Online: Finding Faith on the Internet*, eds. L. L. Dawson and D. E. Cowan. New York: Routledge.

Dawson, L. L., and Cowan, D. E. (2004a). "Introduction." In *Religion Online: Finding Faith on the Internet*, eds. L. L. Dawson and D. E. Cowan. New York: Routledge.

Dawson, L. L., and Cowan, D. E., eds. (2004b). *Religion Online: Finding Faith on the Internet*. New York: Routledge.

Dawson, L. L., and Hennebry, J. (1999). "New Religions and the Internet: Recruiting in a New Public Space." *Journal of Contemporary Religion* 14 (1): 17–39.

Dewdney, C. (1999). "Advanced Thinking." *Advanced Manufacturing* (June); retrieved from www.advancedmanufacturing.com/june99/advanced.htm, November 11, 2003.

Dibbell, J. (1994). "A Rape in Cyberspace: or, How an Evil Clown, a Haitian Trickster Spirit, Two Wizards, and a Cast of Dozens Turned a Database into a Society." In *Flame Wars: The Discourse of Cyberculture*, ed. M. Dery. Durham and London: Duke University Press.

DiBona, C., Ockman, S., and Stone, M., eds. (1999). *Open Sources: Voices from the Open Source Revolution*. Sebastopol, CA: O'Reilly & Associates.

Dixon, T. (1994). "Yule Ritual"; retrieved from www.notelrac.com/whuups.dir/rituals.dir/yule_compuserve, August 5, 2003.

DiZerega, G. (2001). *Pagans & Christians: The Personal Spiritual Experience*. St. Paul, MN: Llewellyn Publications.

Doerksen, L. J. (1995). Book Review of *New Age Cults* by Texe Marsden [*sic*]. *Hecate's Loom* 29 (Lammas): 37–38.

Donath, J. S. (1999). "Identity and Deception in the Virtual Community." In *Communities in Cyberspace*, eds. M. A. Smith and P. Kollock. London and New York: Routledge.

Donath, J., Karahalios, K., and Viégas, F. (1999). "Visualizing Conversation." *Journal of Computer-Mediated Communication* 4 (4); retrieved from www.acsusc.org/jcmc/vol4/issue4/donath.html, April 9, 2003.

Drury, N. (2002). "Magic and Cyberspace: Fusing Technology and Magical Consciousness in the Modern World." *Esoterica* 4: 96–100.

Durkheim, E. ([1895] 1982). *The Rules of Sociological Method*, ed. S. Lukes, trans. W. D. Halls. New York: Free Press.

_____. ([1912] 1995). *The Elementary Forms of Religious Life*, trans. K. E. Fields. New York: Free Press.

Ebersole, G. L. (1989). *Ritual Poetry and the Politics of Death in Early Japan*. Princeton, NJ: Princeton University Press.

Eddy, M. B. ([1875] 1971). *Science and Health with Key to the Scriptures*. Boston: The First Church of Christ, Scientist.

Ehrman, B. D. (1993). *The Orthodox Corruption of Scripture: The Effect of Early Christological Controversies on the Text of the New Testament*. New York: Oxford University Press.

Elder, J. (1996). "A Midsummer's Pagan Internet Dream." *Circle Network News* 62 (Winter): 14.

Eliade, M. (1958). *Patterns in Comparative Religion*, trans. R. Sheed. Lincoln and London: University of Nebraska Press.

_____. (1964). *Shamanism: Archaic Techniques of Ecstasy*, trans. W. R. Trask. Rev. ed. New York: Pantheon Books.

_____. (1969). *Yoga: Immortality and Freedom*, trans. W. R. Trask. Second edition. Princeton, NJ: Princeton University Press.

Ess, C., and the AOIR Ethics Working Committee. (2002). "Ethical Decision-Making and Internet Research: Recommendations from the AOIR Ethics Working Committee," Association of Internet Researchers; retrieved from www.aoir.org/reports/ethics.pdf, February 11, 2004.

Evans-Pritchard, E. E. (1965). *Theories of Primitive Religion*. Oxford: Oxford University Press.

Evans-Wentz, W. Y. ([1911] 1966). *The Fairy-Faith in Celtic Countries*. New York: Citadel Press.

Faber, M. D. (1996). *New Age Thinking: A Psychoanalytic Critique*. Ottawa, Ontario: University of Ottawa Press.

Fabian, J. (1983). *Time and the Other: How Anthropology Makes Its Object*. New York: Columbia University Press.

Farrar, S. (1991). *What Witches Do: A Modern Coven Revealed*. Third edition. Blaine, WA: Phoenix Publishing.

Farrar, J., and Farrar, S. (1981). *Eight Sabbats for Witches and Rites for Birth, Marriage, and Death*. Custer, WA: Phoenix Publishing.

_____. (1984). *The Witches' Way: Principles, Rituals and Beliefs of Modern Witchcraft*. Custer, WA: Phoenix Publishing.

Festinger, L., Riecken, H. W., and Schachter, S. (1956). *When Prophecy Fails: A Social and Psychological Study of a Modern Group that Predicted the Destruction of the World*. New York: Harper & Row.

Firefox, L. (2003). "Getting What You Need with Solo Sex Magick." *newWitch: not your mother's broomstick* 4 (Summer): 11.

Firesilk. (n.d.). "The Origins of Moonfire"; retrieved from www.geocities.com/moonfirecoven/mission.html, December 29, 2003.

Fisher, A. L. (2002). *Philosophy of Wicca*. Toronto, Ontario: ECW Press.

Fisher, B. (2002). Review of *The Wiccan Web: Surfing the Magic on the Internet* by Patricia Telesco and Sirona Knight (Citadel Press, 2001). *newWitch: not your mother's broomstick* 2 (Winter): 73.

Foucault, M. (1970). *The Order of Things: An Archeology of the Human Sciences*. New York: Vintage Books.

_____. (1978). *The History of Sexuality, Volume 1: An Introduction*, trans. R. Hurley. New York: Vintage Books.

_____. (1982). *The Archaeology of Knowledge, and The Discourse on Language*, trans. A. M. Sheridan Smith. New York: Pantheon Books.

Freud, S. ([1913] 1950). *Totem and Taboo: Some Points of Agreement Between the Mental Lives of Savages and Neurotics*, trans. J. Strachey. New York: W.W. Norton & Company.

Frew, D. H. (1998). "Methodological Flaws in Recent Studies of Historical and Modern Witchcraft." *Ethnologies* 20 (1): 33–65.

Gage, M. J. ([1893] 1980). *Woman, Church, & State*. Watertown, MA: Persephone Press.

Galangal, L. [n.d., a]. "Frequently Asked Questions"; retrieved from www.geocities.com/saahiramoon/letter.html, December 28, 2003.

_____. [n.d., b]. "Letter from Our Founder"; retrieved from www.geocities.com/saahiramoon/letter.html, December 28, 2003.

_____. [n.d., c]. "Saahira Moon Coven"; retrieved from www.geocities.com/saahiramoon/membership.html, December 28, 2003.

_____. [n.d., d]. "Saahira Moon Coven Statement of Beliefs"; retrieved from www.geocities.com/saahiramoon/belief.html, December 28, 2003.

Gardner, G. B. [1949] 1996. *High Magic's Aid*. Hinton, WV: Godolphin House.

_____. (1961). *The Gardnerian Book of Shadows*; retrieved from www.sacred-texts.com/pag/gbos, December 6, 2003.

Geertz, C. (1973). *The Interpretation of Cultures*. New York: Basic Books.

_____. (1974). "'From the Native's Point of View': On the Nature of Anthropological Understanding." *Bulletin of the American Academy of Arts and Sciences* 28 (1): 26–45.

_____. (1983). *Local Knowledge: Further Essays in Interpretive Anthropology*, Third ed. New York: Basic Books.

Gillies, J., and Cailliau, R. (2000). *How the Web Was Born: The Story of the World Wide Web*. Oxford: Oxford University Press.

Gilmartin, R. (2001). "Online Coven Initiation"; retrieved from www.shadow-witch.com/inanna_onlineritual.html, November 29, 2003.

Glassner, B. (1999). *The Culture of Fear: Why Americans Are Afraid of the Wrong Things*. New York: Basic Books.

Goffman, E. (1959). *The Presentation of Self in Everyday Life*. New York: Anchor Books.

_____. (1967). *Interaction Ritual: Essays in Face-to-Face Behavior*. New York: Anchor Books.

_____. (1971). *Relations in Public: Microstudies of the Public Order*. New York: Basic Books.

_____. (1983). "Felicity's Condition." *American Journal of Sociology* 89 (1): 1–53.

Goode, E. (2000). *Paranormal Beliefs: A Sociological Introduction*. Prospect Heights, IL: Waveland Press.

Gould, S. J. (1997). "Nonoverlapping Magisteria." *Natural History* 106 (March): 16–22.

Graham, W. A. (1987). *Beyond the Written Word: Oral Aspects of Scripture in the History of Religion*. Cambridge, England: Cambridge University Press.

Grant, C. (2002). "For Forward-Thinking, New Guard Witches," review of *The Cyber Spellbook*, by Sirona Knight and Patricia Telesco; retrieved from www.amazon.com, August 27, 2003.

Green, M. (1991). *A Witch Alone: Thirteen Moons to Master Natural Magic*. London, England: Thorson.

Greene, B. (1999). *The Elegant Universe: Superstrings, Hidden Dimensions, and Quest for the Ultimate Theory*. New York: W. W. Norton.

Greenwood. S. (2000). *Magic, Witchcraft and the Otherworld: An Anthropology*. Oxford, England: Berg.

_____. (2003). *Contemporary Magic & Witchcraft*. London: Southwater.

Greer, J. M. (1998). *Inside a Magical Lodge: Group Ritual in the Western Tradition*. St. Paul, MN: Llewellyn Publications.

Grieve, G. P. (1995). "Imagining a Virtual Religious Community: Neo-Pagans and the Internet." *Chicago Anthropology Exchange* 21: 87–118.

Griffiths, B. (1976). *Return to the Center*. Springfield, IL: Templegate.

_____. (1989). *A New Vision of Reality: Western Science, Eastern Mysticism and Christian Faith*, ed. F. Edwards. London, England: Collins.

Groothuis, D. (1997). *The Soul in Cyberspace*. Grand Rapids, MI: Baker Books.

Guiley, R. E. (1999). *The Encyclopedia of Witches and Witchcraft*. Second ed. New York: Facts on File.

Gutstein, D. (1999). *E.con: How the Internet Undermines Democracy*. Toronto, Ontario: Stoddart.

G'Zell, O. (1971). "Theagenesis: The Birth of the Goddess." *Green Egg: The Journal of the Neo-Pagan Movement* 5 (4); revised edition retrieved from www.caw.org/articles/theagenesis.html, March 5, 2004.

Hadden, J. K. (1989). "Desacralizing Secularization Theory." In *Secularization and Fundamentalism Reconsidered*, eds. J. K. Hadden and A. Shupe. New York: Paragon House.

Hadden, J. K., and Cowan, D. E. (2000a). "The Promised Land or Electronic Chaos? Toward Understanding Religion on the Internet." In *Religion on the Internet: Research Prospects and Promises*, eds. J. K. Hadden and D. E. Cowan. Amsterdam and London: JAI/Elsevier Science.

Hadden, J. K., and Cowan, D. E., eds. (2000b). *Religion on the Internet: Research Prospects and Promises*. Amsterdam and London: JAI/Elsevier Science.

Hafner, K., and Lyon, M. (1996). *Where Wizards Stay Up Late: The Origins of the Internet*. New York: Simon & Schuster.

Hafner, K., and Markoff, J. (1991). *Cyberpunk: Outlaws and Hackers on the Computer Frontier*. New York: Simon & Schuster.

Hanegraaff, W. J. (1996). *New Age Religion and Western Culture: Esotericism in the Mirror of Secular Thought*. Leiden and New York: E.J. Brill.

Hansen, T. B. (1999). *The Saffron Wave: Democracy and Hindu Nationalism in Modern India.* Princeton, NJ: Princeton University Press.

Harakas, M. (2002). "Hits and Myths." *The Houston Chronicle* (July 10): 5.

Hare, J. B. (2001). "The Works of Margaret Murray"; retrieved from www.sacred-texts.com/pag/murray.htm, December 6, 2003.

Harms, D., and Gonce, J. W., III. (2003). *The Necronomicon Files: The Truth Behind Lovecraft's Legend.* Rev. ed. Boston: Weiser Books.

Harris, J. (2003). "You're Being Watched." *The Advertiser* (April 26): 89.

Harrold, F. B., and Eve, R. A. (1995). *Cult Archeology and Creationism: Understanding Pseudo-scientific Beliefs About the Past.* Iowa City, IA: University of Iowa Press.

Harvey, G. (1997). *Contemporary Paganism: Listening People, Speaking Earth.* New York: New York University Press.

Harvey, G., and Hardman, C., eds. (1996). *Paganism Today.* London: Thorsons.

Hauben, M., and Hauben, R. (1997). *Netizens: On the History and Impact of Usenet and the Internet.* Los Alamitos, CA: IEEE Computer Society Press.

Hawkins, C. S. (1996). *Witchcraft: Exploring the World of Wicca.* Grand Rapids, MI: Baker Books.

_____. (1998). *Goddess Worship, Witchcraft and Neo-Paganism.* Grand Rapids, MI: Zondervan.

Heelas, P. (1996). *The New Age Movement: The Celebration of the Self and the Sacralization of Modernity.* Oxford, England: Blackwell Publishers.

Heim, M. (1993). *The Metaphysics of Virtual Reality.* New York: Oxford University Press.

Heinlein, R. A. (1961). *Stranger in a Strange Land.* New York: Putnam.

Helland, C. (2000). "Online-Religion and Religion-Online: Virtual Communitas." In *Religion on the Internet: Research Prospects and Promises,* eds. J. K. Hadden and D. E. Cowan. Amsterdam and London: JAI/Elsevier Science.

Herring, S. (1999). "Interactional Coherence in CMC." *Journal of Computer-Mediated Communication* 4 (4); retrieved from www.acsusc.org/jcmc/vol4/issue4/herring.html, April 9, 2003.

Hess, D. J. (1995). *Science and Technology in a Multicultural World: The Cultural Politics of Facts and Artifacts.* New York: Columbia University Press.

Højsgaard, M. T., and Warburg, M., eds. (Forthcoming). *Religion and Cyberspace.* London: Routledge.

Hopman, E. E., and Bond, L. (1996). *People of the Earth: The New Pagans Speak Out.* Rochester, VT: Destiny Books.

Hubbard, L. R. ([1950] 1990). *Dianetics: The Modern Science of Mental Health.* Los Angeles: Bridge Publications.

Hume, L. (1998). "Creating Sacred Space: Outer Expressions of Inner Worlds in Modern Wicca." *Journal of Contemporary Religion* 13 (3): 309–19.

Hutton, R. (1991). *The Pagan Religions of the Ancient British Isles: Their Nature and Legacy.* Oxford, England.: Blackwell.

_____. (1996). *Stations of the Sun: A History of the Ritual Year in Britain.* Oxford: Oxford University Press.

_____. (1999). *The Triumph of the Moon: A History of Modern Pagan Witchcraft.* Oxford, England: Oxford University Press.

_____. (2003). *Witches, Druids and King Arthur.* London: Hambledon and London.

Iacchus. (2001). "What Is the Church of All Worlds?"; retrieved from www.caw.org/articles/WhatIsCaw.html, September 25, 2003.

Iannaccone, L. (1994). "Why Strict Churches Are Strong." *American Journal of Sociology* 99: 1180–1211.

Ihejirika, M. (2004). "Identity theft is tops among consumer complaints." *Chicago Sun-Times* (January 23): 16.

Ivy. (2003). "Start Your Own Online Coven." *newWitch: not your mother's broomstick* 5 (October 03–January 04): 61–62.

Jacobs, J., coll. ([1892] 1968). *Celtic Fairy Tales.* New York: Dover Publications.

_____. ([1894] 1968). *More Celtic Fairy Tales.* New York: Dover Publications.

Jaffrelot, C. (1993). *The Hindu Nationalist Movement in India.* New York: Columbia University Press.

James, W. ([1892] 1948). *Psychology.* Cleveland, OH: World Publishing Company.

Jeanne (1997). "Letter to the editor." *Sagewoman* 39 (Autumn): 81.

Jones, S. C., ed. (1998). *Cybersociety 2.0: Revisiting Computer-Mediated Communication and Community.* Thousand Oaks, CA: Sage Publications.

Jones, S. G. (1995). "Understanding Community in the Information Age." In *Cybersociety: Computer-Mediated Communication and Community,* ed. S. G. Jones. Thousand Oaks, CA: Sage Publications.

_____. (1997). "The Internet and Its Social Landscape." In *Virtual Culture: Identity and Communication in Cybersociety,* ed. S. G. Jones. Thousand Oaks, CA: Sage Publications.

_____. (1999). "Studying the Net: Intricacies and Issues." In *Doing Internet Research: Critical Issues and Methods for Examining the Net,* ed. S. G. Jones. Thousand Oaks, CA: Sage Publications.

Jordan, T. (1999). *Cyberpower: The Culture and Politics of Cyberspace and the Internet.* London and New York: Routledge.

Judy. (1997). "Autumn Storm Frightened Me." *SageWoman* 39 (Autumn): 82.

Justice. (n.d. [a]). "Coven Info/Members"; retrieved from http://endlessforest.freewebspace.com/about.html, December 28, 2003.

_____. (n.d. [b]). "B.O.S."; retrieved from http://endlesssforest.freewebspace.com/custom4.html, December 28, 2003.

_____. (n.d. [c]). "B.O.S.(2)"; retrieved from http://endlessforest.freewebspace.com/photo4.html, March 8, 2004.

Kaczynski, R. (2002). *Perdurabo: The Life of Alister Crowley.* Tempe, AZ: New Falcon.

Kaplan, J. (1996). "The Reconstruction of the Asatru and Odinist Traditions." In *Magical Religion and Modern Witchcraft,* ed. James R. Lewis. Albany, NY: State University of New York Press.

Kaplan, N. (2000). "Literacy Beyond Books: Reading When All the World's a Web." In *The World Wide Web and Contemporary Cultural Theory,* eds., A. Herman and T. Swiss. New York: Routledge.

Kathi. (1997). "Making a sardine's head your god." *SageWoman* 39 (Autumn): 84.

Kelly, A. (1991). *Crafting the Art of Magic: Book 1.* St. Paul, MN: Llewellyn Publications.

_____. (1992). "An Update on Neopagan Witchcraft in America." In *Perspectives on the New Age,* eds. J. R. Lewis and J. G. Melton. Albany, NY: State Univeristy of New York Press.

Knight, S. (2002). *Faery Magick: Spells, Potions, and Lore from the Earth Spirits.* Franklin Lakes, NJ: New Page Books.

Knight, S., and Telesco, P. (2002). *The Cyber Spellbook: Magick in the Virtual World.* Franklin Lakes, NJ: New Page Books.

Komito, D. R. (1987). *Nagarjuna's "Seventy Stanzas": A Buddhist Psychology of Emptiness.* Ithaca, NY: Snow Lion Publications.

Krasskova, G. (2003). "Care and Feeding of Your (Magical) Computer." *newWitch: not your mother's broomstick* 3 (Spring): 15–16.

Kraut, R., Patterson, M., Kiesler, S., Mukopadhyay, T., and Scherlis, W. (1998). "Internet Paradox: A Social Technology That Reduces Social Involvement and Psychological Well-Being?" *American Psychologist* 53 (9): 1017–31.

Kraut, R., Kiesler, S., Boneva, B., Cummings, J., Helgeson, V., and Crawford, A. (2002). "Internet Paradox Revisited." *Journal of Social Issues* 5 (1): 49–74.

Krogh, M., and Pillifant, B.A. (2003). "Kemetic Orthodoxy: Ancient Egyptian Religion on the Internet." Unpublished manuscript; photocopy of typescript.

_____. (2004). "The House of Netjer: An Online Religious Community." In *Religion Online: Finding Faith on the Internet,* eds. L. L. Dawson and D. E. Cowan. New York: Routledge.

Lady Moon Willow. (n.d.) "Write Your Own Spells"; retrieved from www.dreamwater.org/moonshae/spells/Writeown.htm, August 31, 2003.

Lady Raya. (n.d. [a]). "13 Lessons for Pleasing the Divine"; retrieved from www.ladyraya.org/books, December 23, 2003.

_____. (n.d. [b]). "Lady Raya's Spells of Empowerment," retrieved from www.ladyraya.org/magick, December 23, 2003.

_____. (n.d. [c]). "Meet Lady Raya"; retrieved from www.ladyraya.org/meet0.html, December 29, 2003.

_____. (n.d. [d]). "Temple FAQ"; retrieved from www.ladyraya.org/religion/tempfaq.html, March 13, 2004.

_____. (2001). *13 Lessons for Pleasing the Divine: A Witch's Primer.* Boston: Red Wheel/Weiser.

Larsen, E. (2001). *CyberFaith: How Americans Pursue Religion Online.* Washington, DC: Pew Internet & American Life Project.

Larson, B. (1999). *Larson's Book of Spiritual Warfare*. Nashville, TN: Thomas Nelson.

Lazlow. (2003). "Online Treachery." *Playboy* (March): 93, 142.

Lenhart, A. (2003). "The Ever-Shifting Internet Population: A New Look at Internet Access and the Digital Divide"; retrieved from www.pewinternet.org/reports, September 1, 2003.

Lévi, E. ([1855] 1923). *Transcendental Magic: Its Doctrine and Ritual*, trans, ann., and ed. A. E. Waite. Middlesex, England: Senate.

Levin, C. (2003). "Phishing for Online IDs." *PC Magazine* (December): 27.

Lévi-Strauss, C. (1962). *The Savage Mind*. Chicago: University of Chicago Press.

Levy, S. (1997). "Blaming the Web." *Newsweek* (April 7): 46.

Lew, A. (2001). *One God Clapping: The Spiritual Path of a Zen Rabbi*. Woodstock, VT: Jewish Lights Publishing.

Liddell, S., and Mathers, M., trans. (1995). *The Goetia: The Lesser Key of Solomon the King (Clavicula Salomonis Regula)*, ed. A. Crowley. Second edition. York Beach, ME: Red Wheel/Weiser.

Lightbringer, I. (n.d.). "Inanna's Witchy Ways"; retrieved from www.shadow-witch.com/inanna_spiritualpath.html, February 18, 2004.

Lincoln, B. (1989). *Discourse and the Construction of Society: Comparative Studies of Myth, Ritual, and Classification*. New York: Oxford University Press.

_____. (1994). *Authority: Construction and Corrosion*. Chicago: University of Chicago Press.

Littman, J. (1997). *The Watchman: The Twisted Life and Crimes of Serial Hacker Kevin Poulsen*. Boston: Little, Brown and Company.

Liu, G. Z. (1999). "Virtual Community Presence in Internet Relay Chatting." *Journal of Computer-Mediated Communication* 5 (1); retrieved from www.ascusc.org/jcmc/vol5/issue1/liu.html, January 1, 2004.

Loader, B. D., ed. (1998). *Cyberspace Divide: Equality, Agency, and Policy in the Information Society*. London and New York: Routledge.

Lockard, J. (1997). "Progressive Politics, Electronic Individualism and the Myth of Virtual Community." In *Internet Culture*, ed. D. Porter. New York: Routledge.

Lövheim, M., and Linderman, A. G. (Forthcoming). "Constructing Religious Identity on the Internet." In *Religion and Cyberspace*, eds. M. T. Højsgaard and M. Warburg. London, England: Routledge.

Luhrmann, T. M. (1989). *Persuasions of the Witch's Craft: Ritual Magic in Contemporary England*. Cambridge, MA: Harvard University Press.

Lujan, J. (n.d. [a]). "5.page"; retrieved from www.geocities.com/lightofthegoddess/5.html, December 18, 2003.

_____. (n.d. [b]). "What is LOG?"; retrieved from www.geocities.com/lightofthegoddess/whatis-log.html, December 18, 2003.

Lukes, S. (1982). "Introduction." In E. Durkheim, *The Rules of Sociological Method*, ed. S. Lukes, trans. W. D. Halls. New York: Free Press.

Lurking Bear, I. (1994). "Ritual Reality?" *The Green Egg*; retrieved from www.feri.com/lurking-bear/antiweb/reality.html, August 26, 2003.

MacCulloch, J. A. ([1911] 1992). *The Religion of the Ancient Celts*. London: Constable.

Madden, M. (2003). *America's Online Pursuits: The Changing Picture of Who's Online and What They Do*. Washington, DC: Pew Internet & American Life Project.

Magick Media Group. (2003a). *Mastering Sex Magick*. Decatur, OH: Magick Media Group.

_____. (2003b). "Ordering the Book of Shadows"; retrieved from www.freebookofshadows.com/order.asp, August 30, 2003.

_____. (2003c). "Who Are We?"; retrieved from www.freebookofshadows.com/aboutus.asp, August 30, 2003.

Malinowski, B. (1948). *Magic, Science and Religion and Other Essays*. Garden City, NY: Doubleday Anchor Books.

Mannheim, K. (1952). "The Problem of Generations." In *Essays on the Sociology of Knowledge*, ed. P. Kecskemeti. London: Routledge & Kegan Paul.

Markale, J. ([1981] 1995). *Merlin: Priest of Nature*, tr. B.N. Burke. Rochester, VT: Inner Traditions.

Markoff, J. (1997). "Death in a Cult: The Technology." *The New York Times* (March 28): A20.

Marrs, T. (1990). *Texe Marrs Book of New Age Cults and Religions*. Austin, TX: Living Truth Publishers.

Marvin, L. E. (1996). "Spoof, Spam, Lurk, and Lag: The Aesthetics of Text-based Virtual Realities." *Journal of Computer-Mediated Communication* 1 (2); retrieved from www.ascusc.org/jcmc/vol1/issue2/marvin.html, January 1, 2004.

Maskarinec, G. G. (1995). *The Rulings of the Night: An Ethnography of Nepalese Shaman Oral Texts.* Madison, WI: University of Wisconsin Press.

Matrisciana, C. (1994). *The Pagan Invasion.* Eugene, OR: Harvest House Publishers.

Matthews, C. (1995). *The Celtic Book of Days: A Guide to Celtic Spirituality & Wisdom.* Rochester, VT: Destiny Books.

Matthews, C., and Matthews, J. (1994). *The Encyclopaedia of Celtic Wisdom: The Celtic Shaman's Sourcebook.* Shaftesbury, Dorset, England: Element.

Matthews, J. (1991). *Taliesin: Shamanism and the Bardic Mysteries in Britain and Ireland.* London, England: Aquarian Press.

Mauss, M. ([1902] 1972). *A General Theory of Magic,* trans. R. Brain. London and New York: Routledge.

McCarthy, E. D. (1996). *Knowledge as Culture: The New Sociology of Knowledge.* London and New York: Routledge.

McChesney, R. W. (1999). *Rich Media, Poor Democracy: Communication Politics in Dangerous Times.* New York: The Free Press.

———. (2000). "So Much for the Magic of Technology and the Free Market: The World Wide Web and the Corporate Media System." In *The World Wide Web and Contemporary Cultural Theory,* eds. A. Herman and T. Swiss. New York: Routledge.

McColman, C. (2003). *When Someone You Love Is Wiccan: A Guide to Witchcraft and Paganism for Concerned Friends, Nervous Parents, and Curious Co-workers.* Franklin Lakes, NJ: New Page Books.

McCoy, E. (1994). *Witta: An Irish Pagan Tradition.* St. Paul, MN: Llewellyn Publications.

———. (1995). *Celtic Myth & Magick: Harness the Power of the Gods and Goddesses.* St. Paul, MN: Llewellyn Publications.

McCutcheon, R. T. (2001). *Critics Not Caretakers: Redescribing the Public Study of Religion.* Albany, NY: State University of New York Press.

McLoughlin, M. L., Osborne, K. K., and Smith, C. B. (1995). "Standards of Conduct on Usenet." In *Cybersociety: Computer-Mediated Communication and Community,* ed. S. G. Jones. Thousand Oaks, CA: Sage Publications.

McSherry, L. n.d. [a]. "The Art of Ritual Class"; retrieved from www.jaguarmoon.org/AoRclass.htm, August 26, 2003.

———. n.d. [b]. "An Important Note About the Information in This Web Site"; retrieved from www.jaguarmoon.org/copyright.htm, August 30, 2003.

———. n.d. [c]. "What Is a Cyber Coven?"; retrieved from www.jaguarmoon.org/what.htm, August 26, 2003.

———. n.d. [d]. "What Is JaguarMoon Cyber Coven??"; retrieved from www.jaguarmoon.org/who.htm, August 25, 2003.

———. (2002). *The Virtual Pagan: Exploring Wicca and Paganism Through the Internet.* Boston: Weiser Books.

———. (2003). "CyberCoven.org: Exploring Paganism and Creating Magickal Groups Online"; retrieved from www.cybercoven.org, August 25, 2003.

Mead, G. H. (1962). *Mind, Self, and Society: From the Standpoint of a Social Behaviorist,* ed. C.W. Morris. Chicago: University of Chicago Press.

Merton, R. K. (1968). *Social Theory and Social Structure.* Enl. ed. New York: Free Press.

Merton, T. (1967). *Mystics and Zen Masters.* New York: Noonday Press.

———. (1968). *Zen and the Birds of Appetite.* San Francisco: New Directions.

———. (1985). *The Hidden Ground of Love: Letters,* ed. W. H. Shannon. New York: Farrar, Straus, & Giroux.

Miller, H. (1995). "The Presentation of Self in Electronic Life: Goffman on the Internet." Paper presented at the Embodied Knowledge and Virtual Space Conference, University of London; retrieved from http://ess.ntu.ac.uk/miller/cyberpsych/goffman.htm, January 10, 2002.

Miller, H., and Mather, R. (1998). "The Presentation of Self in WWW Home Pages." Paper presented at the IRISS '98 Conference, Bristol; retrieved from http://ess.ntu.ac.uk/millercyberpsych/millmath.htm, January 10, 2002.

Miller, T., ed. (1995). *America's Alternative Religions.* Albany, NY: State University of New York Press.

Monroe, D. (1992). *The 21 Lessons of Merlyn: A Study in Druid Magic and Lore*. St. Paul, MN: Llewellyn Publications.

_____. (1998). *The Lost Books of Merlyn: Druid Magic from the Age of Arthur*. St. Paul, MN: Llewellyn Publications.

Morrison, D. (1996). "Magical Aids for Cyberspace Travel." *Circle Network News* 62 (Winter): 21.

Mosco, V. (2000). "Webs of Myth and Power: Connectivity and the New Computer Technopolis." In *The World Wide Web and Contemporary Cultural Theory*, eds. A. Herman and T. Swiss. New York: Routledge.

Mossberger, K., Tolbert, C. J., and Stansbury, M. (2003). *Virtual Inequality: Beyond the Digital Divide*. Washington, DC: Georgetown University Press.

Murray, M. A. (1921). *The Witch-cult in Western Europe: A Study in Anthropology*. Oxford, England: Clarendon Press.

_____. (1931). *The God of the Witches*. London: Oxford University Press.

_____. (1954). *The Divine King in England: A Study in Anthropology*. London: Faber & Faber.

Myers, D. (1987). "'Anonymity Is Part of the Magic': Individual Manipulation of Computer-Mediated Communication Contexts." *Qualitative Sociology* 10 (3): 251–66.

Nahmad, C. (1998). *Fairy Spells: Seeing and Communicating with the Fairies*. London, England: Souvenir Press.

Negroponte, N. (1995). *Being Digital*. New York: Vintage Books.

Nichols, R. (1975). *The Book of Druidry*, eds. J. Matthews and P. Carr-Gomm. London, England: Aquarian Press.

NightMare, M. M. (2001). *Witchcraft and the Web: Weaving Pagan Traditions Online*. Toronto, Ontario: ECW Press.

Niven, A. N. (1996). "Living the Dream: Editorial Musings." *SageWoman* 35 (Autumn): 3–4.

_____. (1997). "The Rattle begins with a response from Anne to the ongoing controversy about Jesus and the Goddess . . ." *SageWoman* 39 (Autumn): 80–81.

Noble, C. (2003). "Magic"; retrieved from http://wicca.timerift.net/magic.html, September 10, 2003.

Norris, P. (2001). *Digital Divide: Civic Engagement, Information Poverty, and the Internet World-wide*. Cambridge: Cambridge University Press.

O'Leary, S. D. (1996). "Cyberspace as Sacred Space: Communicating Religion on Computer Networks." *Journal of the American Academy of Religion* 64 (4): 781–808.

Orion, L. (1995). *Never Again the Burning Times: Paganism Revived*. Prospect Heights, IL: Waveland Press.

Palmer, S. J. (1999). "Frontiers and Families: The Children of Island Pond." In *Children in New Religions*, eds. S. J. Palmer and C. Hardman. New Brunswick, NJ: Rutgers University Press.

Palmer, S.J., and Hardman, C., eds. (1999). *Children in New Religions*. New Brunswick, NJ: Rutgers University Press.

Paolillo, J. (1999). "The Virtual Speech Community: Social Network and Language Variation in IRC." *Journal of Computer-Mediated Communication* 4 (4); retrieved from www.ascusc.org/jcmc/vol4/issue4/paolillo.html, January 1, 2004.

Parks, M. R. (1996). "Making Friends in Cyberspace." *Journal of Computer-Mediated Communication* 1 (4); retrieved from www.ascusc.org/jcmc/vol1/issue4/parks.html, January 1, 2004.

Peat, F. D. (1987). *Syncronicity: The Bridge Between Matter and Mind*. New York: Bantam Books.

_____. 1988. *Superstrings and the Search for a Theory of Everything*. Chicago: Contemporary Books.

Peckham, M. (1998). "New Dimensions of Social Movement/Countermovement Interaction: The Case of Scientology and Its Internet Critics." *Canadian Journal of Sociology/Cahiers Canadiens de Sociologie* 23 (4): 317–47.

Peterson, J. H., ed. (2003). *John Dee's Five Books of Mystery: Original Sourcebook of Enochian Magic*. Boston: Weiser Books.

Pew Internet & American Life Project. (2003). "Daily Internet Activities"; retrieved from www.pewinternet.org/reports, September 1, 2003.

Picknett, L., and Prince, C. (1999). *The Stargate Conspiracy*. New York: Berkley Books.

Pike, S. M. (2001). *Earthly Bodies, Magical Selves: Contemporary Pagans and the Search for Community*. Berkeley and Los Angeles: University of California Press.

Pittman, N. C. (2003). *Christian Wicca: The Trinitarian Tradition*. Bloomington, IN: First Books Library.

Postman, N. (1986). *Amusing Ourselves to Death: Public Discourse in the Age of Show Business*. New York: Viking Press.

_____. (1992). *Technopoly: The Surrender of Culture to Technology*. New York: Vintage Books.

Postman, N., and Powers, S. (1992). *How to Watch TV News*. New York: Penguin USA.

Price, S. (2002). *The Journey into Witchcraft: Step Inside a Witch's World*. nN.p.: WitchesWay.Net Publishing.

Rabinovitch, S., and Lewis, J. (2002). *The Encyclopedia of Modern Witchcraft and Neo-Paganism*. New York: Citadel Press.

Raeburn, J. (2001). *Celtic Wicca: Ancient Wisdom for the 21st Century*. New York: Citadel Press.

Raël. (1986). *Let's Welcome Our Fathers From Space: They Created Humanity in Their Laboratories*. Tokyo: AUM Corporation.

Rafaeli, S., and Sudweeks, F. (1997). "Networked Interactivity." *Journal of Computer-Mediated Communication* 2 (4); retrieved from www.ascusc.org/jcmc/vol2/issue4/rafaeli.sudweeks .html, January 1, 2004.

Rampton, S., and Stauber, J. (2003). *Weapons of Mass Deception: The Uses of Propaganda in Bush's War on Iraq*. New York: Jeremy P. Tarcher/Penguin.

RavenWolf, S. (1993). *To Ride a Silver Broomstick: New Generation Witchcraft*. St. Paul, MN: Llewellyn Publications.

_____. (1995). *To Stir a Magick Cauldron: A Witch's Guide to Casting and Conjuring*. St. Paul, MN: Llewellyn Publications.

_____. (1998). *Teen Witch: Wicca for a New Generation*. St. Paul, MN: Llewellyn Publications.

_____. (1999). *To Light a Sacred Flame: Practical WitchCraft for the Millennium*. St. Paul, MN: Llewellyn Publications.

_____. (2003). *Solitary Witch: The Ultimate Book of Shadows for the New Generation*. St. Paul, MN: Llewellyn Publications.

Ravetz, J. (1998). "The Internet, Virtual Reality and Real Reality." In *Cyberspace Divide: Equality, Agency and Policy in the Information Society*, ed. B. D. Loader. London and New York: Routledge.

Raymond, E. S. (1999). *The Cathedral & The Bazaar: Musings on Linux and Open Source by an Accidental Revolutionary*. Sebastopol, CA: O'Reilly & Associates.

Religious Technology Center. (2003a). "Guaranteeing the Future of Dianetics & Scientology"; retrieved from www.rtc.org/guarant/page06.htm, September 14, 2003.

_____. (2003b). "The Guarantor of Scientology's Future"; retrieved from www.rtc.org/guarant/ page01.htm, September 14, 2003.

Reverend, B. (1996). "Priestess and Pastor: Serving Between the Worlds." In *Living Between Two Worlds: Challenges of the Modern Witch*, ed. C. S. Clifton. St. Paul, MN: Llewellyn Publications.

Rheingold, H. (1993). *The Virtual Community: Homesteading on the Electronic Frontier*. Rev. ed. Cambridge, MA: The MIT Press.

Richardson, J. T. (1995). "Manufacturing Consent About Koresh: A Structural Analysis of the Role of Media in the Waco Tragedy." In *Armageddon in Waco: Critical Perspectives on the Branch Davidian Conflict*, ed. S. A. Wright. Chicago: University of Chicago Press.

Richardson, J. T., and van Driel, B. (1997). "Journalist' Attitudes toward New Religious Movements," *Review of Religious Research* 39 (2):116–36.

Ritual Room. (1999). "Ritual"; available upon request from the site administrator, http://thedance.com/rituals; January 23, 2004.

Robinson, B. A. (2000). "Evolution of a Religious Web Site Devoted to Tolerance." In *Religion on the Internet: Research Prospects and Promises*, eds. J. K. Hadden and D. E. Cowan. Amsterdam and London: JAI/Elsevier Science.

_____. (2003). "How Many Wiccans Are There in the U.S.?"; retrieved from www.religioustoler-ance.org/wic_nbr.htm, March 19, 2004.

Robinson, T. A. (1988). *The Bauer Thesis Examined: The Geography of Heresy in the Early Christian Church*. Lewiston, PA: Edwin Mellen Press.

Rochford, E. B., Jr. (1985). *Hare Krishna in America*. New Brunswick, NJ: Rutgers University Press.

Rowling, J. K. (1998). *Harry Potter and the Philosopher's Stone*. New York: A.A. Levine Books.

Roszak, T. (1994). *The Cult of Information: A Neo-Luddite Treatise on High-Tech, Artificial Intelligence, and the True Art of Thinking*. Berkeley and Los Angeles: University of California Press.

216 • Cyberhenge

Russell, C. T. (1906–1917). *Studies in the Scripture*. Allegheny, PA: Watch Tower Bible & Tract Society.

Rutter, J., and Smith, G. (1999). "Presenting the off-line self in an everyday, online environment"; retrieved from http://les1.man.ac.uk/cric/JasonRutter/papers/Self.pdf, October 28, 2003.

Salomonsen, J. (1999). "Methods of Compassion or Pretension? Conducting Anthropological Fieldwork in Modern Magickal Communities." *The Pomegranate: A New Journal of Neopagan Thought* 8 (Spring): 205–13.

_____. (2002). *Enchanted Feminism: The Reclaiming Witches of San Francisco*. London and New York: Routledge.

Sannicolas, N. (1997). "Erving Goffman, Dramaturgy, and On-Line Relationships." *Cybersociology Magazine* 1; retrieved from www.socio.demon.co.uk/magazine/1/is1nikki.html, February 23, 2002.

Sant. (1996). "Paganism and the Net: Oil and Water?" *Circle Network News* 62 (Winter): 18.

Sapphire [T. Parnell]. (2000). *Book of Shadows and Advanced High Magick*. Decatur, OH.: Magick Media Group.

Sarah. (1997). "Letter to the Editor." *SageWoman* 38 (Summer): 85–86.

Schroeder, R. (1996). *Possible Worlds: The Social Dynamic of Virtual Reality Technology*. Boulder, CO: Westview Press.

Segaller, S. (1999). *Nerds 2.0.1: A Brief History of the Internet*. New York: TV Books.

Shanks, J. (2003). Review of *The Cyber Spellbook* by Sirona Knight and Patricia Telesco (New Page Books, 2002). *newWitch: not your mother's broomstick* 4 (Summer): 69–70.

Sharf, B. F. (1999). "Beyond Netiquette: The Ethics of Doing Naturalistic Discourse Research on the Internet." In *Doing Internet Research: Critical Issues and Methods for Examining the Net*, ed. S. Jones. Thousand Oaks, CA: Sage Publications.

Shaw, T. (2000). "Don't Let the Hoax Be On You." *Plain Dealer (Cleveland, Ohio)* (March 13): 1F.

Shields, R. (2000). "Hypertext Links: The Ethic of the Index and Its Space-Time Effects." In *The World Wide Web and Contemporary Cultural Theory*, eds. A. Herman and T. Swiss. New York: Routledge.

Shirky, C. (1995). *Voices from the Net*. Emeryville, CA: Ziff-Davis Press.

Shweder, R. A. (1991). *Thinking Through Cultures: Expeditions in Cultural Psychology*. Cambridge and London: Harvard University Press.

Silvermoon, C. (n.d.). "FAQS"; retrieved from http://celticshamaness1.tripod.com/faq.html, March 13, 2004.

_____. (1996a). "Overview of Celtic Shamanism"; retrieved from http://celticshaman. cjb.net, December 27, 2003.

_____. (1996b). "Overview of Courses"; retrieved from http://celticshaman.cjb.net, December 27, 2003.

_____. (1996c). Rev. Cougar Silvermoon; retrieved from http://celticshaman.cjs.net, March 15, 2004.

_____. (2002). "FAQ"; retrieved from http://cougarshaman.tripod.com/faq.html, March 13, 2004.

Simmel, G. (1906). "The Sociology of Secrecy and of Secret Societies." *American Journal of Sociology* 11 (4): 441–98.

_____. (1950). *The Sociology of Georg Simmel*, tr. and ed. K. H. Wolff. New York: Free Press.

Simon, L. D. (2000). *NetPolicy.Com: Public Agenda for a Digital World*. Washington, DC: Woodrow Wilson Center Press.

Simpson, D. P., ed. (1968). *Cassell's Latin Dictionary*, fifth ed., s.v. "*veritas.*" New York: Macmillan Publishing Company.

Simpson, J. (1994). "Margaret Murray: Who Believed Her, and Why?" *Folklore* 105: 89–96.

Sitchin, Z. (1976). *The 12th Planet*. New York: Avon Books.

_____. (1985). *The Wars of Gods and Men*. New York: Avon Books.

_____. (1990). *Genesis Revisited: Is Modern Science Catching Up With Ancient Knowledge?* New York: Avon Books.

_____. (1995). *Divine Encounters: A Guide to Visions, Angels, and Other Emissaries*. New York: Avon Books.

Skelton, R. (1997). *The Practice of Witchcraft*. Vancouver, British Columbia: Beach Holme.

Slatalla, M., and Quittner, J. (1995). *Masters of Deception: The Gang that Ruled Cyberspace*. New York: HarperCollins.

Slevin, J. (2000). *The Internet and Society*. London: Polity Press.

Slouka, M. (1995). *War of the Worlds: Cyberspace and the High-Tech Assault on Reality*. New York: Basic Books.

Smith, C. B., McLaughlin, M. L., and Osborne, K .K. (1997). "Conduct Control on Usenet." *Journal of Computer-Mediated Communication* 2 (4); retrieved from www.ascusc.org/jcmc/vol2/issue4/smith.html, January 10, 2004.

Smith, J. Z.. (1982). *Imagining Religion: From Babylon to Jonestown*. Chicago: University of Chicago Press.

———. (1987). *To Take Place: Toward Theory in Ritual*. Chicago: University of Chicago Press.

———. (1993). *Map Is Not Territory: Studies in the History of Religion*. Chicago: University of Chicago Press.

Smith, M. A., and Kollock, P., eds. (1999). *Communities in Cyberspace*. London and New York: Routledge.

Softley, I., dir. (1995). *Hackers*. Hollywood, CA: MGM Studios.

Sommerville, C. J. (1999). *How the News Makes Us Dumb: The Death of Wisdom in an Information Society*. Downers Grove, IL: InterVarsity Press.

Srinivasan, S. (2002). "Religion Online: Hindus Turn to the Internet for Prayer," Associated Press (June 27); retrieved from www.wwrn.org, March 13, 2004.

Starhawk. (1988). *Dreaming the Dark: Magic, Sex and Politics*. Rev. ed. Boston: Beacon Press.

———. (1989). *The Spiral Dance: A Rebirth of the Ancient Religion of the Great Goddess*. Second ed. San Francisco: Harper & Row.

Starhawk, NightMare, M. M., and the Reclaiming Collective. (1997). *The Pagan Book of Living and Dying: Practical Rituals, Prayers, Blessings, and Meditations on Crossing Over*. New York: HarperCollins.

Stark, R. (2001). "Reconceptualizing Religion, Magic, and Science." *Review of Religious Research* 43 (2): 101–20.

Stark, R., and Bainbridge, W. S. (1979). "Cult Formation: Three Compatible Models." *Sociological Analysis* 40: 283–95.

———. (1985). *The Future of Religion: Secularization, Revival, and Cult Formation*. Berkeley and Los Angeles: University of California Press.

———. (1987). *A Theory of Religion*. New Brunswick, NJ: Rutgers University Press.

———. (1997). *Religion, Deviance, and Social Control*. New York: Routledge.

Sterling, B. (1992). *The Hacker Crackdown: Law and Order on the Electronic Frontier*. New York: Bantam Books.

Stevenson, R., dir. (1971). *Bedknobs and Broomsticks*. Hollywood, CA: Walt Disney Studios/Buena Vista.

Stewart, R. J. (1999). *The Living World of Faery*. Lake Toxaway, NC: Mercury Publishing.

Stoll, C. (1990). *The Cuckoo's Egg: Tracking a Spy Through the Maze of Computer Espionage*. New York: Pocket Books.

———. (1995). *Silicon Snake Oil: Second Thoughts on the Information Highway*. New York: Doubleday.

———. (1999). *High-Tech Heretic: Reflections of a Computer Contrarian*. New York: Anchor.

Sutin, L. (2000). *Do What Thou Wilt: A Life of Aleister Crowley*. New York: St. Martin's Press.

Sutton, M. M., and Mann, N. R. (2002). *Druid Magic: The Practice of Celtic Wisdom*. Rev. ed. St. Paul, MN: Llewellyn Publications.

Swiss, T., and Herman, A. (2000). "Introduction: The World Wide Web as Magic, Metaphor, and Power." In *The World Wide Web and Contemporary Cultural Theory*, eds. A. Herman and T. Swiss. New York: Routledge.

Talbot, M. (1991). *The Holographic Universe*. New York: HarperCollins.

Tarot.com. (2003). "Karma Coins®"; retrieved from www.tarot.com/karma, September 4, 2003.

Tarryn. (2003). "What Is Penumbra Veritas?"; retrieved from members.cox.net/penumbraveritas/AboutPenumbraveritas.htm, December 16, 2003.

Telesco, P. (1996). "Technological Magic." *Circle Network News* 62 (Winter): 17.

———. (1998). *365 Goddess: A Daily Guide to the Magic and Inspiration of the Goddess*. New York: HarperCollins.

Telesco, P., and S. Knight. (2001). *The Wiccan Web: Surfing the Magic on the Internet*. New York: Citadel Press.

Temple, R. (1998). *The Sirius Mystery: New Scientific Evidence for Alien Contact 5,000 Years Ago*. London: Arrow.

Temple of Duality. (2001). "Who We Are"; retrieved from www.silverstormlavenderdawn.home-stead.com, November 20, 2002.

Thomas, K. (1971). *Religion and the Decline of Magic: Studies in Popular Beliefs in Sixteenth- and Seventeenth-Century England*. Harmondsworth, England: Penguin Books.

Thomas, P. B. (2004). "Re-Imagining Inanna: The Gendered Reappropriation of the Ancient Goddess in Modern Goddess Worship." *The Pomegranate: The International Journal of Modern Pagan Studies* 6(1): 53–69.

Tillich, P. (1957). *Dynamics of Faith*, ed. R. N. Anshen. New York: Harper.

Tönnies, F. ([1887] 1955). *Community and Association*, trans. C. P. Loomis. London: Routledge & Paul.

Torassa, U. (2001). "Web Sites Extend the Reach of Quacks." *San Francisco Chronicle* (February 25): 8.

Toulson, S. (1993). *The Celtic Year: A Month-by-Month Celebration of Celtic Christian Festivals and Sites*. Shaftesbury, England: Element.

Turkle, S. (1995). *Life on the Screen: Identity in the Age of the Internet*. New York: Touchstone.

Turner, V. (1969). *The Ritual Process: Structure and Anti-Structure*. Ithaca, NY: Cornell University Press.

Turoff, M., et al. (1999). "Collaborative Discourse Structures in Computer Mediated Group Communications." *Journal of Computer-Mediated Communication* 4 (4); retrieved from www.acsusc.org/jcmc/vol4/issue4/turoff.html, April 9, 2003.

Urban, H. (2000). "The Devil at Heaven's Gate: Rethinking the Study of Religion in the Age of Cyber-Space." *Nova Religio: The Journal of New and Emergent Religions* 3 (2): 269–302.

Vale, V., and Sulak, J. (2001). *Modern Pagans: An Investigation of Contemporary Pagan Practices*. San Francisco: Re/Search Publications.

Van der Veer, P. (1994). *Religious Nationalism: Hindus and Muslims in India*. Berkeley and Los Angeles: University of California Press.

Van Gennep, A. ([1908] 1960). *The Rites of Passage*, tr. M. B. Vizedom and G. L. Caffee. Chicago: University of Chicago Press.

Varshney, A. (2002). *Ethnic Conflict and Civic Life: Hindus and Muslims in India*. New Haven, CT, and London: Yale University Press.

Von Adams, F. (2003). "I Roomed with a Muggle!" *newWitch: not your mother's broomstick* 5 (October 03–January 04): 63–64.

Von Däniken, E. (1969). *Chariots of the Gods: Unsolved Mysteries of the Past*, trans. M. Heron. New York: Putnam.

_____. (1970). *Gods From Outer Space: Return to the Stars, or Evidence for the Impossible*, trans. M. Heron. New York: Bantam Books.

Wachowski, A., and Wachowski, L., dirs. (1999). *The Matrix*. Hollywood, CA: Warner Bros.

Walker, B. G. (1983). *The Woman's Encyclopedia of Myths and Secrets*. New York: HarperCollins.

Wallace, N. (2003). "The Pagans of Suburbia." *Sydney Morning Herald* (January 9): Metro, 13.

Wallis, R. (1976). *The Road to Total Freedom: A Sociological Analysis of Scientology*. New York: Columbia University Press.

Watson, N. (1997). Why We Argue About Virtual Community: A Case Study of the Phish.Net Fan Community." In *Virtual Culture: Identity and Communication in Cybersociety*, ed. S. G. Jones. London: Sage Publications.

Weber, M. (1964). *The Sociology of Religion*. Boston: Beacon Press.

Wellman, B., and Gulia, M. (1999). "Virtual Communities as Communities: Net Surfers Don't Ride Alone." In *Communities in Cyberspace*, eds., M. A. Smith and P. Kollock. London and New York: Routledge.

Wellman, B., and Haythornthwaite, C., eds. (2002). *The Internet in Everyday Life*. Oxford, England: Blackwell.

Wertheim, M. (1999). *The Pearly Gates of Cyberspace: A History of Space from Dante to the Internet*. New York: W.W. Norton & Company.

Whispering Brook. n.d. [a]. "About Us"; retrieved from www.whisperingbrook.org/public/index.html, August 26, 2003.

_____. n.d. [b]. "Our Beliefs"; retrieved from www.whisperingbrook.org/public/index.html, August 26, 2003.

Wilbur, S. (1997). "An Archeology of Cyberspaces: Virtuality, Community, Identity." In *Internet Culture*, ed. D. Porter. New York: Routledge.

Willowroot, A. (2003). "Spiral Goddess Grove"; retrieved from www.spiralgoddess.com, March 5, 2004.

Willson, M. (2000). "Community in the Abstract: A Political and Ethical Dilemma?" In *The Cybercultures Reader*, eds. D. Bell and B. M. Kennedy. London and New York: Routledge.

Wilson, B. K. (1954). *Scottish Folk-tales and Legends*. Oxford: Oxford University Press.

Wilson, C. (1978). *Mysteries: An Investigation into the Occult, the Paranormal and the Supernatural*. London, England: Grafton Books.

Wilson, M. K. (1996). "Magickal Computers." *Circle Network News* 62 (Winter): 20.

Winkelman, M. (1982). "Magic: A Theoretical Reassessment." *Cultural Anthropology* 23 (1): 37–66.

_____. (1992). *Shamans, Priests and Witches: A Cross-Cultural Study of Magico-Religious Practitioners*. Anthropological Research Papers No. 44. Tempe, AZ: Arizona State University.

Winkler, I., dir. (1995). *The Net*. Hollywood, CA: Columbia/Tristar Studios.

WitchVox Staff. (1997). "Our Mission Statement"; retrieved from www.witchvox.com/twv/mission_statement.html, September 3, 2003.

_____. (2003). "What is the Witches' Voice?"; retrieved from www.witchvox.com/twv/whatis.html, September 3, 2003.

Wolf, F. A. (1988). *Parallel Universes: The Search for Other Worlds*. New York: Simon & Schuster.

Wresch, W. (1996). *Disconnected: Haves and Have-nots in the Information Age*. New Brunswick, NJ: Rutgers University Press.

Wright, S. (2000). "Instant Genius! Just add the Net." *net* (June): 50–58.

Wright, S. A. (1997). "Media Coverage of Unconventional Religion: Any 'Good News' for Minority Faith?" *Review of Religious Research* 39 (2): 101–115.

Wulfslaird. (2002). "Beltaine/Self Healing Ritual"; retrieved from the files section of Online Wiccan Rituals (groups.yahoo.com/group/OnlineWiccanRituals), December 31, 2003.

WulfWuman. (1998). "Temple of Sekhmet"; retrieved from www.geocities.com/sekhmets_dawn/temple.html, September 15, 2003.

Wynn, E., and Katz, J. E. (1997). "Hyperbole over Cyberspace: Self-Presentation and Social Boundaries in Internet Homepages and Discourse." *The Information Society: An International Journal* 13 (4): 297–328.

York, M. (1995). *The Emerging Network: A Sociology of the New Age and Neo-Pagan Movements*. Lanham, MD: Rowman & Littlefield Publishers.

Young, G. A. (2004). "The Mainline Online: Christianity on the Internet." In *Religion Online/Online Religion: Finding Faith on the Internet*, eds. L.L. Dawson and D. E. Cowan. New York: Routledge.

Young, J. I., trans. (1971). *The Prose Edda of Snorri Sturluson: Tales from Norse Mythology*. Berkeley and Los Angeles: University of California Press.

Zickmund, S. (1997). "Approaching the Radical Other: The Discursive Culture of Cyberhate." In *Virtual Culture: Identity and Communication in Cybersociety*, ed. S. G. Jones. London: Sage Publications.

# Index